Mexico's Indigenous Past

The Civilization of the American Indian Series

Mexico's Indigenous Past

ALFREDO LÓPEZ AUSTIN
AND LEONARDO LÓPEZ LUJÁN

TRANSLATED BY
BERNARD R. ORTIZ DE MONTELLANO

UNIVERSITY OF OKLAHOMA PRESS : NORMAN

ALSO BY THE AUTHORS

Alfredo López Austin

The Human Body and Ideology: Concepts of the Ancient Nahua (Salt Lake City, 1988)
The Myths of the Opossum: Pathways of Mesoamerican Mythology (Albuquerque, 1993)
The Rabbit on the Face of the Moon: Mythology in the Mesoamerican Tradition (Salt Lake City, 1996)
Tamoanchan, Tlalocan: Places of Mist (Niwot, Colo., 1997)

Leonardo López Luján

The Offerings of the Templo Mayor of Tenochtitlan (Niwot, Colo., 1994)

Library of Congress Cataloging-in-Publication Data

López Austin, Alfredo
    [Pasado indígena. English]
    Mexico's indigenous past / Alfredo López Austin and Leonardo López Luján; translated by Bernard R. Ortiz de Montellano.
    p. cm. — (The civilization of the American Indian series; v. 240)
    Includes bibliographical references and index.
    ISBN 0-8061-3214-0 (alk. paper)
    1. Indians of Mexico—Antiquities. 2. Mexico—Antiquities. I. López Luján, Leonardo. II. Title. III. Series

    F1219 .L85813 2001
    972'.01—dc21

    20011027133

Mexico's Indigenous Past is Volume 240 in The Civilization of the American Indian Series.

The paper in this book meets the guidelines for permanence and durability of the Committee on Production Guidelines for Book Longevity of the Council on Library Resources, Inc.∞

1 2 3 4 5 6 7 8 9 10

To Martha Rosario and Laura

Contents

Illustrations

Squash-shaped ceramic vessel with anthropomorphic supports, Colima
Mezcala-style anthropomorphic statuettes found in Tenochtitlan,
　Distrito Federal
Talus walls of the defensive system of La Quemada, Zacatecas
Mural fragment at Las Higueras, Veracruz
"Yugo"-type stone sculpture, Veracruz
Representation of a Maya ruler on a stele, Copán, Honduras
Panel with the image of a ruler of Palenque, Chiapas

Following page 225
Aerial view of Tikal, Guatemala
Maya cylindrical vessel found in Teotihuacan, Estado de México
Tripod vase from Tomb 1, Calakmul, Campeche
Vessel with anthropomorphic lid, Guajilar, Chiapas
Ball court, Copán, Honduras
Mural from the Red Temple at Cacaxtla, Tlaxcala
Main ball court, Xochicalco, Morelos
Relief of a mythological feline, Teotenango, Estado de México
Panel from the southern ball court at El Tajín, Veracruz
Monumental columns representing armed warriors, Pyramid B, Tula,
　Hidalgo
Mexica monolith used for human sacrifice, Tenochtitlan, Distrito
　Federal
Mexica feline sculpture used for depositing human hearts,
　Tenochtitlan, Distrito Federal
Mexica bas-relief with the glyph of the ruler Ahuitzotl, Tepoztlán,
　Morelos

Following page 292
Pyramid of Tenayuca, Estado de México
Pyramid of Malinalco, Estado de México
Tableros decorated with mosaic greques, Mitla, Oaxaca
Lord 8 Deer Jaguar Claw with two allies, *Nuttall Codex*
Tarascan yácatas in Tzintzuntzan, Michoacán
Totonac Quetzalcoatl temple, Cempoala, Veracruz
Pyramid called "El Castillo," Teayo, Veracruz
Stele with the image of Tlaloc, Teayo, Veracruz

Huaxtec stone sculpture, the Gulf Area
Codz Pop Palace, Kabah, Yucatán
Atlante from the Temple of the Jaguars, Chichén Itzá, Yucatán
View of Iximché, Guatemala

FIGURES

MAPS

PLANS

TABLES

Preface

This book was originally published in Spanish as part of a series entitled *Hacia una nueva historia de México.* We were honored when, in 1994, Alicia Hernández Chávez, director of the Center for Historic Studies at the Colegio de México, invited us to participate in the series, because this institution has developed a tradition of historiographic excellence over the years. Prime examples, among its many published works, are the Center's prior books in the Mexican history series, which are indispensable reference works for both general readers and scholars. Each book in the series, including this one, has its own theme. The theme for this book was particularly attractive to us, as it involved a long historical period and broad geographical area. We happily agreed to participate, because the project would allow us to leave our ivory towers to take a panoramic view of the precolonial past of Mexico.

Through a series of conversations we came to understand both the goals of the series as a whole and our particular task. Books in the series have a unified vision, are concisely written, and act as critical guides rather than simply providing a plethora of facts. The books are written for scholars as well as for a wider audience but without footnotes and with a limited bibliography and a minimal number of tables and maps.

Although we agreed to these conditions, we must confess that meeting them, once we began to work, was not easy. One of the biggest problems arose from the topic itself. We were commissioned to write a history of ancient Mexico, which forced us to deal not only with the Native societies that once inhabited the geographical space encompassed by Mexico's present borders but with all the peoples in three cultural superareas—Aridamerica, Oasisamerica, and Mesoamerica—that greatly surpassed these borders. Although it was not an insurmountable problem, the title of the book was problematic because we were to write a history of Mexico at a time when Mexico did not exist as a cultural or political entity. In the Spanish edition we avoided the problem by calling the book *The Indigenous Past,* tacitly referring to the name of the series, *Towards a New History of Mexico.* But in the English edition we had to include the name of Mexico and, furthermore, to suggest in the most general way a past that unfolded for more than thirty thousand years, from the arrival of the first settlers in this area to the end of independent existence for the Native peoples.

The prehispanic area north of Mexico is given more space in this book than it is normally given in general surveys. We wanted to avoid the erroneous idea that the historical importance of a people is in proportion to their cultural achievements or level of sociopolitical organization. However, we had to be realistic about the disproportionate amount of material available on Mesoamerica; thus, we emphasize those societies that are most easily accessible because more information about them is available. Nor is our vision of the Native past as unified as we would have wished, as the existence of three cultural superareas indicates the existence of three different histories. Even though it is true that there were permanent, at times very intense, contacts between Aridamerica, Oasisamerica, and Mesoamerica, each superarea had a high degree of autonomy from the others. We tried to find a sense of historical continuity within each of the superareas, although—due to the scarcity of information about hunter-gatherer societies, their diversity, and their limited interactions—it is difficult to understand Aridamerica as a whole.

Despite our exceeding the stipulated length of the book, we are satisfied that we have not sacrificed comprehensibility for the sake of brevity. For each chapter we chose the topics that we felt were indispensable, those that we could summarize, and those that we had to eliminate because of space considerations. We know that many topics were not addressed or were drastically summarized.

During the writing we changed our minds about dispensing with dates, phases, site names, and ceramic types. We realized that a plain narrative without minimal temporal, spatial, or cultural parameters would not give the reader a historical view of the events. Ancient Native history is a chain of successive scenes and simultaneous happenings; if they are not anchored in place, the reader may drown in an amorphous mass of facts. We only included maps and tables that we considered essential and tried to make them as clear and concise as possible.

In writing for historians as well as for a wider educated public interested in history we tried to avoid the magisterial style that proffers every piece of information as absolute truth. Thus, the reader will find—and we hope will not judge it excessive—a hypothetical flavor that we trust will reflect the perennial debate and progress of the academic world. In many chapters we describe ongoing debates and at least some of the solutions that we consider most feasible, if not the arguments on both sides of the question.

Undoubtedly the most difficult task was to eliminate references to the innumerable authors whom we consulted and without whom our approach to most of these topics would have been impossible. Both of us, like our colleagues, specialize in narrow areas of knowledge about the past; nevertheless, a general work must be built on an array of research, proposed hypotheses, and opinions of others. We have been able to mention only a few scholars, and we are conscious of our injustice. The brief bibliography does not reflect the immense literature that has been produced in the last decades. Yet we would like to offer our thanks here to all the scholars we consulted for their contributions to scientific consensus and debate.

It may be useful to situate our book within this abundant material. There are two kinds of general works on the Indian past: collections of monographs by diverse authors that fully cover a topic and single-author comprehensive studies. The two complement each other, collections of monographs revealing the latest results of the research of specialists on particular topics while general studies provide a general sense of the great eras of the past. Some of the best monographic works published in the last decades are: *The Handbook of Middle American Indians,* edited by Robert Wauchope; the *Historia de México,* edited by Miguel León-Portilla; the *Historia general de México,* edited by the Centro de Estudios Históricos in the Colegio de México, the predecessor to *Hacia una nueva historia de México; México: Panorama histórico y cultural,* edited by Ignacio Bernal; *The Handbook of North American Indians,* edited by William C. Sturtevant; and the *Historia antigua de México,* edited by Linda Manzanilla and Leonardo López Luján. Notable single-author comprehensive surveys include: *Una visión del México prehispánico,* by Román Piña Chan; *Mesoamerica: The Evolution of a Civilization,* by William T. Sanders and Barbara J. Price; *The Aztecs, Maya, and Their Predecessors,* by Muriel Porter Weaver; *Mexico: From the Olmecs to the Aztecs,* by Michael D. Coe; *Prehistoric Mesoamerica,* by Richard E. W. Adams; *México prehispánico: Origen y formación de las clases sociales,* by Enrique Nalda; and *Ancient Mesoamerica,* by Richard E. Blanton, Stephen A. Kowalski, Gary Feinman, and Jill Appel.

Finally, though it may seem immodest to say so, our book has the advantage that all of it is the product of a dialogue between a historian and an archaeologist. Every single line has been written by both authors, who used different criteria to achieve unity. It would have been much easier for each of us to write his part alone in the peace and quiet of his own office before we integrated the two into a whole. Even though the process we chose was slow and difficult, however, it proved to be a happy and rewarding experience for both of us, resulting, we hope, in a useful and enjoyable book for the reader.

We thank William T. Sanders for his meticulous reading of the text and his erudite comments; Laura Filloy for her detailed revision of the manuscript; Davíd Carrasco for his support; *Arqueología Mexicana,* Mónica del Villar, Lorenzo Ochoa, Fernando Botas Vera, Salvador Guilliem, and Mari Carmen Serra Puche for their permission to publish illustrative materials; and John Drayton, director of the University of Oklahoma Press, Alice K. Stanton, managing editor at the Press, and Bernard Ortiz de Montellano, translator of the text, for all their work on the project. We especially want to thank Alicia Hernández Chávez for her trust in us and for having given us the opportunity to share moments that will be talked about by our children and grandchildren for years to come.

Alfredo López Austin
Leonardo López Luján

Tepoztlán and Princeton

Translator's Note

The text has been revised to some extent and the bibliography has been updated. All Nahuatl words are accented in the next-to-last syllable, so I have not followed Spanish rules for accents in those words. The ethnic plural is used for names of Native peoples.

Mexico's Indigenous Past

Introduction

ANCIENT MEXICO

The historic present of modern Mexico is like a river fed by many streams, both recent and remote in origin, which make up the complex reality of the country today. Each of the historical periods survives in contemporary Mexicans; no matter how distant they may seem, they merge in the present.

The first of these periods, that of ancient Mexico, is characterized by its isolation as a continent. Lasting more than thirty-four thousand years, the period began with the arrival of hunting-gathering bands and ended, after great social transformations, with the European occupation. Ancient Mexico was never a historical unit. Its limits have been artificially defined on the basis of present political borders. Nevertheless, it is useful to think of ancient Mexico as an entity, because the different indigenous societies that once lived inside the present borders of Mexico are some of the ancestors of Mexicans today.

In antiquity three cultural superareas occupied this territory (see map 1). Even though the societies that formed each one did not comprise a political unit, they did result in certain historical connections inside those superareas. The three cultural superareas—Aridamerica, to the Northeast, also including the Baja California peninsula; Oasisamerica, to the Northwest; and Mesoamerica, the southern half of Mexico—all extended beyond present-day Mexico. The first two occupied

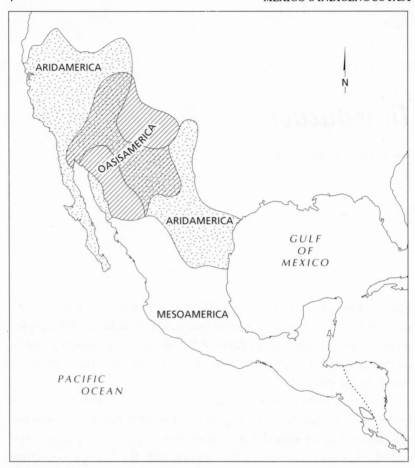

N

ARIDAMERICA

OASISAMERICA

ARIDAMERICA

GULF
OF
MEXICO

MESOAMERICA

PACIFIC
OCEAN

Map 1. Ancient Mexico and its three cultural superareas.

a significant part of the United States, while the third extended to
Guatemala, Belize, Honduras, El Salvador, Nicaragua, and Costa Rica.

By definition a cultural superarea includes groups of humans bound
to each other by a complex and heterogenous set of relationships.
Across the millennia these relationships are established between societies that live next to each other, resulting in shared traditions and
history. Relationships are established through the constant interchange
of goods; permanent or transitory movements of individuals and groups
within the superarea; the shared interests of the elites that govern the
different political entities; and the dominance of one society by another

through acts of war, as much by alliances as by conflicts. The traditions that characterize a cultural superarea should be considered as a particular set of ideas and practices that have evolved continuously over the centuries, with clear regional characteristics, rather than as a set of elements impervious to time and space.

Ancient Mexican societies in the same cultural superarea sometimes differ in their level of development, but relationships within them were relatively permanent and had some formal organization. On the other hand, commercial relationships and the imitation of artistic styles among the three cultural superareas were not enough to unite their peoples into a single tradition. This can be seen, for example, in the intense interchange between Oasisamerica and Mesoamerica, which did not make the sociocultural bases of both areas homogeneous.

CHAPTER ONE

The Great Divisions

ARIDAMERICA, OASISAMERICA, AND MESOAMERICA

THE LITHIC AGE

According to the latest archaeological findings, humans have been in what is now called Mexico for about thirty-five thousand years. For 80 percent of Mexico's past, however, plants were not cultivated. Before the historical milestone of the domestication of maize about seven thousand years ago, the territory was occupied by similar groups who lived from hunting, gathering, and fishing yet had little interaction with each other. The time during which differences developed between them as well as the period of interaction among the three cultural superareas, on a millennial scale, was brief.

The First Hunter-Gatherers

Unfortunately, we know very little about the long pre-agricultural period. There are few material remains from that era for several reasons: the low population density and the dispersion of hunter-gatherers; the inevitable effects of time on their ancient vestiges; and the limited number of archaeological excavations relating to these early people. What we do know about the hunter-gatherer societies has to do primarily with their technology. The information available to archaeologists is composed mostly of stone utensils, remains of hearths, bones of animals eaten, and a few human bones.

Based on the available data, José Luis Lorenzo named this long period the Lithic Age and subdivided it into two periods: the Archaeolithic horizon (33,000–12,000 B.C.) and the Cenolithic horizon (12,000–5000 B.C.). Approximately ten sites belonging to the first horizon are known, including El Cedral, San Luis Potosí, which has the oldest C¹⁴ dates. Societies in the Archaeolithic ("old lithic"), like those of their Asian ancestors, did not have specialized tools. Their basic technique was to strike cobblestones, pebbles, or flakes a few times with a stone in order to obtain cutting edges or sharp angles. What resulted were large, clumsy tools with one or two worked faces that had multiple functions: scraping, scratching, cutting, mashing, and striking. Undoubtedly, people of this period also used objects made from hard fibers, hide, bone, and wood.

All of the Archaeolithic horizon is included in the latter part of the Pleistocene epoch. The area was colder and wetter at that time than at the present, with rain in areas that are now deserts. The lakes were bigger and deeper, and numerous rivers supported a multitude of grasslands where herds of horses, mastodons, camelids, bisons, and mammoths fed.

According to archaeologists such as José Luis Lorenzo and Lorena Mirambell, around 12,000 B.C. there were innovations in stone technology fundamental enough to justify establishing a new horizon, the Cenolithic ("new lithic"). To the Archaeolithic technique of hitting stone against stone were added percussion with softer objects of wood and stone, the use of an intermediary between the hammer and the stone (indirect percussion), and the use of pressure with stone chips to remove small flakes. These techniques produced smaller and more uniform objects for specific functions. Among the new objects were projectile points, knives, razors, and scrapers. The predominance of arrowheads during the Cenolithic leads archaeologists to suppose that humans spent a good deal of time hunting prey of all sizes, although they probably devoted a comparable amount of time to gathering food.

The Cenolithic horizon has been divided into two phases: the Lower Phase (12,000–7000 B.C.) and the Upper Phase (7000–5000 B.C.). Traces of the first phase have been found at more than forty sites in Mexico. Most of these materials have not been found in excavations but above ground. Typical artifacts of the Lower Cenolithic are leaf-shaped projec-

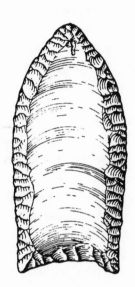
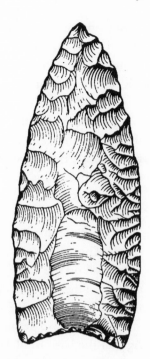

Fig. 1. Projectile points of the Lithic Age (Lower Cenolithic): (a) Folsom-type point; (b) Clovis-type point. (Drawing by Fernando Carrizosa Montfort)

tile points worked on both faces with grooves for a shaft (see fig. 1). Clovis-type points from four to twelve cm long are the most common. Their weight and size are congruent with their being spearheads launched by spear throwers. Bows and arrows were not introduced until much later and were not as widely dispersed as spear throwers.

The transition from the Pleistocene to the Holocene epoch corresponds to the boundary between the two phases of the Cenolithic horizon, because the change of the climate, flora, and fauna had a significant effect on the life of the hunter-gatherers. The end of the Pleistocene was characterized by increasing aridity, which eliminated many forests and extensive pastures as well as many of the large animals. Most sites of the Lithic Age, including shell mounds—permanent coastal settlements whose people lived by gathering and consuming shellfish—correspond with the Upper Cenolithic.

Societies in the Upper Cenolithic made much more delicate and varied tools than those of the earlier phase. The edges of projectile points were delicately reworked with soft burins to achieve sharper edges. Grooved or fluted points almost completely disappeared from artifacts made during this time. Among the new types were what we call Lerma foliated points, which have protrusions or wings at the bottom that allow a much more efficient hafting to a handle. Polished tools such as axes and grinding stones also appeared at this time. The use of these tools implies an increase in the consumption of seeds.

Given such limited remains, what can we know of the lives of these hunter-gatherers? The available archaeological information does not allow us to reconstruct the most basic aspects of these societies in any detail. There are only a few studies, such as that done by Richard S. MacNeish on the Valley of Tehuacán, that have attempted an in-depth analysis of the seasonal movements and exploitation of different ecosystems by these groups. For this reason, some scholars use ethnographic analogies to try to deduce the lifeways of hunter-gatherers in the Lithic Age on the basis of lifeways of hunter-gatherers who lived in different parts of the world less than a century ago. Those who make such hypothetical projections recognize the risks of overdrawn and hasty comparisons, but, if used with caution, such speculations can give us a richer picture of what life was probably like for the early hunter-gatherers.

Using this approach, we can assume that between 33,000 and 5000 B.C. humans in ancient Mexico lived in bands that rarely exceeded one hundred individuals. Internal relationships were based on kinship and the assumption of a common ancestor. Several bands formed alliances of as many as one thousand individuals who came together seasonally during periods of abundance or when conflict arose with other groups. These gatherings also facilitated the exchange of women, which was necessary because the small size of the bands gave no assurance that there would be an even number of males and females to form couples within each band. This interchange strengthened kinship ties. Apparently the societies were basically egalitarian, although—primarily in economic activities—there were differences based on sex and age. Thus, males went on sporadic but intense hunts, while women were more regularly but less strenuously occupied with food gathering. Children and old people performed auxiliary tasks.

Groups did not move randomly but in predetermined circuits. Existence was based on transhumance patterns, the group's movement depending on the season in order to make the maximum use of natural resources in the appropriate territories. In this life-style it was impossible to have many possessions; hunter-gatherers are generally characterized by their sparse and light baggage. The people lived in caves or under rock shelters or built homes of perishable materials. They preferred to set up camp in well-protected sites, with fresh water and basic supplies nearby from which they could reach different ecosystems, in order to reduce to a minimum the risks caused by variations in weather. As they moved, bands tried to avoid territories exploited by their neighbors.

While it is commonly thought that hunter-gatherers suffer constant hardships and spend a major part of the day obtaining food, this is far from the case. Ethnographic studies have shown that hunter-gatherers generally spend a few hours each day getting abundant food and that their diet is more diverse than that of agriculturalists.

The Transition to Sedentary Agriculture

Though it is not clear why, the lives of some hunter-gatherers in ancient Mexico began to change almost imperceptibly. The relationship between humans and their surrounding flora began to shift from one based on gathering to one based on agricultural production. This process has a dual historical significance. It is one of the great achievements of human evolution in Mexico as elsewhere, and it led to the three distinct cultural superareas of ancient Mexico. While some societies continued to develop within a hunter-gatherer economy, others began to change their subsistence basis, their social organization, and, presumably, their conception of the universe.

José Luis Lorenzo calls this long transition the Protoneolithic. Its chronological boundaries are diffuse, but it apparently began around 5000 B.C. and ended around 2500 B.C., the approximate date for the birth of Mesoamerica. Contrary to common belief, the slowness of the change is due to the enormous complexity of the process. Some think, mistakenly, that sedentariness and plant cultivation go hand-in-hand and that observing plant reproduction led humans first to cultivation and then to permanent settlement. Hunter-gatherers are generally quite familiar with the germination of plants, however, and those in ancient Mexico must have often intervened in the cycle of plant growth. Further, sendentariness is not unique to agriculturalists. Along the coasts of Mexico there are remains of early sedentary populations who depended primarily on collecting shellfish and left their remains in shell mounds. Other examples can be found in the lifeways of societies that inhabited the Basin of Mexico around 5000 B.C.. According to Christine Niederberger, a variety of rich adjacent ecosystems, including a lake, meant that inhabitants of the riverine site of Zohapilco did not have to move as the seasons changed. A diametrically opposite case can be seen in the hunter-gatherers who cultivated plants during their seasonal migrations. Kent V. Flannery and Joyce Marcus, for example, found the remains of a domesticated squash in a nomad shelter dating to about 8000 B.C. in Guilá Naquitz Cave.

In order to understand the Protoneolithic it is necessary to look at the steps that lead from simple cultivation to agriculture (see table 1). Cultivation implies a deliberate intervention in the plant cycle with the purpose of producing food. This action, repeated over many centuries, can lead to the domestication of plants; that is, to a genetic modification that benefits humans and makes plants dependent upon them. There are many advantages to the biologic transformation of plants: they yield more and better grains and fruits, they adapt to different climates and soils, they do not scatter grains when they are ripe, and parts of the plant that previously were not usable become so. At the same time, plants lose their capacity to reproduce and disperse naturally.

Societies can be defined as agricultural when they acquire a subsistence pattern in which the production and consumption of cultivated foods predominate. In short, agriculture is not just a technique but a way of living and thinking with its own disadvantages as well as advantages. Compared to hunter-gatherers, for example, early agricultural peoples put in more hours of daily work to acquire their food. Crops were vulnerable to the vagaries of weather. Even more important, the diminished number of cultivated plants contrasted with the variety in flavors and nutritional values provided by collected and captured species.

What, then, caused the gradual transition to agriculture? We still do not know, though many theories have been developed in an attempt to answer this question. Some theories emphasize social causes, others

Table 1. The Periods

Epoch	BP	AD/BC	Period	Sub-period		Description
HOLOCENE	Present		MESOAMERICA	POSTCLASSIC		INDEPENDENT MEXICO / COLONIAL ERA
	500 BP					SEDENTARY FARMERS
		AD		CLASSIC		
		BC		PRECLASSIC		
	4,500 BP	2500	PROTONEOLITHIC			HUNTER-GATHERERS WHO ALSO PLANT — DOMESTICATION OF MAIZE
	7,000 BP	5000	LITHIC	CENOLITHIC	UPPER	
	9,000 BP	7000			LOWER	
	14,000 BP	12,000		ARCHAEOLITHIC		HUNTER-GATHERERS
PLEISTOCENE	35,000 BP	33,000				ARRIVAL OF HUMANS

ecological changes leading to fewer available wild foods, and still others genetic mutations in plants such as those discussed above. The social cause most often cited is that of inexorable population growth. The population of ancient Mexico must have reached such a level that hunting and gathering were no longer sufficient to maintain it, forcing the adoption of agriculture. However, there are no indications of substantial population growth in Oaxaca or Tehuacán, for example, though there was a shift to agriculture there.

Most of the information we have about the Protoneolithic comes from four regions with long occupation sequences: the Valley of Tehuacán in Puebla (studied by MacNeish); the Sierra of Tamaulipas and the Sierra Madre southeast of Tamaulipas (also studied by MacNeish); the Valley of Oaxaca (studied by Flannery and Marcus); and the southern part of the Basin of Mexico (studied by Niederberger at Zohapilco). These investigations provide a fairly complete developmental picture of the Protoneolithic. During the 2,500 years of this horizon we see a gradual increase in population, as demonstrated by the number and size of settlements in each of the regions. Archaeological remains suggest that as time went by, the length of time that bands got together at the same places to form macrobands grew longer. Caves, camps, and shelters continued to be occupied for the duration of the Protoneolithic, but remains show that by 3000 B.C. there was a small semisubterranean house with an oval floor plan in the Tehuacán Valley.

Along the path toward sedentariness the importance of domesticated plants, as opposed to wild plants, increased. At first genetic changes, possibly related to human selection, occurred in the flora; later, slowly, the number of domesticated plants increased. A parallel process took place among animals, although on a much smaller scale and limited to the dog, the turkey, the macaw, the parakeet, and the bee.

As Emily McClung de Tapia points out, the botanical remains that document this transition are scarce and were found in only a few areas of the Mexican territory. Most of them are materials that were preserved in dry caves or in carbonized form in the subsoil. The species found are evidence of independent regional domestications rather than a single process of domestication, because the oldest cultigens in each of the four areas investigated are different. It is possible that the entire region was enriched by a diffusion of all the various cultivated species.

Remains of gourds and squash found in Mexico that date from the end of the Cenolithic indicate that they are two of the oldest cultivated plants in the New World. In time, different species of beans, maize, agave, nopal, *coyol* palm, manioc, tomato, avocado, amaranth, chile pepper, white zapote, black zapote, plum, and cotton were domesticated. Maize, the principal food of ancient Mexico, was domesticated between 5000 and 4000 B.C. New dating of maize remains in the Coxcatlán and Abejas Phases in Tehuacán places them at 3000 B.C. However, experts consider that this discrepancy with the earlier date is due to the late introduction of an already domesticated maize into Tehuacán.

The identity of the wild ancestor of maize has been debated for decades. The most solidly supported hypothesis at present is that *teocintle* (*Zea mexicana*) was the predecessor that mutated to produce maize (*Zea mays*). A large part of the high semiarid and semitropical area from Chihuahua to Guatemala has been proposed, at one time or another, as the place where maize was first domesticated. The similarity of maize to one of the races of teocintle called Chalco suggests that the place of origin was Central Mexico.

The transformation of life during the Protoneolithic was also reflected in the stone industry. Objects become smaller and more functional due to refined retouching and polishing. Carefully polished necklace beads, pipes, axes, and adzes from this age have been recovered. As in earlier times, plant fibers were used to make ropes, baskets, nets, and cloth.

A transcendental historical event, the invention of pottery, marks the end of the Protoneolithic.

ARIDAMERICA

In the northern regions of ancient Mexico, where the dry climate did not allow the Protoneolithic transformation to agriculture, hunter-gatherers continued their old way of life for thousands of years longer than was the case further to the south. Conventionally, the birth of Mesoamerica and Aridamerica is given as 2500 B.C., the time of the division between nomadic and agricultural societies. Two thousand years later, about 500 B.C., the vast Aridamerican territory shrank, probably due to encroachment by farmers coming from the south to the current territories of

Chihuahua, Sonora, New Mexico, and Arizona. Thus, a new cultural superarea, Oasisamerica, was created in the middle of Aridamerica.

Contacts between farmers and hunter-gatherers of the three super-areas were intense—sometimes peaceful, sometimes hostile. Often, complementary relationships developed between the two economic groups. This created wide and diffuse border areas in which groups with different social organizations coexisted, and in which communities with mixed economies and cultures developed. The borders themselves varied over time in response to changes in rainfall. The advances and retreats of the agriculturalists were roughly determined by fluctuations in the limits of two climate zones: BShw (dry, hot steppes with summer rains) and Cw (humid, temperate areas with summer rains).

European colonization had a drastic effect on the Aridamericans. The expansion of colonists that began in the sixteenth century meant that some nomadic groups were forced to become sedentary, others were driven to seek refuge in inhospitable areas, and yet others were pursued militarily and exterminated. The governments of Mexico and the United States would later continue these genocidal practices, declaring open warfare on remaining hunter-gatherers. Despite this, even at the beginning of the twentieth century nomadism had not completely disappeared from Mexico.

Paul Kirchhoff defined Aridamerica in 1954 as a cultural superarea whose societies lived mostly in arid and semiarid regions and whose livelihood was primarily based on plant gathering rather than hunting. He also included fishing peoples and incipient cultivators in this super-area. Based on these economic criteria, he distinguished Aridamericans from other nomadic societies in North America such as the expert hunters of the Plains, who depended primarily on the buffalo. Kirchhoff included nine areas in Aridamerica: Central California, Southern California, the Great Basin, Northwest Arizona, the Apache Region, Baja California, the Coast of Sonora and Sinaloa, North Mexico, and South Texas (see map 2).

We must point out that characterizing Aridamerica is problematic. Despite the fact that they have similar economies, the gathering societies of the arid and semiarid regions have very different cultural traditions. In contrast with the peoples of Mesoamerica, they did not maintain the permanent and intensive contact among themselves that would be

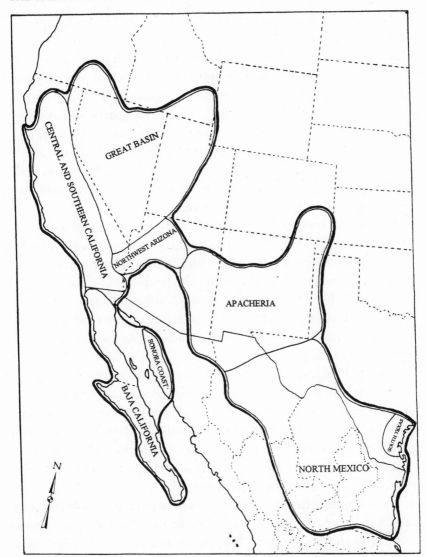

Map 2. Aridamerica and its cultural areas.

needed to develop a solid common culture. A complicating factor is that we know very little about many of these groups, such as the Coahuiltecans, the Tobosos, and the Mansos. Following Kirchhoff's work, little scientific debate about the concept of an Aridamerica cultural super-area has taken place. Works that critique, expand, or modify Kirchhoff's concept are practically nonexistent. Consequently, the model must be used with caution.

Aridamerica is a geographic mosaic. Even though aridity is its dominant feature, the landscape includes mountains, steppes, plateaus, deserts, and coastal areas. Generally, the vegetation fluctuates among short grasses, xerophytes, cacti, and conifers. The variety and availability of resources varies widely from one region to another. For example, in certain areas of California thick oak forests provided humans with acorns, whereas—as old documents attest—during hard times the inhabitants of the Coahuila desert were forced to eat dirt, wood, and deer excrement to appease their hunger.

Aridamerica bordered six other cultural superareas: to the south, the Mesoamerican civilizations; to the east, in a narrow strip, the peoples of the southeastern United States and, along a long corridor, the hunters of the prairies; to the north, the peoples of the Great Plains plateau and the fishing peoples of the Northwest Coast; and, in its center, the Oasisamerican farmers. Aridamerica had extensive coastlines on the Pacific and the Gulf of California but just a short stretch on the Gulf of Mexico.

The little information we have about the peoples of Aridamerica comes primarily from archaeology, descriptive colonial documents, and modern ethnographies. There have been few systematic archaeological digs, and the results of those excavations often have not been published. This problem is particularly acute in Mexico, where the study of the high cultures of Mesoamerica has been favored and that of the less developed northern groups neglected.

Historical records referring to Aridamericans are notably less accurate than those referring to Mesoamericans. There were enormous misunderstandings between Europeans and Natives, because most nomadic groups resisted the colonial domination that was forcing them to settle down and contacts were frequently limited to military engagements. When the Europeans forced the Indians into missions, presidios, or mines, they knew little of their previous nomadic existence. Missionaries, who are the source of much of our information about the Indians, were prejudiced against people who did not till the earth, did not have permanent settlements, and had few possessions. Their ethnographic descriptions were usually superficial, generalized, and vague. They lumped together societies with different economies and social organizations under the rubric of "savages" or "barbarians." Their scorn was even greater for the religion and ethics of these societies. It is not surprising that their reports emphasize the inferiority of the Natives or are limited to lists of names of groups that are difficult to identify today. In short, the information that we have about Aridamerica from documentary sources does not cover all the territory in a systematic or uniform way.

For the period after the Cenolithic, archaeology can provide cultural sequences for a number of regions of Aridamerica. The following information, for example, is available regarding sequences in northern Mexico, Baja California, and the Great Basin.

The ancient inhabitants of northern Mexico belonged to the so-called Desert Archaic Culture, which persisted with few significant changes for nine thousand years. The principal settlements of this culture were on the well-irrigated and relatively vegetation-rich inner slopes of the Sierra Madre Occidental. People migrated from camps on the slopes to the caves and shelters of the Highlands in search of seasonal harvests.

Other groups remained in the semidesert zones of the high plateau, where life was more difficult. Major sources of food for desert dwellers were agaves, cacti, mesquite, pine, oak trees, and many other plants that provided fruits, roots, seeds, and berries. Their consumption was made possible by the use of hand axes, flat grinding stones (metates), and stone hammers with which desert peoples cut and ground the tough plant fibers needed to make sandals, fishing and carrying nets, bags, and tumplines. At that time gourds were an important resource for transporting water.

The most important finds of hunting implements are in the high zones of the Sierra Madre. The scarcity of stone projectile points leads us to think that the people often used sticks with fire-hardened points. Two kinds of spear throwers have been found. Other techniques involved the use of long rods to probe the dens of rodents, clubs, and traps. By 2000 B.C. the use of bows and arrows changed hunting techniques fundamentally and provided greater resources.

Archaeological excavations in Coahuila allow us to divide the ancient history of this region into three complexes, though their exact dates are hard to determine. The first, the Ciénegas Complex, which extended from 8000 to 5000 B.C., is outside our time line. The second, the Coahuila Complex, extends from 7500 B.C. to A.D. 200. During this period, catastrophic arid climactic changes took place. These changes must have forced desert dwellers into specific responses, such as increasing the radius of their migrations and their use of long-fiber plants. Their settlements moved to the mouths of canyons and to sites next to alluvial plains. The Jora and Mayrán Complexes (A.D. 200–1500) vary from the previous complex in details of their artifacts, but there is a continuity in the practices employed.

Archaeological studies of Baja California divide the peninsula into three cultural zones. The northern zone was culturally linked to southwestern Arizona and the lower basin of the Colorado River. About A.D. 800 the Cocopas adopted agriculture and made ceramics. The central zone, which was the largest, corresponded to the Comondú Complex and included the central desert and the San Francisco and Giganta Sierras. The differing plant and animal life of the region was very favorable for hunters, gatherers, and fishermen. Metates and wooden hooks for the harvesting of *pitahaya* cactus (*Cereus* sp.) are proof of the consumption of fruits and seeds. Objects made from tough fibers—primarily baskets and sandals—were found, as were tubular stone pipes and boards with drawings that, by analogy, were attributed to ritual use.

The most distinctive characteristics of the central zone are its petroglyphs and rock paintings, for which more than 250 sites have been reported in the San Francisco Sierra. Most of the petroglyphs in this area are geometric, although there are some figures of animals (such as deer, lizards, and rabbits) and of humans (both full bodies and hands and feet). In contrast, the rock paintings are mostly naturalistic images of humans as well as of wild sheep, pumas, manta rays, whales, sea lions, and other animals. It is interesting to note that the animals are drawn in motion, while the humans are drawn in still poses. Men are painted longitudinally, half black and half red, which might be due to a dualistic conception of the human body. The team directed by María de la Luz Gutiérrez has obtained radiocarbon dates for Cueva Pintada, Baja California Sur, that range from 2350 B.C. to A.D. 1480, giving some indication of the astonishing antiquity of pictorial activity in the area.

The third Baja California cultural zone, lying at the southernmost region, is referred to as the Palmas Culture. This area also has great ecological diversity, including mountains, plains, and beaches, and has many petroglyphs. Wooden spear throwers, palm-bark containers, and bone spatulas were found in excavations there.

According to Jesse D. Jennings, the precontact history of the Great Basin cultural area can be divided into five major periods, two of which belong to the era we are discussing: the Middle Archaic (2000 B.C.–A.D. 500) and the Late Archaic (A.D. 500–1700). Generally, during these 3,700 years the area was inhabited by nomads who ate grass seeds, tubers, nuts, and fruits as well as the local animals, large and small. They were peoples who lacked domesticated animals, permanent settlements, and horticulture. Nevertheless, after A.D. 400 in the eastern half and southwest of the Great Basin, centered in Utah, the gatherers modified their economy in the direction of a more or less sedentary agriculture, resulting in the Fremont Culture. Even though the Fremont Culture never attained the complexity of its southern neighbors due to the scarcity of resources in the area, it is almost certain that they were stimulated to change by Anasazis from Oasisamerica. The Fremont Culture ended about A.D. 1300, perhaps due to a change in climate, and subsequently throughout the region there was a return to the characteristic subsistence techniques of Aridamerica. Even though we know they are flawed, most information about the societies of Aridamerica is found in documents from the time of first contact with Europeans. In our discussions that follow, we will broadly use the area categories proposed by Kirchhoff.

Central and Southern California Area

The central and southern parts of what we now call California were exceptionally rich in natural resources. This extensive territory, which had a high population density in comparison to the rest of Aridamerica, was inhabited by societies with very different origins who spoke about one hundred distinct languages. Each group occupied a specific area and engaged in a particular enterprise, making possible a peaceful coexistence based on an intense trade of small shell disks and snail columela that were used as media of exchange. For example, among the Yuroks and Hupas the accumulation of wealth was the basis of an individual's social rank. Both slavery and social stratification existed among the Yuroks and Hupas.

Natives of this area did not prosper through agriculture but by their magnificent adaptation to their environment. Acorns were their principal sustenance. In order to use them, and particularly to eliminate the acorns' high tannic-acid content, they used a leaching process that included grinding, washing, drying, and roasting. The flour that was produced was used to make porridge and bread. The Indians also made syrup from the sap of the sugar pine. They caught large quantities of fish and marine mammals off the Pacific coast. The Chumash Indians went to sea in wooden boats, which were quite different from the reed boats they used in lakes and rivers. During the winter the people stopped moving around and settled in hamlets composed of huts made from perishable materials. Three to thirty hamlets made up what specialists have called a "tribelet", a social unit that occupied the same territory under the limited rule of a chief.

Basketry is the distinctive mark of these societies. It is said that no people have ever attained the mastery of basket weaving achieved by the California Indians. The fine creations of the Pomos stand out particularly, including baskets made with thin fibers adorned with beads and the feathers of hummingbirds, woodpeckers, and other birds.

As a part of their religious practices, the old inhabitants of Central and Southern California, like some of their neighbors, communed with their deities through visions often produced by consuming jimson weed (*Datura stramonium*). Their complex mythology featured the coyote as a trickster who caused the evils and the imperfections of the world. Included in these intricate world views is the belief of the Gabrielinos that righteous humans, after death, became stars in the heavens.

Great Basin Area

East of the rich California soil beyond the Sierra Nevada lies the area known as the Great Basin, which can be distinguished by its paucity of resources. It is an arid territory unfit for cultivation. Its Numic-speaking inhabitants of the Middle and Late Archaic periods—Utes, Paiutes, and Shoshones among others—lived scattered among an almost interminable succession of mountains and valleys. The paucity of a vegetation composed of grass, brush, and small trees that were adapted to extreme and dry conditions allowed only small family groups to subsist. Because of this hostile environment, the Shoshones and Paiutes had a precarious existence. Thus, the Shoshones were known as the "root diggers." The primary occupation of the Great Basin was the harvest of pine nuts. In the autumn these and other seeds were collected and stored in caves and rock shelters where humans would later seek protection from the rigors of winter.

Although elk, bear, and bison could be hunted in the north and the east of the Great Basin, the normal prey of the rest of the territory were small game species such as prairie dogs, moles, birds, reptiles, and mice. Hunting techniques included poisoning arrows with rattlesnake venom, rotten entrails, and the sap of poisonous plants. There were also much simpler and more common techniques such as catching and roasting grasshoppers with fire "surrounds." Families joined together at propitious times such as antelope hunts. Tribes, in a political sense, did not exist; rather, people in this area lived in small groups, each claiming a piece of land as their territory.

Northwestern Arizona Area

In the northwestern corner of Arizona, southeast of the Great Basin, lived three peoples of the Yuman language family during the Middle and Late Archaic periods: the Havasupais, the Yavapais, and the Walapais. These peoples were geographically and culturally transitional, since they lived between the Great Basin and Oasisamerica. In a climate that resembled that of the Colorado Plateau, they practiced hunting-gathering during the winter and an incipient form of cultivation during the summer. Thus, during the cold months their diet relied on deer, antelope, and rabbit meat in addition to pine nuts, sunflower seeds, wild grasses, and cooked agave. During the hot months they lived on corn, beans, and squash. The culture of northwestern Arizona also had hybrid aspects. Their technology and artifacts are almost identical to those of the Paiutes of the Colorado Plateau. They were also slightly influenced by the Californian Indians and the Apaches.

Apache Area

At the end of the nineteenth century, in the states of Sonora, Chihuahua and Coahuila, the Apaches fought their final battles to defend their nomadic way of life from the Mexican army. Similarly, to the north in Arizona, New Mexico, Colorado, Oklahoma, and Texas, the government of the United States was pushing the Natives onto small reservations. The popular image of the Apaches is far from reality. Their warlike character was a late development due to pressure from the expansion of the Western world. Unlike the culture of the prairie tribes, the culture of the Apaches was not traditionally shaped by war. It is true that the Apaches were notorious for their raids, pillage, and skill in battle, but their tradition was not built upon war and the search for human trophies.

About A.D. 1300 the Apaches constituted a single linguistic group. They were Athapaskan peoples whose origin was far to the north in the Mackenzie River basin. Once they settled in the Southwest, they split into seven tribes: the Chiricahuas, Jicarillas, Kiowas, Mescaleros, Western Apaches, Lipans, and Navajos. With the exception of the Lipans, who lived in the great prairies, and the Navajos, who were incorporated into Oasisamerica, the Apaches generally hunted deer and antelope and gathered agave, yucca, mesquite, sunflower, and various grasses. Like many other Indian peoples, the Apaches were economically transformed by the acquisition of the horse in the seventeenth century. Traditionally, there was a division of labor based on gender. While the men spent most of their time hunting, the women gathered food, cared for the children, prepared the skins, made clothing, and built the homes. On the other hand men collected agave, while women hunted rabbits.

The basic social unit was the matrilocal extended family, each family living in home groups that differed depending on the locale. On the plains they lived in tepees, conical tents on poles covered with skins. In the Highlands they lived in wickiups, dome-shaped shelters made from branches and grasses. As in most hunter-gatherer societies, an Apache chief chosen for his personal characteristics had authority over the group. When the chief was no longer able to function due to age, another— not necessarily related—individual was chosen as his successor.

A number of ritual occasions marked the life of an Apache. A woman's reaching puberty was marked by the Dawn Dance. When a member of the community died, the corpse was taken to a distant place after careful funerary ceremonies to prevent the harmful return of the soul of the departed. The ritual launched the departed on a four-day journey to the netherworld in the north. The Apaches had a rich mythology. Two cultural heroes stand out, one associated with water and the other with fire and the sun. One of their best-known myths describes a ball game between beneficent and harmful animals. The outcome of the game was the defeat of perpetual darkness, producing the alternation of day and night.

Baja California Area

Anthropologists have long considered Baja California a cul-de-sac, successively penetrated from the north by the Pericús, Guaicuras, Cochimis, and other groups. The Pericús went through the entire peninsula and settled in the southern tip. The Guaicuras, who belonged to a different linguistic family than their predecessors, occupied territory to their north, from the Todos Los Santos River to the middle of the Sierra de la Giganta. The extensive Cochimi territory, including the San Pedro Mártir Sierra, began north of the Guaicuras' territory. The Cochimis spoke a language distantly related to the Yuman language spoken by Indians in what is today northwestern Arizona. The extreme north of the peninsula was occupied by groups such as the Paipais, the Kiliwas, the Kumiais, the Diegueños, and the Cocopas, all of whom also belonged to the Yuman linguistic family.

With the exception of the Cocopas, the Baja Californians were nonagriculturists, rather exploiting their environment as hunter-gatherers. Colonial missionaries and sailors describe people who went out onto the sea on rafts made of bundles of reeds to catch fish and aquatic mammals. They were surprised by the poverty of these almost naked men and women, who moved around carrying everything they owned: bows and arrows, wicker trays, bone awls, turtle-shell fishhooks, fire drills, tobacco, and agave fiber nets. The people also gathered pitahaya and hunted deer, rabbits, lizards, and snakes. They lived in settlements composed of a few temporary dwellings.

An interesting custom of these Native societies was the ceremony of redistribution of deerskins that had been obtained in the course of a year. The Cochimis celebrated this feast of *cabet* by putting down all the skins of the community like a carpet and then dividing them among the women, who were to make clothing from them. This group divided the year into six parts, characterized as much by different seasonal products as by particular religious feasts. One of the most widely diffused beliefs in Baja California was that an envoy from the celestial deity had come to earth to plant pitahayas, to arrange the estuaries, and to teach humans how to exploit their environment.

Sonora Coast Area

The Seris, who settled on the eastern shore of the Gulf of California (on the coast of the present state of Sonora) as well as in the islands of Tiburón and San Esteban, spoke a language that is purportedly a member of the Hokan-Coahuiltecan language family. This group is well known, not only through seventeenth-century documents but also from recent data, as they kept their nomadic habits until the 1950s. Their coastal desert habitat provided them with a rich variety of animal and plant species but, because of the absence of surface water, was not suitable for cultivation. Nevertheless, the Seris ate maize that they obtained by trading deerskins and salt with their farming neighbors. One of their key dietary items was the meat of the green sea turtle (*caguama*). The Seris, who were expert sailors, built rafts, pointed at both ends, from three bundles of reeds. They hunted and fished using bows up to two meters long and also made finely woven baskets called *coritas.*

Northern Mexico Area

The area known as North Mexico, the most complex of Kirchhoff's areas, is a wide corridor that includes the Mexican Plateau and the coastal Tamaulipas plains. It occupies the mostly semiarid territory of eleven modern-day states: New Mexico and Texas in the United States, and Chihuahua, Coahuila, Nuevo León, Tamaulipas, Durango, Zacatecas, Guanajuato, San Luis Potosí, and Querétaro in Mexico. Many indigenous groups lived in this enormous expanse, including the Janos, Cocomes, Sumas, Jumanos, Conchos, Coahuiltecans, Cacaxtes, Tobosos, Laguneros, Guachichils, Zacatecs, Guamares, and Pames. They differed in their economic life-styles, and their linguistic affiliations are unclear.

Thus, we find gatherers such as the Tobosos, hunters such as the Guachichils, sweet-water fishermen such as the Laguneros, incipient cultivators such as the Conchos, and more advanced cultivators such as the Sumas and the Jumanos.

It is important to mention that some of these groups are so little known that their membership in the Aridamerican culture is uncertain. Ignorance about the groups from northern Mexico led to their all being called "Chichimecs" by the Spanish from the beginning of the colonial era—a name that was also imprecise when it was used by the Mexicas to describe these peoples in prehispanic times. The term is still used to refer to peoples with different ethnicities, economies, and cultures who originated in this region.

Without attempting to generalize, we will mention some of the Chichimec customs described in colonial documents here. Most of the societies of the area were based on the gathering of plants, particularly, cactus, mesquite, agave, tubers, and yucca, which were the preferred foods. The pads, flowers, and fruit of the prickly-pear cactus were eaten, and—properly cut—cactus pads could be used to hold water. The juice of the prickly pear served as a substitute for water in dry times or places; cooked and fermented it yielded an alcoholic beverage. Mesquite pods, seeds included, were dried and ground to make flour, which was eaten as a powder or baked into bread rings that would keep for months. The agave was, without a doubt, the plant least wasted. When the agave pads or hearts were baked underground, they became a confection now called *mescal.* The cooked roots were also edible. The sap was drunk as mead, or as *pulque* when fermented. Cloth and ropes were made from its fibers, and needles from its thorns. Another plant, peyote, was not only consumed but also exported to Mesoamerica. Its hallucinogenic effects were used by the Chichimecs to forecast the outcome of battles. Although hunting deer was important, a larger part of the Chichimec diet consisted of rabbits, jackrabbits, squirrels, frogs, worms, quail, and—in the case of the Laguneros—fish and aquatic birds.

The Chichimecs were famous both before and after the Spanish conquest for their mastery of the bow and arrow, and it was they who introduced these weapons into Mesoamerica. They also used flint knives, *macanas* (war clubs), and slings. In hunting they used beaters, decoys, and men disguised with deer heads. When a hunting party caught a large animal, the hide was awarded to the hunter who had fired the fatal shot and then the meat was distributed among the families of all the participants. Even today, the Chichimecs are famous as experienced, cruel warriors. Colonial documents refer to poisoned arrows, hit-and-run raids, ambushes, the evisceration of captives, and the use of skull tops—war trophies that they used as drinking vessels. War produced a particular social structure. In peaceful times Chichimec bands were fragmented, but when interethnic or intergroup conflict arose, the bands united in federations under a single commander.

We have vague notions about the religious ideas of these societies. We know, for example, that they worshipped the stars, mountains, caves, trees, and animals. Apparently, they did not generally make images of their gods. Their therapeutic practices included letting blood as well as cautery to diminish pain in affected members. Because of their proximity to Mesoamerica, northern Mexican hunter-gatherers had multiple interchange relationships, which led to mutual cultural influences. The northern peoples traded hides, turquoise, and peyote for grains, ceramics, textiles, metals, and adornments from the south.

Southern Texas Area

The last area listed by Kirchhoff is southern Texas, a territory covered by swamps and estuaries full of lotuses, bamboos, legumes, oysters, turtles, fish, porpoises, alligators, deer, bisons, and peccaries. In this fertile setting the Karankawas moved from one camp to another in rhythm with the seasons. Álvar Núñez Cabeza de Vaca, who knew the Karankawas well, relates that in the fall they ate aquatic roots; in the winter, when the roots hardened, they moved to areas full of mollusks; and later yet they moved their camps to places where blackberries had ripened. Some of the customs of this group included the domestication of mute dogs, making of ceramics covered with bitumen, rule by two chiefs (one for peace and one for war), and easy acceptance of homosexual relationships.

OASISAMERICA

Oasisamerica, the last of the three cultural superareas to develop in prehispanic Mexico, began two thousand years after the split between Mesoamerica and Aridamerica, or about A.D. 500 (see map 3). As we

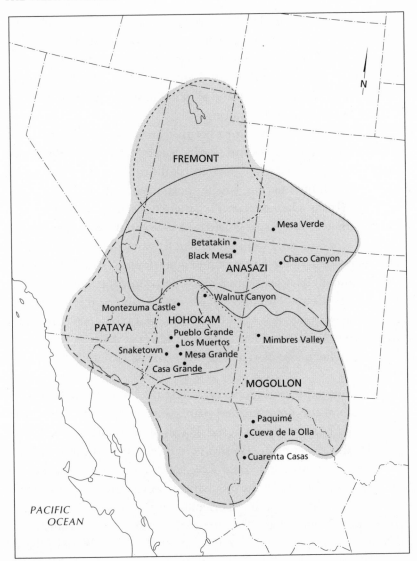

Map 3. Oasisamerica and its cultural areas.

mentioned above, some Aridamerican peoples used cultivation as a
supplementary activity. Many of those belonging to the so-called Desert
Culture were increasingly and more dependent on cultivated plants,
ultimately becoming true agriculturalists. These nascent societies differed

from Mesoamericans in that they lived in an arid environment where successful crops were primarily assured in oases or irrigated locales. The need to construct irrigation systems meant that the expansion of Oasisamerica was gradual and difficult. Some groups adopted this subsistence mode as late as A.D. 600, and all of them still supplemented their economy by hunting and gathering.

At its maximum Oasisamerica occupied what is now known as the southwestern United States and northwestern Mexico, including most of Utah, Arizona, and New Mexico; significant parts of Colorado, Sonora, and Chihuahua; and smaller portions of California, Baja California, and Texas. Oasisamerican is generally a semiarid territory with a harsh climate. Rain is sparse and comes, torrentially, during only a few months of the year. Kirchhoff named this area on the basis of a few oases where some of the larger populations dwelt.

Excavations at Bat Cave, New Mexico, recovered the oldest evidence for maize (pre-chapalote) and squash in Oasisamerica. However, the dating of these remains is quite uncertain, and scholars debate dates ranging from 3500 to 1500 B.C. In upper levels of this site, remains of chapalote, naltel maize, and teosinte dated as older than 500 B.C. were found.

These finds led to arguments regarding the endogenous or exogenous source of the domesticated plants and of agriculture in Oasisamerica. Today, most experts agree that all of the domesticated plants except for the tepary bean (*Phaseolus acutifolius*) were introduced from Mesoamerica. It is also generally accepted that agriculture itself came from the south. Essentially, the only explanation for an abrupt transition from no agriculture to complex agriculture with extensive canal systems is an imported technology. The proposed route of the transmission is the long strip of sedentary societies that inhabited the Western Sierra Madre. Scholars hypothesize that pottery making moved along the same route. Although there is no Mesoamerican prototype for the oldest Oasisamerican ceramics, which date to 300 B.C., it is probable that they derived from the cultures of Zacatecas and Durango.

Despite the probable diffusion of domesticated plants, agriculture, and ceramics from Mesoamerica, over the centuries the societies of Oasisamerica acquired their own characteristics. Great cultures like the Anasazi, the Mogollon, and the Hohokam imprinted a particular pattern on the arid northern landscape by their systems for water and erosion control. Canals, terraces, dams, and ridges transformed the desert. Settlements with multifamily, multistory dwellings arose in the valleys, the plateaus, and the cliffs. At that time extensive roads linked the centers of power with their dependencies.

From A.D. 500 until the collapse of its large centers, Oasisamerica increased its interchanges with the distant Mesoamerican societies. It is likely that the principal contacts to the south were with the peoples of Guanajuato, Michoacán, Jalisco, and Nayarit. The relationship between these two superareas was fundamentally one of trade, as evidenced by the presence of copper hawk bells, pyrite mosaics, and macaw skeletons in Oasisamerica and of the prized northern turquoise in Mesoamerica. Mesoamerican religious traditions came to Oasisamerica along with trade, as shown by the proliferation of ritual mounds and ball courts. Despite the reciprocal influences, the northern cultures always remained autonomous and vigorous.

To a great extent their uniqueness was maintained by the enormous distance between the nuclei of both cultural superareas and the presence of groups between them that did not achieve the complexity of either their northern or their southern neighbors. This has created difficulties for specialists who attempt to delineate precisely the borders between Mesoamerica and Oasisamerica. The succession of farming peoples along the Western Sierra Madre such as the Huichols, Coras, Tepehuans, and Tarahumaras reflects the long transition between the two superareas. On the other hand, the Oasisamericans had intense and frequent contacts with their hunter-gatherer neighbors. As we discussed above, the zones bordering Aridamerica were inhabited by societies with intermediate cultures and economies.

Oasisamerica became a historical unit in its own right. The coexistence of centuries-old societies with different levels of development resulted in a basically homogeneous culture, but one with distinct regional characteristics and different areas with oscillating borders. Around the first century A.D., the agricultural societies that had emerged from the Desert Culture began to differentiate. In 1954 Paul Kirchhoff proposed the division of Oasisamerica into seven areas, based on the sixteenth-century historical record: (1) Tanoan-speaking Pueblos; (2) other Pueblos (Hopi, Zuni, Keres, and Jémez); (3) Navajo; (4) Cahita;

(5) Tohono O'Odham; (6) Tarahumara; and (7) River Yuman. More recently, first- to sixteenth-century Oasisamericans have been grouped in five areas: Anasazi (Kirchoff's areas 1, 2, and 3); Hohokam (Kirchhoff's area 5 minus Ópata); Mogollon (Kirchhoff's areas 4 and 6 and Ópata); Pataya (Kirchhoff's area 7); and Fremont.

Anasazi Area

The most complex societies of Oasisamerica flourished in the Four Corners area where the states of Utah, Colorado, Arizona, and New Mexico meet. Low juniper forests help to give this stark but beautiful region a distinct appearance. Its inhabitants depended for centuries on their ability to store products, because plants were scarce between April and November.

The Anasazi Area is, without a doubt, the most-studied area in the United States. The intense excavations carried out over a century there allow us to divide its contact history accurately into three Basketmaker and four Pueblo phases. The societies of the three Basketmaker phases, which came from the Desert Culture, are characterized by their mixed economy and for making the fine baskets that they used instead of pottery. The transition between nomadic life and a life of sedentary agriculture based on corn, which had been introduced in 750 B.C., took place in Basketmaker Phase I (prior to 100 B.C.). During Phase II (100 B.C. to A.D. 400) most of the inhabitants lived in caves, shelters, and promontories, while in Phase III (A.D. 400–700) they lived in complexes of three to four semisubterranean houses with circular ground plans.

The Pueblo period begins in A.D. 700 with the first pottery making. The Anasazis differed from the peoples of neighboring areas because of the predominance of vessels with red or white bottoms and black geometric patterns or images. The four phases of the Pueblo period are: Phase I (A.D. 700–900), characterized by irrigation agriculture and the replacement of subterranean houses by aboveground stone houses; Phase II (A.D. 900–1100), characterized by large multifamily dwellings with several levels, some of which were built on cliffs; Phase III (A.D. 1100–1300), in which the society achieved its maximum expansion of agriculture and its network of regional roads; and Phase IV (A.D. 1300–1540), in which, after the heights reached in the two previous phases, the

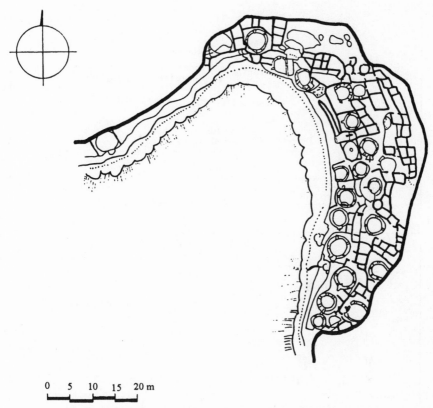

0   5   10   15   20 m

Plan 1. Cliff Palace Archaeological Zone, Colorado. Anasazi Area, Oasis-america. (Based on Fewkes)

system shrank, the large sites were abandoned, and—in some places—people returned to a hunter-gatherer life-style.

Mesa Verde in southwestern Colorado and Chaco Canyon in northwestern New Mexico were the two areas with highest population at the height of the Anasazi culture (see map 4). Mesa Verde includes sites such as Fair View House, Big Juniper House, Badger House, Mug House, and Cliff Palace (see plan 1). Cliff Palace, built in the ample rocky shelter of a cliff to relieve its inhabitants from the threat of enemy attacks, is considered the most important site. Calculations show that the complex housed more than four hundred inhabitants in more than two hundred rooms. It also has numerous granaries and twenty-three subterranean

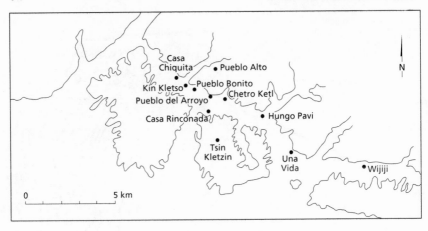

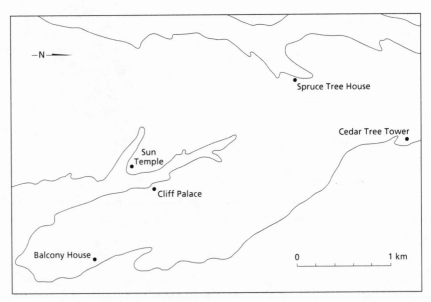

Map 4. Chaco Canyon and Mesa Verde.

chambers, which have been called *kivas* because of their similarity to
the ceremonial chambers of present-day Indian pueblos.

Chaco Canyon includes the closely spaced sites of Casa Rinconada,
Pueblo Alto, Chetro Ketl, Una Vida, Half House, and Pueblo Bonito.
These and numerous other sites were interconnected by an impressive
network of roads that facilitated communication between the large sites

and their satellites. Pueblo Bonito is Chaco Canyon's most impressive architectural complex. This urban nucleus seems to have dominated the entire region between A.D. 950 and 1150. Despite a long-held belief, the main building in Pueblo Bonito was not built room by room over the years. Its complex semicircular design reflects four great building phases that followed strict patterns based on cosmological conceptions. This walled complex has more than 650 rooms distributed in five stepped levels. The architecture of the building, like that of many others at Chaco Canyon, is characterized by the use of rock slabs, low doors, multiple windows, balconies, storage cellars, and large kivas. The size of Pueblo Bonito implies the presence of a large number of people organized by a dominant elite. The magnitude of the project can be demonstrated by the fact that it required beams from 215,000 pines for its floors and roofs, the wood having to be transported from forests that were eighty kilometers away. The size of many settlements in the Chaco Canyon, the length of the irrigation canals, and the extensive network of roads have led scholars to believe that the people of Chaco Canyon belonged to a stratified society, perhaps organized as a chiefdom. This hypothesis is supported by the discovery of sumptuary goods in places such as Pueblo Bonito. Pyrite mirrors, parrots, and pseudocloisonné ceramics from Mesoamerica are evidence of an elite who imported rich products from regions thousands of kilometers to their south.

We do not know the reason for a decadence that occurred in Anasazi societies. The most widely held of the many theories attempting to explain Anasazi decadence attributes it to a long drought that lasted from A.D. 1276 to 1299. It is not clear what took place after this time. It is possible that the Pueblo Indians met by the Spanish in the sixteenth century were the descendants of the Anasazis.

When the Spanish arrived, the Pueblo Indians were not a single linguistic unit. The Zunis were a linguistic isolate; the Hopis belonged to the Uto-Aztecan family; the Tewas and Tiwas were members of the Tanoan family; the inhabitants of Acoma, Zia, and Cochiti Pueblos were Keresans; and the Navajos were Athapaskans. Many of these peoples shared the fertile lands of the Upper Rio Grande, a zone where, like their predecessors, they planted maize, made exceptional ceramics, and built multiroom communal houses.

One of the best-studied aspects of the Pueblos' daily life is their religion, whose principles, literature, and principal rituals are still in force today. Primarily agricultural in character, this religion exalts fertility gods. The supernatural figures of the Pueblo cosmo-vision—which are associated with crops, rain, and hunting—assume the form of kachinas, characters that emerged on the earth's surface from an opening at the center of the world (*sipapu*) at the moment of the creation of humans. The kachinas, believed to be life-giving spirits from whom all creatures of the universe derive, live in a prominent mountain in the west from which they come periodically to help humans. Kachinas such as Crow Mother, Earth God, Ripe Corn, Solstice, Long Ears, the ogre Stone Eater, and the humorous and incestuous Mud Head appear among the people both as living images portrayed by members of the community and as small polychrome wooden statues that are placed on the walls of houses. Pueblo religion is organized around fraternal secret societies that meet privately in the kivas. The Antelope and Snake Societies are appointed to bring rain, at Hopi pueblos through the famous Snake Dance, during which dancers hold live rattlesnakes between their teeth.

We do not know when the Athapaskan peoples reached the Four Corners area. Some of these hunters, the Navajos, converted to a semi-sedentary farming life after they came in contact with the Pueblo Indians, settling in canyons and on cliffs. Their principal contact with the Pueblos was for the purpose of trade in meat, salt, alum, and pelts. This permanent contact led them to adopt aspects of the agricultural religion, which they enriched with their own songs and sand paintings, both of which are still used for therapeutic purposes.

Hohokam Area

In contrast with the Anasazi Area, the Hohokam Area has been little studied. Although its borders shifted over the centuries, it developed mainly in Arizona at the heart of the Gila and Salado River basins, which cross the Sonoran Desert. The Hohokams dominated the semiarid desert regions like no other Oasisamerican civilization. The high temperatures, low humidity, and infrequent—though torrential—rains forced these farmers to canalize the Gila and Salado Rivers. Sometimes these channels were as much as ten km long, becoming deeper and narrower to hinder evaporation as time went by. Although the canalizing techniques required considerable communal effort, they were the means by which the people were able to raise two crops a year in a harsh ecology. Agricultural products were supplemented by pitahayas gathered in the summer and mesquite pods in the fall.

Some of the best-known Hohokam settlements are Snaketown, Casa Grande, Red Mountain, Roosevelt, Pueblo de los Muertos, and Valshni Village. The Hohokams are easily distinguishable from the neighboring Anasazi and Mogollon peoples by a predominance of Red-on-Brown pottery. They lived in villages composed of a few semisubterranean houses with elongated ground plans. Other distinctive archaeological markers include stone tablets for grinding pigments, axes with low notches for the haft, and adornments made from shell etched with an acid that was made by fermenting pitahayas. Most of these shells were imported from the coasts of the Gulf of California, worked by the Hohokams, and exported to the Anasazi and Mogollon Areas.

The origin of the Hohokams is controversial, and there is little agreement about events connected with these people before A.D. 600. While some investigators maintain that Snaketown, the most important site in the area, was begun in 300 B.C., others argue that this took place six hundred years later. It is not known how the Hohokam culture came to be. Some scholars believe that the culture was an endogenous development, although bearing some Mesoamerican influences; others propose that the Hohokams began with a direct migration from Mesoamerica. The latter explanation is more credible given the presence in 300 B.C. of a well-developed ceramic complex, irrigation canals, metates, and funerals involving cremation, none of which had local antecedents.

The Hohokam era is generally divided into five periods, including the Pioneer (300 B.C.–A.D. 550), Colonial (A.D. 550–900), Sedentary (A.D. 900–1100), and Classic (A.D. 1100–1450). The Classic period ended with the disappearance of the great centers of Hohokam power, due perhaps to disease, invasions by nomads, internal warfare, or climatic changes. An unexplained hiatus occurred between A.D. 1450 and the arrival of the Spanish in Arizona.

From the beginning, during the Pioneer period, the Hohokams built irrigation canals near their villages. Their houses were dug into the ground as a protection from the extreme climate. The peak of Hohokam

art and architecture was reached during the Colonial period, when relations with Mesoamerica increased. These contacts led to the Hohokams'
building large sites with ball courts (long, oval ball courts with midfield
markers) and platforms that supported religious structures. The copper
hawk bells and pyrite mosaics imported by the regional elites also came
from Mesoamerica. These facts suggest that, during the Colonial and
Sedentary periods, the Hohokams were organized into chiefdoms
composed of powerful centers and villages dependent upon them.
During the Classic period, the population was concentrated into denser
settlements characterized by multistory buildings. The best-known
example is the four-level Casa Grande.

Relationships with Mesoamerica diminished during the Classic period,
however, and by the time the first Europeans arrived in the Sonoran
Desert, the great Hohokam centers had disappeared. The region, called
Pimería Alta by the Spanish, was occupied by the presumed descendants
of the Hohokams, the Tohono O'Odhams, who spoke a Uto-Aztecan
language. These Piman people practiced seasonal agriculture. In winter
they lived on the high slopes next to permanent streams; in the summer
they moved to the plains between the mountains, where they farmed.
Success in this climate depended on the availability of water from the
mountain slopes, directed by dams. The Tohono O'Odhams, like the
ancient Hohokams, used the pitahaya to make jam, candy, mead, wine,
fruit, oil, and flour.

Mogollon Area

The Mogollon Area, bordering the area of the Hohokams, comprises
an immense territory that includes southeastern Arizona, southwestern
New Mexico, northern Chihuahua, and northeastern Sonora. The
Mogollons adapted better than any other Oasisamerican peoples to the
mountainous, pine-covered terrain; nevertheless, the maximum population densities during the peak period were in well-irrigated open
valleys.

The Mogollons are distinguished from their northern neighbors by
their tradition of burying their dead. Mogollon skeletons found by
archaeologists have been accompanied by the most beautiful ceramics
in Oasisamerica. Their quality has led to tomb robberies, because the

pieces are highly valued by American collectors. The predominant ware of these settlements is brown with red decorations.

At the Mimbres River in southwestern New Mexico, one of the most spectacular ceramic complexes of the prehispanic world developed. This complex, which was only made between the eighth and twelfth centuries, is important not only for its aesthetic worth but also for the ethnographic information contained in its designs. Almost all the pieces are white earthenware bowls with geometric decorations in black, but about a fifth of the total has figurative images that allude to both the supernatural and the natural world. The figures include mythical beings; masked animals; decapitations; warriors and priests; hunting and gathering scenes; fights against bears; and depictions of swimming, wagering, training parrots, making ceramics, and so forth.

Mogollon archaeology differs from archaeology of the two previously described areas in that there is no generally agreed upon chronology. Temporal sequences that have been suggested have been limited to specific regions or sites. Nevertheless, in order to simplify the general description of the Mogollons we will follow Paul S. Martin's proposal of two very long periods, an Early period (500 B.C.–A.D. 1000) and a Late period (A.D. 1000–1500).

During the fifteen hundred years of the Early period, the Mogollons settled on mesas, mountaintops, and mountain ridges, places that were safe from attack by neighboring hunter-gatherers. Usually, settlements in this period did not exceed fifteen semisubterranean houses, the houses having a rounded ground plan. Occasionally, the settlements included a kiva.

Beginning in A.D. 1000, Mogollon sites increased in number and complexity. It is very probable that during this Late period there was less conflict with nomadic peoples, because settlements were now built in places that were open and easy to reach, such as valleys that were well irrigated by rivers and streams. The population increase and the social stratification that characterize this period have been attributed to a greater efficiency in agricultural techniques, particularly the control of water.

In the first part of the Late period, the dwellings were still semisubterranean but with rectangular ground plans and of better quality. During the latter part of the Late period, the dwellings were larger and, perhaps due to Anasazi influence, built on the surface with rock or adobe walls. Like the buildings of Pueblo Bonito or Snaketown, they had more than four rooms, reaching five hundred in the case of Grasshopper Ruin. The average Mogollon village normally housed two hundred to three hundred inhabitants and had plazas and some kivas. After A.D. 1200, some regions were abandoned. Others, among them Grasshopper and Paquimé, continued to exist until the fourteenth or fifteenth century.

In the Mogollon Area in Mexico, one of the most impressive settlements of Oasisamerica, Paquimé—also called Casas Grandes—evolved (see plan 2). This city was built on the western plain of the present-day state of Chihuahua, adjacent to the Casas Grandes River. Its location contrasts with that of its presumed satellites, which were built in shelters or caves in the Sierra Madre Occidental. Their location in cliffs and their adobe construction are similar to the Anasazi Cliff Palace. Some of those including several rooms, silos, and watchtowers are Cuarenta Casas, Valle de las Cuevas, El Segundo, Cueva Grande, and El Potrero.

The ground-breaking work of Charles C. di Peso established the flowering of Paquimé at A.D. 1060–1340, but newer investigations have shifted it forward by several centuries to 1300–1450. The center of Paquimé contains the ruins of a large multifamily complex of at least four stories. Its walls—which today are severely eroded by wind or rain, in some cases reconstructed by archaeologists—were made of adobe enclosures. This resulted in solid one-piece adobe walls covered with a layer of lime that insulated the buildings' interiors from the extreme heat and cold of the desert. Some of the T-shaped doors of the complex remain, built so low that the inhabitants would have had to stoop to go from one room to another. This type of door is typical in Oasisamerica, but there are more of them at Paquimé than anywhere else. Life must have been pleasant in this complex, with its networks distributing drinking water, its stoves, and its granaries. The latter were large silos like the *cuezcomates* of Central Mexico, resembling huge pots with rounded bottoms.

Public ceremonies in Paquimé took place around the large multifamily dwelling, the ceremonial buildings being built around it. Many of the ceremonial buildings have peculiar shapes and unknown functions. The Cross Mound is one of the most interesting, not only because

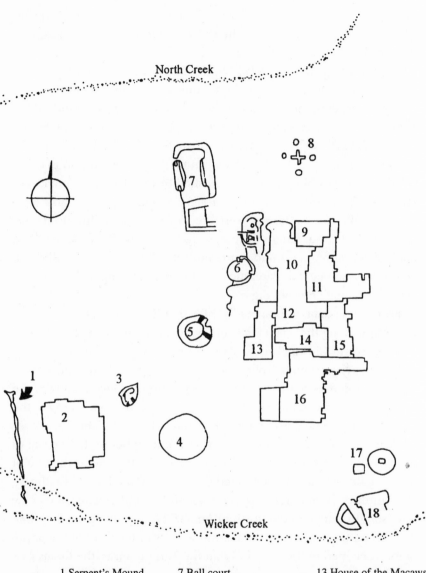

North Creek

Wicker Creek

0 30 m	1 Serpent's Mound	7 Ball court	13 House of the Macaws
	2 House of the Serpent	8 Mound of the Cross	14 House of the Dead
	3 Bird's Mound	9 Housing Unit of the North	15 House of the Skulls
	4 Reservoir	10 Main Plaza	16 House of the Pillars
	5 Heroes Mound	11 House of the Well	17 House of the God
	6 Reservoir	12 Marketplace	18 Ball court

Plan 2. Paquimé Archaeological Zone, Chihuahua. Mogollón Area, Oasis-america. (Based on C. DiPeso)

of its shape but also because of the astronomical orientation of its arms. The two ball courts found on the site also undoubtedly had religious functions.

In excavations in the 1960s, Charles Di Peso discovered Paquimé's commercial trademark. More than 4 million *Nassarius* shells obtained from the shores of the Gulf of California, more than three hundred km away, were excavated in the structured called Casa de la Noria ("House of the Waterwheel"). Mesoamerican pyrite mirrors and pseudocloisonné ceramics as well as New Mexican turquoise were found in other buildings. Archaeologists were astonished by the abundant remains of macaws of the *Ara macao* and *Ara militaris* species, which also have remote origins but in this case were bred locally. The five hundred specimens found so far range from eggs to old birds. Remarkably, even adobe birdcages were found in the multifamily complex. Metallic artifacts were also made in Paquimé, the presence of copper slag offering evidence of ancient smelting ovens.

From these data one can easily infer that Paquimé was a great trading center along the 5,600 km route between the high Central Plateau of Mexico and Chaco Canyon. At one time it was thought that Chaco Canyon had been run by Toltec merchants; however, there is no archaeological evidence whatsoever to support its dependence on any of the great Mesoamerican metropolises. Furthermore, the new dating of the apogee of Paquimé places it after Tula but before Tenochtitlan.

Paquimé and the last Mogollon sites fell long before the arrival of the Spanish. We are not sure of the cause of the decline or the fate of their inhabitants, but it is suspected that they migrated to the southeast, the Mimbres population settling in Coahuila. Other emigrants may have sought refuge to the north in Anasazi lands, some from Paquimé possibly joining the Zunis. What is more likely is that most of the population remained in the area and that the Tarahumaras, the Ópatas, or the Cahitas are their descendants.

The Tarahumaras today live in southwestern Chihuahua, inhabiting the most rugged terrain of the Sierra Madre Occidental, from the high pine forests to the subtropical bottoms of the canyons. They live in settlements composed sometimes of huts, sometimes of caves. The territory of the warlike Ópatas is quite different, including the narrow and fertile valleys of the center and east of Sonora. Like the Tarahumaras and the Ópatas, the Cahitas belong to the Uto-Aztecan linguistic family. The best-known Cahita groups are the Yaquis and the Mayos. They range from Arizona to Sinaloa, using fertile floodplains for planting and rivers and coasts for fishing.

Fremont Area

Between A.D. 400 and 1300, Aridamerica had a peripheral branch in the present-day state of Utah. This branch is known as the Fremont Area. According to several scholars, the societies of the Fremont Area were a northern product of the Anasazi Culture that, due to the rugged environment and contact with hunter-gatherers of the Great Basin, were never able to achieve the level of prosperity of the societies of Chaco Canyon and Mesa Verde. Other investigators maintain that the peoples of the Fremont Area possibly descended from Athapaskan bison hunters who arrived in the territory about A.D. 500. As time went by, they adopted the ceramics and the horticulture of the Anasazis with some modifications, fusing the nomadic cultures of the prairies with those of Oasisamerica. The Anasazi influence is clear, for example, in their semisubterranean masonry dwellings. The Fremont Culture began to decline by A.D. 950, shrank dramatically by A.D. 1150, and disappeared completely 150 years later. Apparently, the Uto-Aztecan-speaking Shoshones are the descendants of the Fremont Area peoples.

Pataya Area

Another area on the periphery of Oasisamerica is Pataya, located in southeastern California, western Arizona, northern Baja California, and northwestern Sonora. Almost the entire region is a succession of mountains and basins that feed the Colorado River, which is the principal water source in this desert ecosystem with extreme temperatures.

The ancient inhabitants of the area were influenced by the Hohokams, from whom, beginning in A.D. 500, they learned agriculture, pottery making, the ball game, and cremation of the dead; nevertheless, they never established large pueblos or permanent settlements. The Pataya peoples followed a seminomadic pattern, living for short periods of time in huts made of perishable materials. They faded between A.D. 1300 and 1400. In the sixteenth century the territory was occupied by the River Yumans, who still cultivated the alluvial plains of the Colorado and Gila Rivers. Like the Ópatas, the River Yumans were noted for their bellicosity and their strong tribal cohesion.

MESOAMERICA

From the earliest colonial times the cultural unity of the vanquished peoples of Mesoamerica was evident to outsiders. In the sixteenth-century *Apologética historia sumaria*, Friar Bartolomé de las Casas described the similarity of the beliefs of the Guatemalans to those of other peoples we now call Mesoamerican. Referring to Guatemala, he said, "All this land and that which properly belongs to New Spain must have had, more or less, one religion and kind of gods which extended down to the provinces of Nicaragua and Honduras and [on the other side] toward Xalisco it reached, I believe, the province of Colima and Culiacán." Evidently, the Indian societies of this huge territory were a single unit.

Las Casas's comments about the unity of the Indians' religious beliefs can be applied to all areas of their thought and action, and, indeed, that is the prevalent view of Mesoamerican culture among scholars today. In the early twentieth century, scholars of the caliber of Miguel Othón de Mendizábal, Clark Wissler, Alfred L. Kroeber, and Wigberto Jiménez Moreno defined the spatial limits of such cultural affinity, articulated some of the concepts in order to allow more precision in the future, and laid down some of the bases for debate on the subject. Simultaneously, anthropology was sharpening its theoretical tools to attack similar questions at the hemispheric level. These included Herbert Spinden's concept of *cultural horizon,* Wissler's concept of *cultural area,* Kroeber's concept of *cultural trait,* and concepts such as that of *cultural complex.*

In view of the perceived need to join these theoretical concepts both to each other and to concrete facts about the prehispanic Mesoamerican cultures, the International Committee for the Study of Cultural Distribution in America was set up as the aftermath to the 27th International Congress of Americanists (1939). This committee delegated the issue of the southern half of Mexico and the western part of Central America to the distinguished anthropologist Paul Kirchhoff. Kirchhoff began his task by identifying the cultural superarea of Mesoamerica and naming its societies as "higher agriculturalists." Noting that these societies were linguistically diverse, he divided them into five groups, one of which was those with unclassified languages. He defined the Mesoamerican territory occupied when the Spanish arrived as an area limited on the north by the Sinaloa, Lerma, and Pánuco Rivers and on the south by a belt that went from the Motagua River to the Gulf of Nicoya, passing through Lake Nicaragua (see map 5). Based on Jiménez Moreno's historical ideas, Kirchhoff said that the superarea had been formed by different migrants who had entered the territory of Mesoamerica at various times and had thereafter been united by a common history.

Kirchhoff compared Mesoamerica with the other American super-areas (the southeastern and southwestern United States, Chibcha, the Andes, and Amazonia), looking for the presence or absence of traits that would culturally distinguish them. He produced a table listing traits that were exclusive to or at least typically Mesoamerican; traits that were common to Mesoamerica and other American superareas; and traits that were significantly absent in Mesoamerica. One example of an exclusively Mesoamerican trait was that of a year composed of eighteen 20-day months with an additional 5 days and the combination of twenty day signs with thirteen numbers, making a period of 260 days. Kirchhoff created subgroups with common traits: all the superareas cultivated the maize/bean/squash triad, while a clan social organization of the *calpulli-ayllu* type only included Mesoamerica and the Andes. Matrilineal clans and poisoned weapons were found in other superareas but were absent in ancient Mesoamerica.

Kirchhoff's ideas appeared in 1943 in a short article that was republished in 1960 and 1967. On many occasions Kirchhoff asked colleagues for constructive criticism, and he was repeatedly disappointed: "I conceived this study as the first of a series of investigations that would successively deal with these problems anticipating that much of this labor would be done by others. This hope was fruitless because although many have accepted the `Mesoamerica' concept, no one, to my knowledge has critiqued it constructively or developed it systematically."

However, even though Kirchhoff's proposals were not soon critiqued, his work was followed by a number of valuable contributions, including those of Pedro Armillas, who tried to unite the concept of Mesoamerica with the idea of socioeconomic formation to create a new, dynamic concept. Other theories influenced by Kirchhoff include Jiménez Moreno's

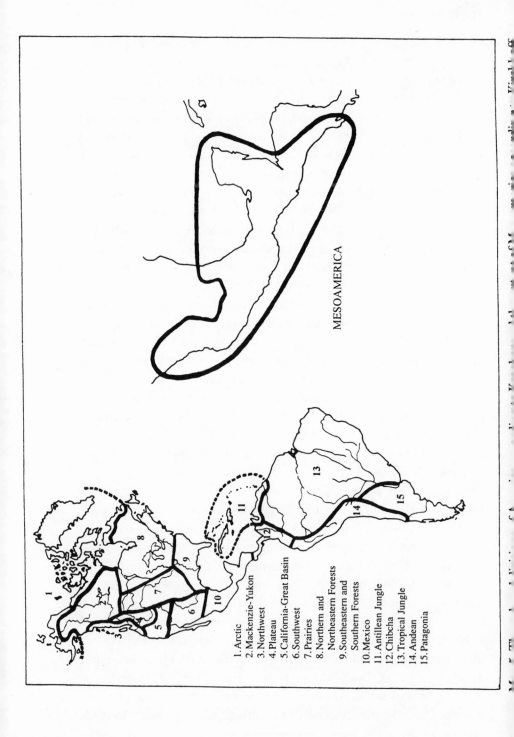

hypothesis of a dialectical relationship between the coast and the High Plateau as the dynamic force explaining the superarea; Ángel Palerm and Eric. R. Wolf's insistence that all the key areas in Mesoamerica had cultivated terraces; and Gordon R. Willey's conception of the superarea as representing a transformation from a village-agricultural culture to an urban culture.

It would be too time-consuming to describe in detail where this debate is today. Many scholars have participated in the theoretical discussion through the years. We will only mention a few, without an extensive description of their contributions. In 1968, for example, Kent V. Flannery emphasized environmental factors, pointing out that a key factor in forming the superarea was the development of a complex arrangement of subsystems composed of societies adapted to specific microenvironments. Also in 1968, William T. Sanders and Barbara J. Price referred to a single, unique Mesoamerican culture, which is manifested synchronically as a cultural area and diachronically as a cotradition. Sanders and Price focused on the sequence in which Mesoamerican social systems developed (bands, tribes, chiefdoms, and civilizations) as the basis for an evolutionary and ecological interpretation. In 1975 Jaime Litvak King highlighted the role of interethnic exchange in the formation of Mesoamerica. This process included establishing a web of normal relationships in an ever-changing balance of different ecozones. Litvak King argued that this involved the simultaneous interaction of different processes involving local, intermediate, and regional forces (ecological, technological, and economic-political) as well as general ones (interethnic and interregional exchanges).

In 1982 Eduardo Matos Moctezuma argued that Mesoamerica is synonymous with a mode of production that existed from the time of the Olmecs and expanded to reach Kirchhoff's territorial limits by the sixteenth century. In this mode of production, based on agriculture and tribute, a double exploitation occurred—the exploitation of one class by another in the same society and of the ruling class over the tributary states. Other models, such as the "world-systems model," were used in the 1980s to try to explain the extremely complex reality of Mesoamerica. Other interesting explanations were presented at the 19th Round Table of the Mexican Anthropological Society, which met in Querétaro in 1985 for the purpose of discussing problems with the concept of Mesoamerica. During the meeting Anne Chapman proposed that the concept of a Mesoamerican superarea should be based on its being either a high culture or a civilization based on two levels—those of society and culture. Chapman argued that the process should begin with the societies of the sixteenth century, because more abundant and intricate information is available about them. The model would then be applied retrospectively to earlier Mesoamerican societies, which arrived at a common identity despite following different paths.

Critiques of Kirchhoff's specific proposal, though delayed, have been very useful in continuing the debate about the theoretical validity of his concept. Other scholars, such as Eduardo Matos Moctezuma and Enrique Nalda, wrote voluminously on this topic years before the 1985 Querétaro Round Table. Some of Kirchhoff's key points were questioned through the years. For example, critics pointed out that the process of classifying by cultural traits itself denatures a culture, because it dismembers its elements as if these were not integrally linked within social systems. Kirchhoff was criticized because he did not systematically choose the defining traits he used or rank them in importance. It was also argued that these traits belonged only to particular areas and that, thus, the result did not reflect a dynamic cultural superarea but only the particular instant of its existence at the eve of the conquest. Despite these criticisms, the Round Table concluded that Kirchhoff's concept has been of immense use in the study of the Mesoamerican superarea and that, despite some obsolescence, it could be reconstituted on a firmer basis.

The reformulation of the concept is an ongoing challenge for Mesoamericanists. Mesoamerica was a historical reality produced by very different interrelationships (economic interchanges, politics, religion, war) that produced different kinds of systems. A new concept of Mesoamerica must, among other things, deal with the causal links that brought societies into the system; the cohesive links that allowed them, once they were a part of the system, to remain permanently tied to it; and the structural links that explained their behavior as components of this complex system.

Peoples, Periods, and Territories

What faces someone wanting to approach this problem from a theoretical viewpoint? The issues are extremely complex. Contributing to

this complexity are: (1) the diverse societies that joined in this historical process over thousands of years; (2) the different paths that they
followed in their development; (3) the extent of the social and political
transformations that took place; and (4) the length of time and size of
the territory involved. As Kirchhoff pointed out, the diversity of the societies of Mesoamerica derives from their origin, because they arrived at
this superarea at very different times and spoke very different languages
(see map 6). Mesoamericans include sixteen different linguistic families, some of which have numerous languages while others have only
one. These linguistic families are:

1. Hokan-Coahuiltecan (Tequistlatec or Oaxacan Chontal)
2. Chinantec (Chinantec)
3. Oto-Pame (Otomí, Mazahua, Matlatzinca, Ocuiltec, Matlame)
4. Oaxacan (Zapotec, Mixtec, Mazatec, Chatino, Papabuco, Cuicatec, Trique, Amuzgo, Popoloca, Ixcatec)
5. Manguean (Chiapanec, Chorotega, Dirián, Maribio, Oritiña,
   Nagranda)
6. Huave (Huave)
7. Tlapanec (Tlapanec, Subtiaba)
8. Totonac (Totonac, Tepehua)
9. Mixe (Mixe, Zoque, Popoluca)
10. Maya (Huastec, Cotoque, Yucatec, Lacandón, Mopán, Chol,
    Chontal, Tzeltal, Tzotzil, Tojolabal, Mam, Kanjobal, Chuj, Kekchí,
    Pokomchí, Ixil, Quiché, Cakchiquel, Pokomam, Rabinal, Tzu-
    tuhil, Aguacatec, Chortí, and so forth)
11. Uto-Aztecan (Cora, Huichol, Tecual, Huaynamota, Teul, Nahuatl,
    Pochutec, Pipil, Nicarao)
12. Tarascan (Tarascan)
13. Cuitlatec (Cuitlatec)
14. Lenca (Lenca)
15. Xinca (Xinca)
16. Misumalpan (Matagalpa, Cacaopera)

Thanks to Morris Swadesh's initial glottochronological studies and
Leonardo Manrique Castañeda's current investigations, it has become
possible to approach the problem of the gradual penetration of language
streams into Mesoamerican territory. Over the course of centuries,

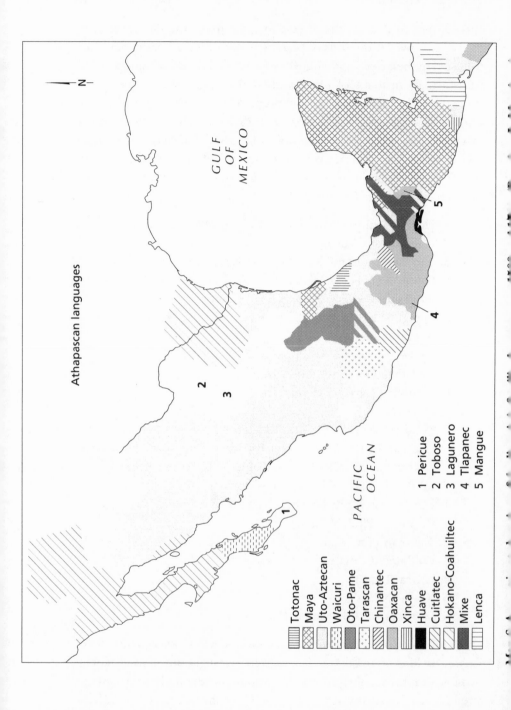

Athapascan languages

| Totonac |
| Maya |
| Uto-Aztecan |
| Waicuri |
| Oto-Pame |
| Tarascan |
| Chinantec |
| Oaxacan |
| Xinca |
| Huave |
| Cuitlatec |
| Hokano-Coahuiltec |
| Mixe |
| Lenca |

1 Pericue
2 Toboso
3 Lagunero
4 Tlapanec
5 Mangue

GULF
OF
MEXICO

PACIFIC
OCEAN

people with diverse origins created a cultural unity based on the cultivation of maize. We can identify the first Mesoamericans as farmers
descended from the nomadic hunter-gatherers who had inhabited the
same territory for thousands of years. As we have discussed, these nomadic
ancestors domesticated and cultivated maize, beans, squash, and chile,
among other plants, this invaluable legacy becoming the basis of the Mesoamerican diet. Farmers who cultivated these plants developed a shared
culture that was independent of influences from outside the continent
until the sixteenth century. The two historical milestones of agricultural
sedentariness and the European irruption are the temporal limits of a
Mesoamerica that began about 2500 B.C. and disappeared as an autonomous cultural tradition after A.D. 1521.

The territorial boundaries of Mesoamerica varied over time. According to Kirchhoff, at the time of the conquest it extended from 25° to 10°
north latitude and from sea to sea for most of that extent. This territory
included high, cold valleys and tropical and rain forests; wide coastal
plains and extensive interior plains; arid lands and lands full of rivers
and lakes. Mesoamericans in this diverse habitat perfected their subsistence techniques and developed their organizational structures, political institutions, and conception of the cosmos. The people moved along
an evolutionary path that began with egalitarian primitive farmers living
in scattered dwellings and culminated in highly stratified societies that
built impressive cities and powerful states. Paradoxically, human and
ecological diversity were important factors in the development of their
common tradition.

In summary, the definition of Mesoamerica must be based on three
interrelated elements: a subsistence pattern based primarily on techniques for cultivating maize; a shared tradition created by the farmers
in this territory; and a common history that allowed this agricultural
tradition to form and transform over the course of centuries. By *tradition* we mean an intellectual inheritance that has been socially created,
shared, transmitted, and modified. It is composed of mental representations and forms of action in which ideas and modes of conduct are
developed with which the members of a society—individually or collectively, in an internalized or an externalized way—confront the different situations that life brings. It is not just a formal and uniform cluster
of social expressions passed on from generation to generation, but the

way that a society responds intellectually to any situation. The elements composing a tradition range from its solid nucleus, which is not immune to historical transformation but is extremely resistant to change, to the most changeable elements, as well as elements evolving at an intermediate pace. The cultural inheritance is continually generated by and structured from the cultural nucleus.

Without diminishing the value of the cultural heritage of the nomadic ancestors, we should point out that the cultural nuclei of the Mesoamerican tradition were lifeways produced by sedentary agriculture. Local Mesoamerican traditions developed from the shared nucleus of the maize cultivators, and the intellectual frameworks produced as time passed were superimposed on this basic nucleus. Consequently, despite regional contrasts and different transformations in social, political, and economic development, Mesoamerican societies established a dialogue on the basis of the common content of their various traditions, and this communication reinforced the common content.

Mesoamerican unity does not necessarily imply the existence of common cultural traits, nor does it derive from a parallel evolution of organizational aspects. Rather, this unity derives from a history shared by societies at different levels of development, an evolution based on intensive relationships that converted this heterogeneous group of peoples into joint producers of a cultural substrate. The ties that led to joint production of culture were not always the same, nor were they uniform and permanent once established. On the contrary, these ties oscillated according to historical processes.

Many of the components of the nucleus of the shared Mesoamerican tradition were created and strengthened during the thirteen centuries of the Early Preclassic period, which lasted from the beginning of agricultural sedentary life to the formation of the first stratified societies. The techniques of production, family structures, and cosmovision and religion that subsequently developed have their roots in the distant thought of these first peasants.

On this Mesoamerican base rose local and regional traditions that derived from ecological, ethnic, cultural, and historical variations in smaller areas. Beyond these local and regional traditions, different and newly generalizing forces occurred. These were "lead actors," societies that for different reasons had a decisive influence over large areas of

Mesoamerica at certain times. In the following chapters we will discuss the characteristics of the globalizing "lead actor" actions of the Olmecs, Teotihuacans, Toltecs, and Mexicas. Nevertheless, it is clear that the historic changes resulting from their intervention were not caused by them alone, because much of what took place depended on how the other actors in this history received, assimilated, rejected, or imitated their influence.

The history of Mesoamerica is woven from three strands: the Mesoamerican (produced by the basic tradition), the local/regional traditions, and the globalizing actions of the "lead actors." The latter are usually seen as unifying forces, but this must be qualified. It is true that the Olmecs, Teotihuacans, Toltecs, and Mexicas spread goods, beliefs, institutions, knowledge, styles, and fashions, but they also imposed systems that did not always produce symmetrical relationships with peoples within their sphere of influence. In many cases they did not encourage the development of a particular model (of which they were the prototype). Further, by their actions they inhibited the economic and creative potential of others. Their globalization often produced a kind of Mesoamericanization that fostered differences as well as similarities. Societies incorporated into their systems had to take the specific roles assigned to them.

Inevitably, the problem of this historical complexity is reflected in the chronological division of Mesoamerica. Every division into periods is based on ideas about classifying societies on the basis of a particular way of looking at history. A full study of the way in which Mesoamerica has been divided into periods is beyond the scope of this book. Countless scholars from diverse philosophical schools have worked on a theoretical approach to the problem and have developed suggestive outlines. We are aware of the injustice done by only mentioning among them Herbert J. Spinden, George Vaillant, Julian Steward, Jorge A. Vivó, Gordon Ekholm, Pedro Armillas, Alfonso Caso, Ignacio Bernal, Julio César Olivé Negrete, Gordon R. Willey, Román Piña Chan, William T. Sanders, Barbara J. Price, Eduardo Matos, and Enrique Nalda, and it is even more unjust not to write a couple of lines about each concrete theoretical proposal.

As a minimum, we include a troublesome substitute based on the previous discussion. A division based on criteria of evolutionary development would produce a different chronology for each cultural area; when tied to a general vision of Mesoamerica, however, it would show considerable gaps. On the other hand, a global historical approach would produce uniform periods but would require novel ways of interpreting the history of both the superarea and its constituent areas. Although we lean more toward the second option, we recognize that a mix of cultural-evolution and historical approaches, despite problems with its theoretical basis and terminology, has long been an important vehicle for communication among specialists.

We will use the most popular periodization (see table 2), although we will return to its theoretical limitations in the last chapter of this book. We have chosen to use it because of its convenience and for custom's sake, but without attributing to it a unilineal evolutionary meaning or implying that characteristics were shared simultaneously by all the societies of Mesoamerica. According to this system, prehispanic Mesoamerica can be divided into the Preclassic, Classic, and Postclassic periods, with the following general characteristics, time spans, and subdivisions:

1. *Preclassic* (2500 B.C.–A.D. 200), which can be divided into Early (2500–1200 B.C.), Middle (1200–400 B.C.) and Late (400 B.C.–A.D. 200). The beginning of agricultural sedentariness and ceramics. A constant growth of population parallelled the development of agricultural techniques. Slow progress in controlling the flow of water. The making of ceramics was perfected. A long journey from egalitarian to hierarchical societies took place. Work became specialized. Sites ranged from hamlets and villages to protourban capitals derived from regional centers. From the beginning the interchange of goods was important, resulting in long commercial routes. Carving of stones, from polished jades to monumental sculptures was very important. At the end of the Preclassic some Mesoamerican peoples had complicated calendars and writing and built monumental buildings.

1-a. *Protoclassic.* Some authors use this term synonymously with the Late Preclassic (400 B.C.–A.D. 200) and others associate it with its second half (100 B.C.–A.D. 200). This transitional intermediate period between the Preclassic and the Classic is identified as the time when the bases for the political and cultural development of the Classic were laid. Some scholars feel that intensive agriculture was practiced at this time, enabling rapid population growth. There were more and larger sites. Rivalries and wars occurred between the regional centers, possibly contributing to the creation of more developed forms of political organization. There was a growing socioeconomic complexity. Monumental architecture, which on occasion could be gigantic, appeared. In certain places complex writing, calculations, and writing were employed. (We chose not to have a separate Protoclassic chapter in this book, because its information is included in the chapters that deal with the Preclassic.)

2. *Classic* (A.D. 200–650/900). With variants in each area, it can be divided into Early (A.D. 200–650/750) and Late (A.D. 650/750–900). Differentiation occured between rural and urban areas, the bulk of subsistence goods being produced in the rural areas while craft, administrative (political and religious), and service activities were concentrated in cities. This period was characterized by the development of vast regional traditions. The notable increase in population produced large agglomerations as well as the development of the intensive agriculture techniques necessary to support such populations. At the end of the period metallurgy was found in only a few places and had no economic importance. Notable social stratification and great occupational specialization occurred. The elites consolidated the government, resulting in general political and ideological control. Institutionalized religion was included in the governmental sphere. Long-distance commerce was organized in complex webs, with considerable influence on local and regional economies and politics. The great capitals controlled cities in their region and extended their influence beyond their territory. Strong political powers associated with the most important cities emerged. Rigorously planned and developed urban centers included massive architectural complexes, some of which were profusely decorated. Strong archaic states arose and frequent warfare occurred. The calendar, writing, mathematics,

and astronomy reached their zenith and the arts flourished. The religious pantheon solidified. At the end of the period, many of the great capitals of the Classic declined and collapsed.

2-a. *Epiclassic.* Some scholars use this term synonymously with the Late Classic (A.D. 650/750–900/1000) and others associate it with its second half (A.D. 850–1000). This transitional period between the Classic and Postclassic is often found in classifications. It is characterized by the rise of cities that benefited from the collapse of the great Classic cities. Commercial links became fragmented and important regional competition developed. Power centers were situated in strategically chosen places. Cities and their architectural features were defensive. Societies had a marked ethnic diversity. There was integration of different regional traditions into new cultural forms. (We have adopted the use of this classification and deal with the Epiclassic period in several chapters of this book.)

3. *Postclassic* (A.D. 900/1000–1520). With variants in each area, it can be divided into Early (A.D. 900–1200) and Late (A.D. 1200–1520). There was group mobility during this period, and the northern frontier shrank. After the farmers abandoned the north, groups of them, along with hunter-gatherers, invaded Mesoamerica. Cultural elements were widely diffused. Metallurgy developed, with the manufacture of gold, silver, and copper objects. Merchandise was distributed widely within the super-area and Oasisamerica. There was political instability, accompanied by the sudden rise and fall of aggressive states and militarism, expansion through conquest, and tribute from the conquered. Cities and their architectural features were defensive. New forms of worship developed in a religion that acquired a strong military and political tone. Human sacrifice increased considerably. Civil architecture became more important. Art was militaristic and referred to death and sacrifice. The end of the Postclassic—and of Mesoamerica—came as a result of the Spanish conquest. A limit of 1521 is tied to the Mexica state, because the last corner of uncolonized Mesoamerica—Tayasal—remained free until 1697.

Table 2. Mesoamerican Periods

Date	Period		SOUTHEAST	GULF	OAXACA	CENTER	WEST	NORTH
1500	POSTCLASSIC	Late	Northern Kingdoms / Quiches	Mexica conquests	Mixtec Kingdoms	Mexica dominance	Tarasca dominance	Abandonment
1200		Early	Splendor of Northern Maya	Toltec presence	Toltec presence	Chichimecs / Dominance of Tula	Independent principalities / Toltec presence	
900	CLASSIC	Epiclassic / Late	Maya splendor	El Tajín	Dominance of Monte Albán	Xochicalco Teotenango Cholula Cacaxtla	Metallurgy / Shaft Tombs	Farmers sharing territory with hunter-gatherers
650		Early	Development of Maya Culture	Presence of Teotihuacan		Dominance of Teotihuacan	Presence of Teotihuacan	
200			Architectural giantism	Complex writing and the long count	Rise of urbanism	Architectural giantism		
AD | BC	PRECLASSIC	Late		First calendric notation — RIVALRIES BETWEEN REGIONAL CENTERS				Advances of the farmers
400		Middle	Olmec presence	Gulf Olmecs		Olmec presence		
1200			EMERGENCE OF HIERARCHICAL SOCIETIES					
		Early	First Pottery	DEVELOPMENT OF EGALITARIAN VILLAGE SOCIETIES		First Pottery		
2500								

Mesoamerica, like every other superarea, varied in size during its existence. The agricultural tradition expanded gradually over the entire area wherever a rainy season assured crops. After A.D. 100, using irrigation techniques and exploiting favorable climatic conditions, farmers expanded into their northernmost position during the Classic. Apparently, a prolonged drought around A.D. 1000 forced them to retreat to their previous borders, which is why Kirchhoff, who took the conditions at the time of the conquest as the limits of Mesoamerica, ignored this wide strip extending northward for 250 km—northern Mesoamerica.

In its totality Mesoamerica included the southern half of Mexico, all of Guatemala, Belize, El Salvador, the western part of Honduras, the Pacific coast of Nicaragua, and northwestern Costa Rica. Its borders had very distinct characteristics. The northwestern border extended to the territory of both mountain and coastal agricultural peoples, who formed a belt with traditions midway between those of Mesoamerica and Oasisamerica, making precise definitions of their border very difficult. The northern border was the most variable of the borders due to advance and retreat of people between the first and the tenth centuries A.D. At the time of their maximum extension, hunter-gatherer and sedentary farmer societies overlapped within the northern area. To the southeast, where the Mesoamerican frontier was more stable, it reached agricultural societies that also cultivated maize but belonged to the tradition of another superarea, that of the Chibchas.

We have divided the Mesoamerican superarea into six areas characterized by particular historical, ethnic, linguistic, or geographical aspects that generated important cultural characteristics (see maps 7–13). These six areas are:

1. The *West*, including the partial or complete territories of the current states of Sinaloa, Nayarit, Jalisco, Colima, Michoacán, and Guerrero.
2. The *North*, including the partial or entire territories of the current states of Durango, Zacatecas, San Luis Potosí, Tamaulipas, Jalisco, Aguascalientes, Guanajuato, and Querétaro.
3. *Central Mexico*, including the partial or entire territories of the current states of Hidalgo, México, Tlaxcala, Morelos, Puebla, and the Distrito Federal.

4. *Oaxaca,* its limits almost coinciding with the present state of Oaxaca although it includes part of the adjacent areas of Guerrero, Puebla, and Veracruz.

5. The *Gulf,* including the partial or entire territories of the current states of Tamaulipas, San Luis Potosí, Hidalgo, Veracruz, Puebla, and Tabasco.

6. The *Southeast,* including the partial or complete territories of the current states of Tabasco, Chiapas, Campeche, Yucatán, Quintana Roo, and the Central American countries of Guatemala, Belize, El Salvador, Honduras, Nicaragua, and Costa Rica.

The borders between these cultural areas were not always the same, because the areas comprising them could move from one cultural-historical context to another at any given time. Nevertheless, the global partition is useful as a classificatory instrument for such an extensive and varied territory.

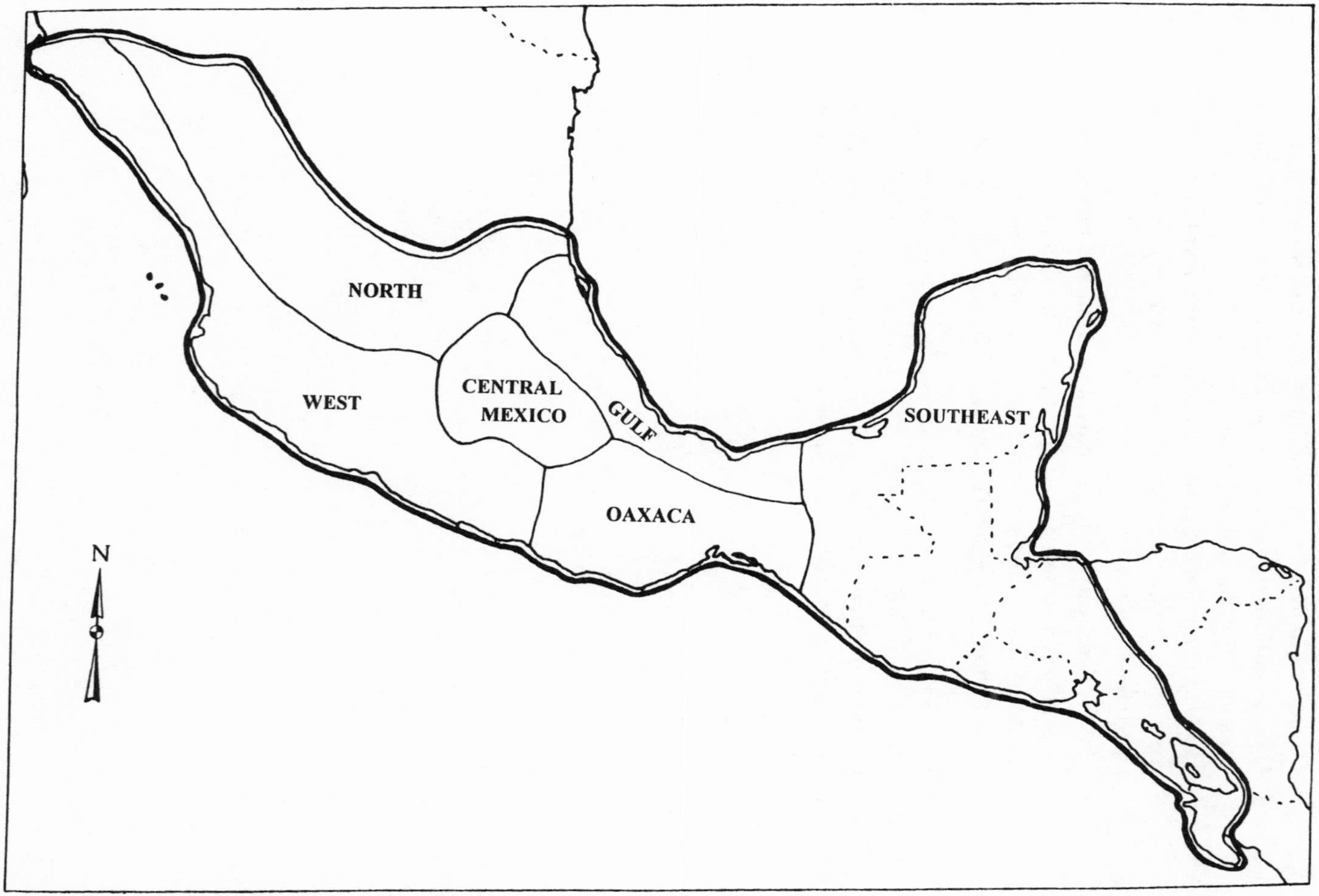

Map 7. Mesoamerica and its cultural areas

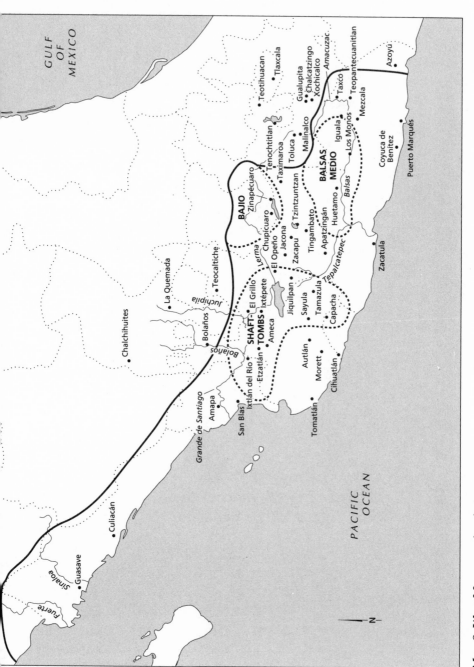

Map 8. West Mesoamerica Area.

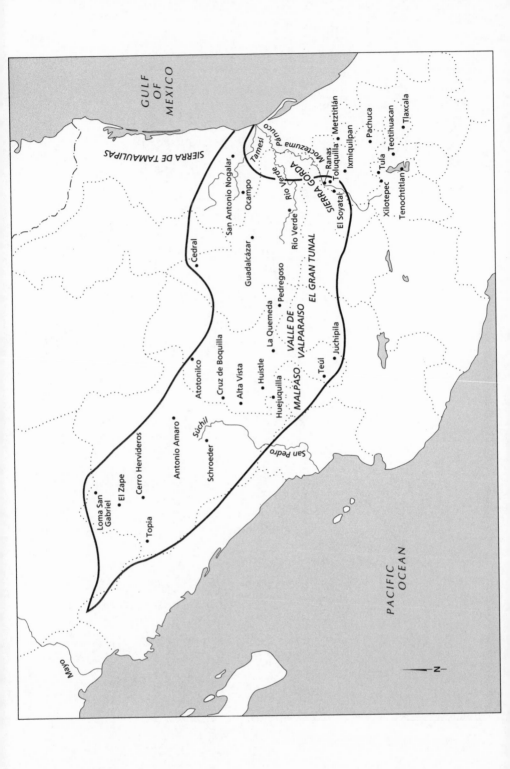

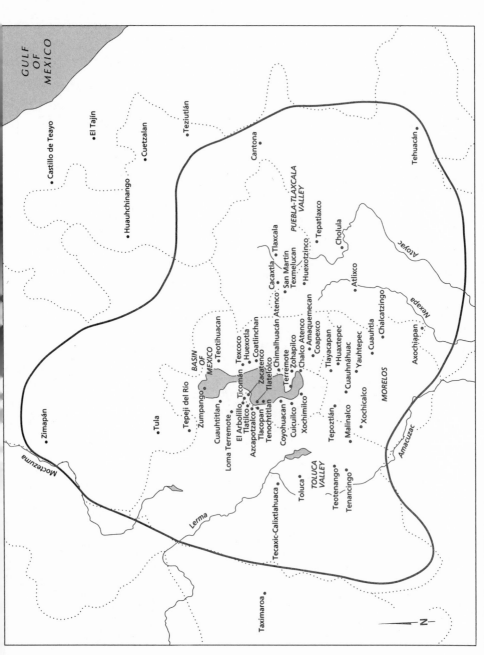

Map 10. Central Mexico Area.

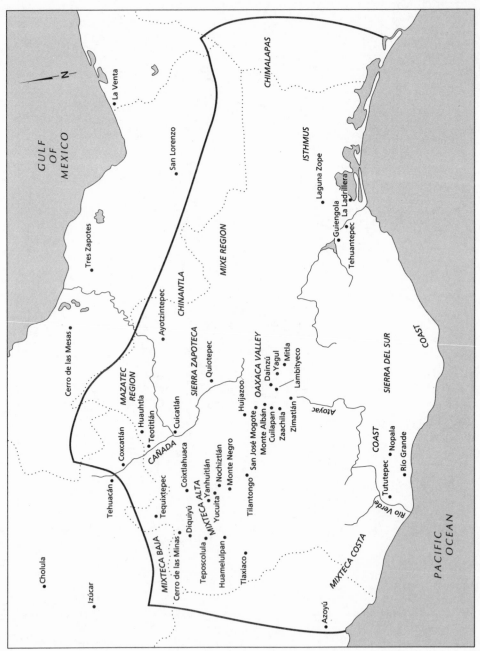

Map 11. Oaxaca Area

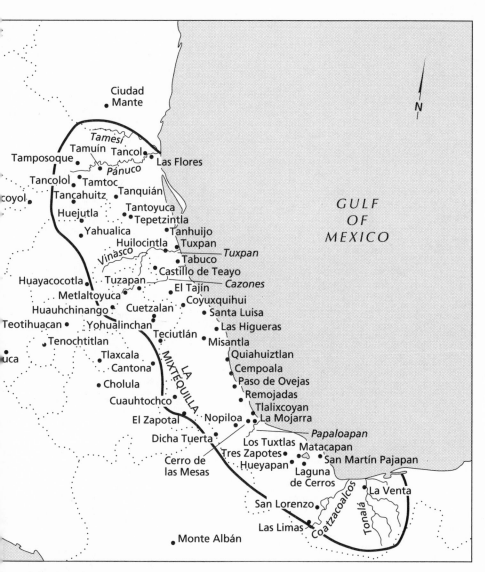

Map 12. Gulf Area.

Map 13. Southeast Mesoamerica Area.

Rock paintings in the San Francisco Sierra, Baja California Area, Arid america. (Photograph: André Cabrioler © *Arqueología Mexicana,* INAH)

Kivas from the multifamily dwelling unit at Pueblo Bonito, Chaco Canyon, New Mexico. Anasazi Area, Oasisamerica, Pueblo III Phase. (Photograph: Leonardo López Luján)

Anthropomorphic vase from Paquimé, Chihuahua. Mogollon Area, Oasis-america, Late Period. (Photograph: Carlos Blanco © *Arqueología Mexicana,* INAH)

Temple half-buried by lava at Cuicuilco, Distrito Federal. Central Mexico Area, Preclassic period. (Photograph courtesy of Aerofotoservicios)

"Danzante" relief at Monte Albán, Oaxaca. Oaxaca Area, Preclassic period. (Photograph: Carlos Blanco © *Arqueología Mexicana,* INAH)

Brazier with the image of the young fire god, Oaxaca. Oaxaca Area, Preclassic period. (Photograph courtesy of Salvador Guilliem)

Waisted tecomate, Capacha type, Jalisco and Colima. West Mesoamerica Area, Preclassic period. (Photograph: Ignacio Guevara © *Arqueología Mexicana*, INAH)

Olmec greenstone ceremonial celt, Gulf Area, Preclassic period. (Photograph: Ignacio Guevara © *Arqueología Mexicana*, INAH)

Aerial photograph of Teotihuacan, Estado de México. Central Mexico Area, Classic period. (Photograph: Carlos Blanco © *Arqueología Mexicana*, INAH)

Murals at Totometla, Teotihuacan, Estado de México. Central Mexico Area, Classic period. (Photograph: Marco Antonio Pacheco © *Arqueología Mexicana*, INAH)

Incense-burner lid found in Oztoyahualco, Teotihuacan, Estado de México. Central Mexico Area, Classic period. (Courtesy of Salvador Guilliem)

Travertine merlon, Teotihuacan, Estado de México. Central Mexico Area, Classic period. (Courtesy of Salvador Guilliem)

Zapotec glyph found in the Oaxaca barrio of Teotihuacan, Estado de México. Central Mexico Area, Classic period. (Courtesy of Salvador Guilliem)

CHAPTER TWO

The Mesoamerican Preclassic Period

A GENERAL VIEW OF THE PRECLASSIC PERIOD

When archaeologists say that they have reached a preceramic stratum, they are referring to the oldest levels of human history. Here we find only remains of hunting-gathering societies. Ceramics in shallower layers differentiate later stages of cultural development in sedentary societies. Pottery is an excellent indicator of sedentariness because nomads, even preceramic peoples, do without utensils that are too voluminous, heavy, or fragile for their way of life. When people do not have to move periodically, however, baked clay containers are more useful than baskets or containers of leather, wood, or stone. The invention of ceramics was an enormous technological advance, because ceramic vessels can be shaped into specialized forms, hold liquids well, withstand high temperatures, and fend off predators and microorganisms.

The birth of Mesoamerica is tied to the appearance of ceramics. The oldest ceramics found in Puerto Marqués, Guerrero, in Tehuacan, Puebla, and in Tlapacoya, México, have radiocarbon dates of 2400–2300 B.C. They are crude pots with rough surfaces caused by the coarse sand mixed into the clay to make it easier to shape. However, we must not equate the beginning of the Preclassic with the appearance of ceramics. Rather, the beginning of the Preclassic and, therefore of Mesoamerica, is defined by the appearance of new forms of social organization. Pottery is simply the trait that is most evident to archaeologists.

This first Mesoamerican period falls between 2500 B.C. and A.D. 200. Its most notable characteristic is the spread of sedentary agriculture. During the Preclassic, societies depended primarily on their harvests; as their numbers increased, they settled in hamlets and villages. As a whole, the Preclassic can be divided into three epochs with different levels of social complexity. The first epoch, the Early Preclassic (2500–1200 B.C.), was a time when only egalitarian tribal communities existed. Hamlets of less than twenty houses were built next to cultivated fields. These huts, made from perishable materials, were as homogeneous as the group itself. Community activities centered on agriculture, which utilized seasonal rains, river floods, and soils moistened by a high groundwater level. Although differences in ecological conditions favored interchanges among villages, each community produced most of the goods it needed for its subsistence. The religious beliefs of the dwellers can be inferred by their frequent burial of their dead under the floors of their houses.

The second epoch is the Middle Preclassic (1200–400 B.C.). Considerable changes, particularly in agriculture, took place during these eight centuries. Dams, canals, terraces, and other systems for controlling water have been found in key regions of Mesoamerica. Through these, people were able to diminish the risk of late or insufficient rains and increase the number of harvests per year. Irrigation systems appeared in Tehuacan about 700 B.C., about one hundred or two hundred years later in the Basin of Mexico, and by 400 B.C. in the Valley of Oaxaca. The variety of domesticated plants expanded at the same time. Advances in other technological areas and increasingly specialized production favored the interchange of raw materials, products, and ideas among hamlets and from one region to another, strengthening the cultural and historical unity of Mesoamerica. As specialization grew, an increasing number of individuals were devoted solely to the production of food.

The most important phenomenon was the appearance of social stratification, which reached its first spectacular heights among the Olmecs in the region of the Gulf of Mexico. Social differences were reflected in the complexity of tombs and the richness of funerary offerings, in iconographic representations, and in the importance that sumptuary goods, particularly foreign ones, acquired. Scholars emphasize the importance of the interchange of sumptuary goods between elites. These goods were often made from materials that came from remote areas. Making most of them required skilled craftsmanship and many hours of labor. These items include fine polychrome ceramics; ilmenite and hematite mirrors; cinnabar powder; greenstone figurines; and jewelry made from bone, shell, and semiprecious stone. The use of these goods was related to rulership, the representation of the community in relation to other groups, and the mediation between humans and supernatural powers.

Various explanations have been proposed for the rise of social stratification. Each theory attributes this transcendental change to a different cause: differential access to natural resources due to population growth, technological development, knowledge of the basic natural phenomena needed for agriculture, coordination of communal hydraulic works, control of regional interchanges or of the distribution of foreign products, or management of the supernatural. Given the meager factual information provided by archaeology, it is difficult to choose a particular theory. In any case most of these explanations posit an increasing specialization of particular segments of the community, most likely kinship groups. As time went by, some of these groups had special access to goods and services, exercised social control functions, and attained a prestigious position.

The development of writing and of the calendar parallels and is tied to the rise of social stratification. From the beginning writing transmitted political information, and chronological registers are often tied to it. According to Joyce Marcus, history, myth, and political propaganda fused and were written down from 600 B.C. until the end of Mesoamerican civilization. The earliest calendrical notations, carved in stone, have been found in the Valley of Oaxaca: Monument 3 of San José Mogote and the carved "*danzantes* (dancers)" and Stelae 12 and 13 at Monte Albán. Some of these artifacts show dates in the 260-day divinatory calendar, while others have year-bearers and year symbols and, possibly, the names of 20-day periods that referred to the solar year of 365 days. Dense population centers with monumental architecture rose in particular regions of Mesoamerica during this period. The best examples are La Venta and San José Mogote.

The third epoch, the Late Preclassic, which lasted from 400 B.C. to A.D. 200, began as the Olmec world fell. During this period some villages grew in size and complexity, becoming major power centers and surrounded by satellites ranked according to their importance. This multiplicity of contending centers generated disputes and outright wars with the purpose of settling political and economic rivalries.

The new centers are characterized architecturally by plazas, platforms, and monumental temples composed of superimposed rectangular or circular bases on top of which was placed a chapel reached by ramps or stairs. Giantism was the hallmark of the period. Never before had pyramids of such dimensions been erected. The Pyramid of the Sun at Teotihuacan (sixty-three meters high) and the main pyramid of the Tigre Complex at El Mirador, Guatemala (fifty-five meters high) are examples.

Archaeologists have found evidence of the importance of trade at these capitals. Thus, we know that Kaminaljuyú, in the Guatemalan Highlands, was a flourishing center of trade and that Teotihuacan was established at the crossroads of exchange routes and adjacent to rich obsidian mines.

Religious sculpture depicting mythical episodes and cosmological scenes proliferated during the Late Preclassic. Some of the most noteworthy, which provide insight into beliefs at the time, can be found at Izapa. Writing also developed during the Late Preclassic, expanding to the vast territory of Oaxaca, Veracruz, Tabasco, Chiapas, and Guatemala. Current knowledge about Mesoamerican writing does not allow us to attribute its invention to a particular ethnic group; nevertheless, inscriptions are found in territories occupied in the past by speakers of Mixe-Zoque and Oto-Manguean languages. Known texts have more complex structures than those of the Middle Preclassic and have an unusual number of glyphs, bearing increasingly elaborate messages. The Long Count, the most developed calendrical system in Mesoamerica, which accurately dated mythical and real events on the basis of a starting date, appeared during the latter half of the Late Preclassic. Stele 2 at Chiapa de Corzo bears the oldest known Long Count date (36 B.C.). Other monuments with early dates are Stele C at Tres Zapotes (31 B.C.), Stele 1 at El Baúl in South Guatemala (A.D. 16 and 36), the Tuxtla statuette (A.D. 162), and Stele 1 at la Mojarra (A.D. 143 and 156). The Mojarra

Stele, with its very long text referring to a richly dressed ruler, prefigures Classic Period Maya writing. It is exceptional because it is apparently written in a Mixe language.

CENTRAL MEXICO IN THE PRECLASSIC

Central Mexico is the best-known Mesoamerican area because of the detailed descriptions of it in written sources and intensive archaeological investigations that have taken place there. The area is basically composed of four geographical units tied together by shared traditions: the Morelos Valley to the south, the Puebla-Tlaxcala Valley to the east, the Basin of Mexico at the center, and the Toluca Valley to the west. The Morelos Valley is the only one of these units that is located in the tropics (*tierra caliente*). The other three, surrounded by high mountains, lie north of the neovolcanic axis and are two thousand meters above sea level. These are large tracts of fertile land that, in prehispanic times, had important systems of lakes and rivers.

The Basin of Mexico played a key role in Mesoamerican history due, among other things, to its central locality, its large size, and the richness and diversity of its ecosystems. A seventh of its area was covered by a system of lakes and swamps that provided abundant animal protein and facilitated human movement. Additionally, it had a benign climate, dense forests, good alluvial soils with a high water table, and a magnificent distribution of seasonal resources. All of these factors led to the existence of sedentary hunter-gatherers in the Basin even before the spread of agriculture.

Like the Preclassic in the rest of Mesoamerica, the Preclassic of the Basin of Mexico can be divided into three long periods: Early (2500–1250 B.C.), characterized by agrarian villages; Middle (1250–600 B.C.), during which many regional centers arose; and Late (600 B.C.–A.D. 150), which began by changing some of these centers into protourban capitals and culminated in the birth of a city with supraregional power—Teotihuacan.

According to studies by Christine Niederberger, David C. Grove, Paul Tolstoy, and others, societies in the Early Preclassic were egalitarian, fully agricultural, and distributed among very similar villages. The Basin lacked a great increase in population in comparison with that of the

Fig. 2. The island village of Terremote, Distrito Federal. Central Mexico Area, Preclassic period. (Reconstructive drawing by Fernando Botas Vera)

prior stage of preagricultural sedentariness. The best-known settlements of this epoch are Chalcatzingo in the Morelos Valley and Loma Torremote (see fig. 2), El Arbolillo, Tlatilco, Tlapacoya, and Coapexco in the Basin of Mexico. With the exception of the latter, it seems that the norm was to settle on the shores of rivers and lakes and on the piedmont.

As mentioned above, evidence of the oldest pottery in Central Mexico comes from the Tehuacan Valley in Puebla (Purrón Phase) and could, according to Richard S. MacNeish, date to 2300 B.C. This type of ceramic, with surfaces so rough that it is called "pox pottery," contrasts sharply with the exquisite ceramic pieces produced a thousand years later in Tlatilco and Tlapacoya. Its Red-on-Brown decor is similar to that of San José Mogote and Chupícuaro, indicating strong contact between the Basin of Mexico and its Mesoamerican contemporaries.

Substantial changes began in 1250 B.C., at the beginning of the Middle Preclassic. Two of the most important characteristics of this period were considerable population growth and agricultural intensification. Vestiges of terraces and canals have been found in the dry zones of the Basin of Mexico as well as in the Puebla and Morelos Valleys. Similarly, there are traces of the building of *chinampas* (artificially constructed raised fields) in the swampy areas of the lakes. Despite the great importance of these techniques, however, it is clear that most agriculture still relied on seasonal rains.

This widespread uniformity among villages became a political reality in the Middle Preclassic. Spatial arrangements changed as regional centers surrounded by numerous satellite villages developed, implying complex political and administrative structures that grew into a pan-Mesoamerican exchange system. The principal sites in the Basin were Tlapacoya at the lake shore, Tlatilco in the piedmont, and Coapexco on the foothills of Iztaccihuatl. Another important site is Chalcatzingo in the Amatzinac Valley of Morelos, which benefited from regional wealth in hematite, kaolin, and lime and a climate favorable for the cultivation of cotton.

A new social group, not directly involved with food production, lived in these places. The benefits this emergent elite obtained from the unequal distribution of prestige, power, goods, and services can be seen today in archaeological remains. These include clay representations of individuals carrying attributes of command or richly attired as well as sumptuous tombs for both children and adults, showing that status was acquired solely by birth into a privileged lineage.

As in many other parts of Mesoamerica, the power of these elites was expressed in sumptuary objects made in the style of or using the symbols of the people generally called Olmecs. This extensive artistic diffusion was one of the consequences of the unusual Mesoamerican interrelationships that developed at the time. One example is the remarkable dissemination of obsidian extracted from mines in the Basin of Mexico to the most remote regions of Mesoamerica. In the new hierarchical arrangement the rulers were in charge of specialized manufacture, interchange with distant regions, and the redistribution of imported goods. Central Mexico's most important contacts were San Lorenzo in the Gulf Area, the Valley of Oaxaca, and Chiapas.

Another defining element of the Middle Preclassic is the proliferation of clay figurines. These give us a hint of some of the religious concepts at the time. Wide-hipped female figurines, which have been associated with agricultural fertility, predominate. Figurines with two heads or two faces, as well as ball players and contortionists are also commonly found. The most impressive array of religious images, Olmec-style bas-reliefs carved into the rocks of a cliff, are found at Chalcatzingo (see fig. 3). The human and divine characters, rampant felines, fantastic animals, and plant motifs of squashes and bromeliads, all connected with agriculture, reveal a rich mythology and a complex cult consecrated to the earth and rain.

Specialists on the Basin of Mexico date the beginning of the Late Preclassic in this area to the disappearance of Olmec influence around 600 B.C. This period, which ended about A.D. 150, was characterized by the transformation of some regional centers into protourban capitals that not only concentrated power but also became magnets for population. For example, in the Puebla Valley different centers developed into capitals with temple platforms, plazas, streets, drainage systems, and ball courts.

Cuicuilco is a notable example of a protourban capital. Established on the western shores of Lake Xochimilco, it became politically and economically powerful enough to erect a majestic complex of public buildings surrounding a temple with a conical platform that measured 135 meters in diameter and 26 meters high. Cuicuilco's attraction for neighboring

Fig. 3. Relief called "The King," Chalcatzingo, Morelos. Central Mexico
Area, Preclassic period.

villages is impressive. According to William T. Sanders et al., in 300 B.C. the
Basin had 80,000 inhabitants, 5,000 to 10,000 of whom lived in Cuicuilco.
During the next two centuries, when the population of the Basin was
140,000, Cuicuilco had at least doubled in size. By then, however, Teotihuacan had equaled its southern rival both in population and in size.

   At the end of the Late Preclassic, Cuicuilco disappeared, probably
due to eruptions of the Xitle Volcano. Because of this, Teotihuacan,
which may have absorbed the people of Cuicuilco, became the absolute

power in the Basin and was able to extend its influence well beyond the region's boundaries. Between 100 B.C. and A.D. 150, Teotihuacan's population was 80,000, about 80 to 90 percent of the total population of the Basin. This population size made possible the erection of the Pyramids of the Sun and the Moon as well as the construction of the monumental Mesoamerican city as a whole.

OAXACA IN THE PRECLASSIC

Of all the areas of Mesoamerica, Oaxaca provides scholars with the clearest evolutionary sequence in the Preclassic. A very long time ago, groups from different linguistic branches of the Oaxaca family established agricultural villages all over the territory. Sites such as El Guayabo in the Mixteca Baja, Yucuita in the Mixteca Alta, San José Mogote in the Valley of Oaxaca, Hacienda de Tecomaxtlahua in the Cañada, Ayotzintepec in the Chinantla, and Laguna Zope in the Isthmus are examples of this pristine village phase. By the fifth century B.C. various villages, among them Yucuita, Huamelulpan, Cerro de las Minas, and Monte Albán, developed into the precursors of Mesoamerican urbanism.

Archaeologists in Oaxaca have concentrated primarily on the Valley of Oaxaca, which has three lobes: Etla, Tlacolula, and Zimatlán. The Valley, which has an area of more than two thousand square km, is bordered by the Sierra Madre del Sur to the south and the mountains of the Mixteca Alta to the north. The region has a temperate semiarid climate with great agricultural potential, as most of it is composed of alluvial soils irrigated by the Atoyac and Salado Rivers. During the Preclassic it had abundant forests and minerals, such as quartz, flint, magnetite, ilmenite, and clay.

Thanks to the systematic efforts of the group headed by Kent V. Flannery and Joyce Marcus, we know that during the Preclassic a continuous transformation of egalitarian village societies into stratified urban societies took place in the Valley of Oaxaca. Excavated archaeological remains allow us to reconstruct life in the Valley from its preceramic stages to the emergence of the city of Monte Albán.

The Early Preclassic in the Oaxaca Valley, which extends from 1900 to 1150 B.C., is divided into the Espiridión and Tierras Largas Phases. A coarse, undecorated ceramic resembling the Purrón ceramics of

Teotihuacan was manufactured during the first phase. By 1400 B.C. in the Etla Valley, there were five hamlets surrounding the small village of San José Mogote, which had a population of 150 and an area of more than seven hectares. In the center of the village stood a stuccoed public building with an interior altar, while around it clustered wattle-and-daub houses with ovens and conical pits for storing grain.

The Middle Preclassic in Oaxaca, which lasted from 1150 to 500 B.C., is divided into the San José, Guadalupe, and Rosario Phases. The epoch is characterized by a surprising population growth, a multiplication of settlements in the Valley, and the development of social differentiation. In the first three hundred years of the Middle Preclassic, San José Mogote grew to seven hundred inhabitants, distributed in four residential quarters. By that time there were dwellings with larger dimensions and stone-and-adobe construction as well as burials with rich offerings. The presence of ceramics and greenstone sculptures from the Gulf, pottery from Morelos and Guatemala, and products from the coast such as manta-ray spines, shark teeth, and conch shells are evidence of strong contacts with other Mesoamericans, particularly the Olmecs of San Lorenzo. In exchange for these goods San José Mogote exported ceramics, stone axes, and, above all, magnetite and ilmenite mirrors like those that have been found in sites in Morelos and in the so-called Olmec metropolitan zone. Nuggets of ilmenite iron ores found in creeks of the Etla lobe were used to manufacture mirrors that were used as pendants or inlaid in wood or shell.

A slow diminution of the interchange between Oaxaca and the nuclear Olmec area began in the ninth century B.C. According to Marcus Winter, the area began to regionalize, as shown by an increasing variety in ceramics. At that time the Mixteca Bajas developed strong ties with the Puebla-Tlaxcala Valley peoples, the Chinantlas with those of the Gulf Area, and the people of the Isthmus of Tehuantepec with the Olmecs and inhabitants of the Soconusco region and the Guatemalan Highlands.

In the ninth century irrigation techniques that increased production emerged in the Valley of Oaxaca, such as the canals and terraces found at Hierve el Agua. This increase in harvests paralleled the multiplication of villages. Some investigators have categorized settlements into three levels of complexity, placing San José Mogote at the top of the pyramid and its rival, Huitzo, at the second level, with hamlets at the bottom.

San José Mogote attained its maximum splendor near the end of the Middle Preclassic. By that time, it is calculated that it had a population of fourteen hundred people as well as twenty subordinate villages. Several public buildings were built upon masonry platforms at San José Mogote. At the entrance of one of the buildings, a human figure similar to those that would appear later at Monte Albán (the so-called "danzantes") is carved on a stone monument. This figure is important for two reasons. First, it seems to show a sacrificed captive, which bolsters the concept of a warlike atmosphere at the time; second, its glyph, 1-Earthquake, is the oldest evidence for the 260-day divinatory calendar.

During the Late Preclassic (500 B.C.–A.D. 250), San José Mogote lost the preeminence it had held for centuries. Its place was taken by a new power center, Monte Albán, which made San José Mogote a subordinate. The rise of what is considered by some to be the oldest city in Mesoamerica—placed atop a four-hundred-meter-high uninhabited and hard-to-reach hilltop with very difficult access to sources of water—remains controversial. Richard E. Blanton attributes the choice of location to the fact that Monte Albán's hill is exactly at the confluence of the three valley lobes and dominates them. According to Blanton it is probable that Monte Albán was the result of the union of three formerly autonomous political entities that established a new common capital in a strategic neutral location.

The Preclassic history of this site has been divided into three phases: Early Monte Albán I (500–300 B.C.), Late Monte Albán I (300–200 B.C.), and Monte Albán II (200 B.C.–A.D. 250). Its urbanization began in the first phase with a population of five thousand. Archaeologists can distinguish four levels of social hierarchy at settlements in the Valley during this period. Late Monte Albán I had an impressive growth in population, with a estimated population of sixteen thousand. Social differentiation is clearly marked by luxurious stone tombs. The Danzantes building, famous for its walls decorated with approximately three hundred slabs representing naked men in diverse positions—usually with elaborate hairdresses, ear spools, eyes closed, open mouths, distorted legs, and strange volutes on their chests or genital areas—dates to this time. Depending on their vertical or horizontal position, the figures have been called, respectively, "dancers" or "swimmers." Many of these images are accompanied by glyphs, some of which may be names. Among the many hypotheses regarding the meaning of this assemblage, we prefer the one that suggests they represent sacrificial conquered enemy rulers, some of whom have been emasculated.

The urban plan of Monte Albán was established in Phase II with the leveling and paving of the Great Plaza, the architectural complex that organizes space at the site. Around it were erected the first two-room temples. Building J, a strange construction with an arrow-shaped base pointing to the point where—according to Anthony F. Aveni's calculations—the star Capella rose, was built in the middle of the Great Plaza. A total of forty plaques commemorating conquests are embedded in this building, which is believed to be an observatory. Some of the toponyms on the plaques have been deciphered as today's Cuicatlan, Miahuatlan, Tututepec, Sosola, Ocelotepec, and Chiltepec. If we suppose that these names have lasted for centuries, we can see a corridor of Zapotec influence that extended from Cuicatlan all the way to the northern coast of the Pacific Ocean. The seat of government and royal residence was apparently on the North Platform. At the end of the Preclassic, the city had almost three thousand houses divided into four quarters. A small area containing public buildings was located in the center of each quarter.

WEST MESOAMERICA IN THE PRECLASSIC

In contrast with the other Mesoamerican areas, western Mexico never formed a clear cultural unit. The societies that lived in the extensive territory that includes the center and south of Sinaloa, Nayarit, Jalisco, Colima, Michoacán, and parts of Guanajuato and Guerrero lacked the common history that is so evident in Central Mexico, the Gulf, the Southeast, and Oaxaca. We classify this enormous corridor as an area partly because of the scarcity of archaeological investigations, which hinders the development of a more precise subdivision. This ignorance is compounded by the fact that West Mexican ceramics are greatly desired by collectors, this demand encouraging systematic looting of sites. As information about the period prior to A.D. 250 is limited to a few regions, we do not have a total image of the area. Perhaps the only clear common denominator among West Mexican Preclassical societies is an adherence to village life and a slow evolution, differing from that in other areas, toward more complex forms of social organization.

A monochromatic ceramic, called Capacha by Isabel Kelly, was made in Colima and Jalisco. Radiocarbon dating indicates that it is surprisingly old, dating from approximately the eighteenth century B.C. The most typical forms of Capacha ceramics are earthenware bowls (*tecomates*) decorated with incising and punctation. The narrow waists of some containers makes them look like two vessels placed one on top of the other; in extreme cases they really are two different vessels, united by three curved vertical tubes.

Without a doubt, the Shaft Tomb Tradition (Tumbas de Tiro) was one of the most vigorous cultures in West Mexico. It occupied Nayarit, Jalisco, Colima, and Michoacán beginning in 200 B.C. and lasting for eight hundred years. Peoples from this culture buried their dead amid rich offerings in subterranean cavities dug out of the hardpan subsoil, which were reached by shafts that were frequently four to six meters deep. El Opeño in Michoacán is one of the few places where archaeologists have found unlooted tombs. One of these contained the remains of ten individuals, ceramic figurines, and vessels. Another undisturbed tomb, found in Huitzilapa, Jalisco, contained a multiple burial with traces of the reed mats (*petates*) in which the corpses were wrapped. One of the individuals in this tomb was accompanied by a rich offering of shells and ceramics. A third tomb, recently excavated in San Martín de Bolaños, Jalisco, was dated at about 135 B.C. It is interesting to note that these societies and some of the contemporaneous cultures of northeastern South America both used shaft tombs and vessels with stirrup-shaped handles, implying that these two groups were in contact by sea.

Further south, in the state of Guerrero, significant Olmec influence existed between 1400 and 600 B.C. The biggest site in this region is Teopantecuanitlan, which is located at the confluence of the Amacuzac and Balsas Rivers. The size of the structures at this site, excavated by Guadalupe Martínez Donjuán, show that it was home to a complex society. Among the structures are a stone aqueduct that carried water from a dam to the cultivated fields, a sunken rectangular precinct surrounded by heavy stone blocks, and four anthropomorphic sculptures with characteristic jaguar traits. Two other Olmec sites in Guerrero, famous for their polychrome paintings, are the caves of Juxtlahuaca and Oxtotitlan.

The remains of the Mezcala Culture in the upper Balsas River are much more recent. This region has also been heavily looted by people searching for its desirable greenstone sculptures. Because of their spare style, the sculptures have been compared to those of the Cyclades Islands. In Mezcala art a few short, straight strokes suffice to form beautiful full-figure human figures, masks, animals, temples, and ritual objects. Ahuiná-huac is the only Preclassic site in the region where these works have been excavated in an archaeological context. Louise I. Paradis has shown that they date to between 700 and 200 B.C. The Ahuinahuac stone carvers lived together in dwelling complexes with several rooms.

Finally, we would like to mention Chupícuaro, a Late Preclassic village that disappeared about A.D. 300. Located on the banks of the Lerma River in Guanajuato, it is famous because more than four hundred tombs with rich offerings were excavated there. The offerings found include musical instruments, dogs, crania with the brain removed, and rich ceramics that were unpainted or decorated with Red-on-Cream and Black-on-Cream designs. Chupícuaro pottery resembles that of contemporaneous sites in eastern, northern, and central Mesoamerica.

SOUTHEAST MESOAMERICA IN THE PRECLASSIC

Until recently, our reconstructions of the Preclassic civilizations of Southeast Mesoamerica were quite limited. The great gaps in our knowledge were a direct result of the problems of preserving the earliest remains of agricultural peoples in a tropical context; of the obstacles that existed and still exist in identifying small sections of the first public buildings that have been buried under the massive fill of later structures; and of the apathy of many archaeologists who are more interested in establishing the cultural sequence of grandiose sites than in the regional study of older epochs with more modest remains. Fortunately, the growing interest in the Preclassic and the resulting proliferation of archaeological digs in the last few years have made a global view possible and have produced a number of theories that try to explain the rise of the Olmec and Maya cultures. These recent theories still have to be submitted to rigorous scientific critiques.

One of the most influential factors in the development of societies in Southeast Mesoamerica was geographical diversity. During the Preclassic the most important cultural foci developed in four completely different environments in the area: the southern coastal plains of Chiapas and Guatemala, the Guatemalan Highlands, the tropical jungles of Petén, and the extensive chalky plains of the Yucatán Peninsula. These were the settings for the two great cultural complexes that scholars connect with the Mixe-Zoque and Maya linguistic families.

The Mixe-Zoque complex, named the Great Isthmus Tradition, was recently studied by John E. Clark and Michael Blake. According to their controversial proposal, the complex developed in the territory of Chiapas and later expanded beyond the limits of Southeast Mesoamerica, reaching southern Veracruz and eastern Tabasco. During the Early Preclassic— between 1800 and 1325 B.C., during the Barra, Locona, and Ocós Phases— village people devoted to farming fishing, hunting, and pottery making lived in the fertile coastal plains of Soconusco and Guatemala. Sites from this period include Altamira, La Victoria, Salinas la Blanca, and Paso de la Amada. The high level of technical and artistic achievements of these people distinguishes them from those of the contemporaneous cultures of Oaxaca and Tehuacán. Their ceramics, decorated with iridescent pigment and cord-and-shell impressions, resembles that of Ecuador.

By 1600 B.C. the societies of Soconusco had expanded across the isthmus to the area that would be the Olmec nuclear area beginning in 1200 B.C. Based on glottochronology, it appears that this group penetrated like a wedge into an area inhabited by proto-Maya speakers. According to Clark and Blake, the result of this process was the birth of Olmec culture on the Gulf Coast as a fusion of these Mixe-Zoques with the Proto-Mayas and the people of Oaxaca.

During the Middle Preclassic (1200–400 B.C.), the Great Isthmus Tradition flowered at places such as Tzutzuculi, Pijijiapan, Chiapa de Corzo, La Blanca, Bilbao, Chalchuapa, and Quelepa, along a corridor that extended from Mexico to El Salvador. Influenced by contact with the Olmecs, these societies seem to have been independent political units with Olmec cultural traits that are visible as much in their ceremonial mounds, more than twenty meters high, as in their important sculpted monuments.

A second complex, named the Lower Maya Tradition, began to develop between 1200 and 900 B.C. in the tropical jungles of Guatemala and Belize and in Yucatán. The oldest villages were inhabited by maize farmers. A significant find from these remote times are the old burials found in Group 9N-8 of Copán, which were accompanied by vessels with motifs similar to those of Tlatilco, Tlapacoya, and San José Mogote. The origin of the Lower Maya Tradition is debatable. Authors such as E. Wyllys Andrews V propose a dual origin. Around 1000 B.C. the southern Petén was inhabited by a non-Maya group, whose principal sites were Seibal and Altar de Sacrificios and who made the so-called Xe ceramics. The similarity of these ceramics to others found further south indicates that their precursors came from the Chiapas or the Guatemalan Highlands and perhaps, even earlier, from the Pacific Coast. The second group were Maya speakers concentrated in northern Belize in sites such as Cuello. About 600 B.C. these Mayas began to expand throughout the Petén and even reached El Salvador. At this time a completely different ceramic called Mamom appeared. The principal sites of this Maya culture were Uaxactún and Tikal. The best-studied Maya sites of the Middle Preclassic are the egalitarian village of Cuello in Belize and much more complex localities with several stone temples and greater social differentiation, such as Nakbé and El Mirador in Guatemala and Calakmul in Campeche. Innumerable hamlets dating from that period have been found in the Yucatán Peninsula at Dzibilchaltún, Aké, Maní, Dzibilnocac, and Edzná.

About 400 B.C. transcendental changes took place that marked the beginning of the Late Preclassic. One of the distinctive characteristics of this epoch, which ended by A.D. 250, was an atmosphere of violence and competition between the principal power centers, which is illustrated by the massive burials of sacrificed victims in places such as Cuello and Chalchuapa. Some scholars propose that the continuous skirmishes and open warfare of the period are among the causes of the florescence and collapse of Preclassic capitals such as El Mirador and also served to catalyze the emergence of state societies. Another characteristic of the Late Preclassic are architectural works requiring several thousand workers and organized specialists for their construction. What had been the residential areas of Middle Preclassic villages became the sites of impressive architectural works. Some of the most notable examples are the fifty-five-meter-high complex called El Tigre at El Mirador; Structure II at Calakmul (also fifty-five meters high); the North Acropolis at Tikal; the thirty-three-meter-high pyramid at Lamanai; the two-kilometer-long defensive moat that surrounded Becán; and the pier and canal at Cerros. On the other hand, public architecture at sites in Yucatán such as Dzibilchaltún and Komchén never reached such dimensions.

Many of the temples in the lower central territories were beautifully decorated with great stucco masks, images of the deities at the end of the Preclassic. Among them were the sun and the planet Venus studied by Linda Schele and David Freidel at Structure 5C-2nd at Cerros. The same passion for representing the supernatural can be clearly seen much further south at Izapa and Abaj Takalik, although the images there appear on stelae and stone altars. Mythical images that were to be repeated for centuries to come such as the sacred tree that joins the sky, the surface of the earth, and the underworld as well as depictions of adventures of gods can be seen. The artistic style, the mythological themes, and the use of Long Count calendrical notation has led many scholars to propose that both centers are a link between the Olmec and Maya Cultures. From this perspective, the ideology of the Mayas is seen to have originated on the Pacific Coast near the present border between Mexico and Guatemala.

THE GULF IN THE PRECLASSIC

Little remains of the lush environment where the villagers of the Barí River lived in the third millennium B.C. and which still existed when Matthew W. Stirling explored the capitals of the Olmec world in the 1940s. Today, cattle raising and petroleum drilling and exploration have ravaged the jungles of Veracruz and Tabasco, turning them into savannas. Nevertheless, in this enormous coastal plain a wide hydrological network containing large rivers and extensive swamps still survives. The climate is tropical, with torrential rains. The area of widest cultural activity included almost eighteen thousand km² and surpassed the basins of the Papaloapan and Tonalá Rivers. In the center of this area of uniform altitude rise the Tuxtla Mountains. The oldest Preclassic settlements yet found in the area are in Tabasco, near La Venta. About 2250 B.C., people cultivated the shores of the Barí River and utilized the resources of the mangrove swamp, this rich environment suppling them with fish, mollusks, turtles, fish, and deer that—together with maize and, probably, manioc—sustained them. The people first manufactured pottery between 1750 and 1400 B.C. During this period migrants from Soconusco belonging to the Great Isthmus Tradition may have arrived in the Gulf region. These peoples would make ceramics in San Lorenzo between 1500 and 1150 B.C. (Ojochi, Bajío, and Chicharras Phases) that were similar to the ceramics of Ocós on the coast of the Pacific.

The Middle Preclassic is associated with the seven-century (1150–400 B.C.) history of the Olmecs. Debate continues regarding the origin of Olmec civilization, which has been primarily associated with the Maya and Mixe linguistic families. Recently, it has been proposed that the Olmecs were a fusion of peoples of the Maya, Mixe, and Oaxaca linguistic families, all of which were united in advanced chiefdoms.

Olmec art is so beautiful that many scholars have chosen to do stylistic and iconographic studies of it and have paid less attention to the social and economic aspects of the people who made it. The number of publications on topics such as agricultural production, the use of resources, and settlement patterns is relatively small. Nevertheless, a study of the complex symbols portrayed in very different works ranging from huge basalt monoliths to small greenstone sculptures is a magnificent way to learn basic aspects of the social organization, legitimation of hierarchy, and religious concepts of the people who made them (see fig. 4). The sculptures reaffirm the social position and wealth of the elites. Supernatural beings are depicted next to the images of the rulers, thus giving the latter a semidivine aspect. Servants and war captives are also depicted next to kings, alluding to the material aspects of power. Olmec art depicts a complex pantheon, with deities acquiring fantastic forms that meld human and animal traits. The mythic world is expressed in a vigorous style along with natural figures such as alligators, sharks, serpents, birds of prey, and, above all, jaguars. Often, schematic anatomical elements—jaws, wings, claws, eyebrows, skin spots—suffice to represent these beings. There is a seemingly obsessive fusion of human and jaguar in representations of chubby-cheeked infants with long fangs, feline lips, and even claws.

As F. Kent Reilly points out, the symbols reproduce the topology of the universe. The Olmecs conceived the surface of the earth as a plane

Fig. 4. Examples of Olmec iconography. Preclassic period.

defined by four corners and a center that was the axis of the world. The earth was personified as a mythical being with a V-shaped cut on its head. From this cut emerged a maize plant, a polyvalent symbol of royal power and of the cosmic tree that linked the sky with the underworld. The other four points of the plane were similar columns supporting the cosmos. This five-pointed design was repeated in the sky in the shape of a St. Andrews Cross.

Examples of Olmec art come from archaeological sites such as San Lorenzo, La Venta, Tres Zapotes, El Manatí, Laguna de los Cerros, Potrero Nuevo, and Las Limas, San Lorenzo being the major Olmec center between 1150 and 900 B.C. San Lorenzo was located between the Highlands and the fertile plains watered by the Coatzacoalcos and Chiquito Rivers. Most of its buildings were erected atop a great natural platform 45 meters high and 50 hectares in area that had been made uniform by humans. The predominant shapes are earthen mounds enclosing rectangular plazas, and there are also numerous dwellings. Among the most important urban-planning works in San Lorenzo was

an aqueduct made from large carved basalt pieces that has been excavated along a stretch of 170 meters. Even more remarkable when one
considers the amount of labor involved in making them are the beautiful monuments sculpted during the apogee of this site. Hundreds of
men were probably needed to transport the enormous stones from
Mount Cintepec in the Tuxtla Mountains 70 kilometers away, taking
them on rafts through the currents of the Coatzacoalcos River. Some
of the ten monoliths found so far are colossal male heads covered with
tight-fitting helmets. Because there are differences in their features,
they probably are portraits of actual rulers. Other monoliths have been
called altars because they have flat tops. Some of the sculptural motifs
of these altars include that of a ruler sitting in a niche that represents
the mouth of the earth, holding a small child with jaguar aspects on his
knees.

During San Lorenzo's peak, other sites such as La Venta and Tres
Zapotes were also actively being built. They too carved colossal heads.
Four have been found in La Venta and two in Tres Zapotes. Nor was
cultural homogeneity limited to colossal sculptures at this time. The
buildings at La Venta are oriented on the same axis as those in San
Lorenzo (see plan 3). Both sites have altars, underground aqueducts,
offerings with greenstone figurines, and hematite mirrors. San Lorenzo
declined about 900 B.C., while La Venta reached its maximum splendor
during the following four centuries, although monumental sculptures
were no longer carved. Contrary to long-held opinion, La Venta was
not merely a ceremonial center. It is true that the large public buildings were located on an island, but there was an extensive population
distributed in the surrounding territory, which was traversed by rivers
and swamps. Several plazas form the center of La Venta. The principal
plaza (Complex C) is bordered by two elongated structures, a low
mound and a large thirty-four-meter-high pyramid. As Rebecca González
Lauck's investigations show, the pyramid has a radial base with turned-
in corners. To the north, on the same axis, lies another rectangular
plaza (Complex A), which at one time was surrounded by several buildings and a wall of two-meter-high prismatic basalt columns. Under its
superimposed pink, purple, and red clay floors were found massive
offerings of serpentine, mosaic pavements forming geometric masks of
telluric beings, axes, and greenstone figurines. At the northern end of

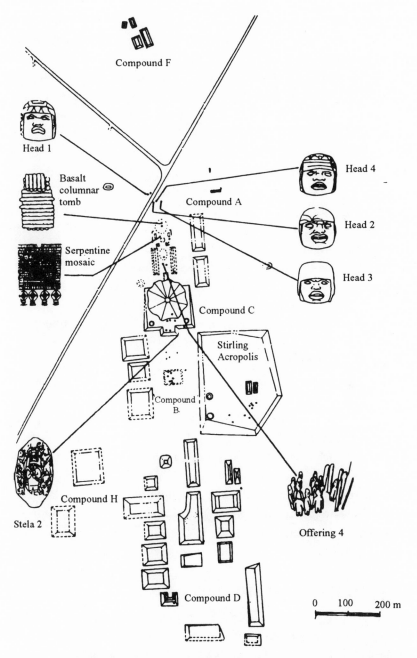

Compound F

Head 1

Basalt
columnar
tomb

Compound A

Head 4

Head 2

Serpentine
mosaic

Head 3

Compound C

Stirling
Acropolis

Compound
B

Compound H

Stela 2

Offering 4

Compound D

0   100   200 m

Plan 3. La Venta Archaeological Zone, Tabasco. Gulf Area, Preclassic period. (Redrawn by Marco Antonio Pacheco © *Arqueología Mexicana*, INAH) this plaza lies a clay mound under which was found a tomb with a roof and walls made of basalt pillars in which two juvenile bodies lay. According to archaeologists, La Venta came to a violent end as San Lorenzo had centuries before. About 400 B.C., twenty of the twenty-four large stone monuments known to date at La Venta were mutilated.

Tres Zapotes, the third of the great Olmec centers, was located on the hills surrounding a swampy basin of the Papaloapan and San Juan Rivers. In Tres Zapotes there are more than fifty buildings and numerous stone monuments. The long sculptural tradition continued at Tres Zapotes for several centuries after the fall of the Olmec world, which is dated by archaeologists at 400 B.C. We do not know with any certainty what happened at that time, but scholars consider that after that date one can no longer speak of the Olmecs as a cultural unit. Afterward, during the Late Preclassic, Tres Zapotes continued to be inhabited by peoples supposedly from the linguistic family of the Olmecs—the Mixes. Even its artistic production resembled that of the great disappeared culture, which has led to the period's being called the Epi-Olmec. Stele C, the most famous monument from this period, combines a style clearly derived from Olmec art with a Long Count calendrical date of 31 B.C. It is one of the earliest examples of the use of this calendrical system.

Other early examples of Long Count dates accompanied by long hieroglyphic inscriptions come from the Gulf Area. The most notable are the Tuxtla Statuette (A.D. 162) and La Mojarra Stele 1 (A.D. 143 and 156) (see fig. 5). The latter shows the richly attired figure of a ruler accompanied by an extraordinarily long text describing the principal political events of his life, proving that this calendrical system and complex writing were not unique to the Classic Maya period, which were preceded by those developed by Mixe-Zoque peoples.

THE OLMECS AND THE PRECLASSIC

Three great epochs can be synthesized in the Preclassic. The first period, which established Mesoamerica, was characterized by a number of similar agricultural villages linked by barter and inhabited by egalitarian groups. In the second crucial period a chain of related villages became a complex multiethnic web. Centers of political, economic, and

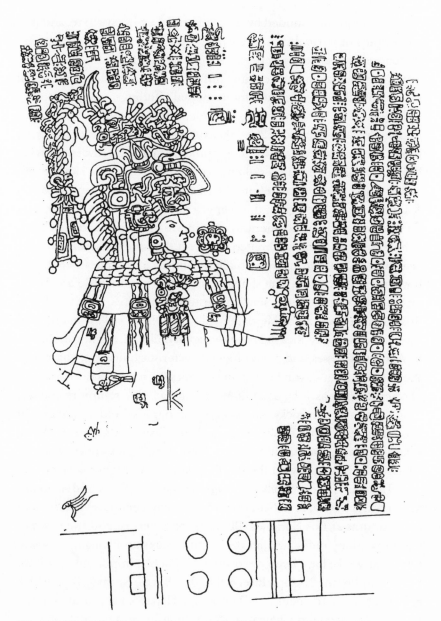

Fig. 5. Stele 1, La Mojarra, Veracruz. Gulf Area, Preclassic period.

religious power surrounded by villages popped up everywhere, and new techniques of agricultural intensification arose. From that time on, Mesoamerican societies were stratified. The third and final period of the Preclassic was one of regional differentiation, the development of writing and the calendar, and monumental buildings.

If we look at Mesoamerica as a whole, it is clear that the second or Middle Preclassic period (1200–400 B.C.) was one of maturation, during which the barriers set up by geographic or linguistic diversities were broken, leading to the universalization of Olmec dynamism. However, we first face the problem of defining the Olmecs. Very different historical realities have all been given this name: a people from the Gulf Area, an art style, and a pan-Mesoamerican culture. We have discussed the Olmec people, whose habitat was limited to the southeast of Veracruz and western Tabasco, but the art style usually attributed to them transcends the borders of this region. The shapes and symbols of this style are found on crags, caves, monoliths, small greenstone sculptures, and clay objects disseminated over all of Mesoamerica, The Olmec style is manifested from Jalisco to Costa Rica in images of jaguar-children, flaming eyebrows, St. Andrews Crosses, and many other characteristic traits. As we have said, the Olmec presence can be seen in ceramics from the Pacific Coast and Oaxaca as early as 1150 B.C. Olmec-style megalithic sculptures, stelae, bas-reliefs carved in rocky outcroppings, and household art abound in the State of Chiapas at sites such as Xoc, Tzutzuculi, Ojo de Agua, Altamira, Izapa, and Aquiles Serdán. Similar examples are common in Guatemala, principally on the Pacific Coast and at higher sites such as Abaj Takalik. There are rock paintings in Cañón Muñeca, and sites exist in Central America, in El Salvador at Chalchoapa and Las Victorias and in Honduras at Los Naranjos, Playa de los Muertos, and the caves of Cuyamel. Many miles away, in the Central Mexican Plateau, extensive Olmec artworks have been discovered. In Puebla, important sites have been found in the Nexapa River Valley, Las Bocas, Necaxa, Tepatlaxco, and San Martín Texmelucan. Tlatilco and Tlapacoya are located in the Basin of Mexico, and Chalcatzingo, Atlihuayán, and Guadalupita are important sites in Morelos. Guerrero has an impressive archaeological site at Teopantecunitlán as well as the cave paintings of Juxtlahuaca and Oxtotitlan. Many artifacts in the purest Olmec style, primarily ceramics and objects of polished greenstone, have been excavated in peripheral regions, probably having reached them as prized exchange goods. Clear examples of this are a celt discovered in Etzatlán, Jalisco, and numerous objects now found in private and public collections in Costa Rica.

Who, then, were the creators of the style that, since the 1920s, we have called "Olmec"? The customary reply is that they were the inhabitants of the Gulf who spread their culture to peoples of lesser cultures. Guerrero and Morelos have also been proposed as sources of diffusion. This view, which assumes a direct influence of culturally active societies over less evolved and more malleable populations, creates a new problem, however. The term *influence* is vague and can include a great range of types of events. In an effort to be more precise, scholars have proposed various vehicles for the spread of culture, such as military conquests; commercial expansion that distributed sumptuary objects in exchange for raw materials such as obsidian, cinnabar, greenstones, and the iron ores needed to make mirrors; colonization or the migration of groups who taught the local populations a new life-style; and the diffusion of religious doctrine by missionaries.

According to a new view that is presently gaining support, Olmecs of the Gulf Area set up a trading network with many different ethnic groups that were located in distant territories. According to Flannery, these ethnic groups had incipient elites who reinforced their hierarchical position by adopting the Olmec ideology and using prestige goods imported from places such as La Venta and San Lorenzo. The ideas, symbols, adopted customs, and, perhaps, interchange of women among the elites must have reinforced social and political contrasts within chiefdoms in most of Mesoamerica.

It would be difficult to evaluate these hypotheses empirically today. It is difficult, on the basis of archaeological evidence, to distinguish between past processes of conquest, commercial expansion, colonization, and evangelization. Although there are data that support some of the proposals at some of the sites, we do not have archaeological methods and techniques accurate enough to convert such data into proofs. In addition, it is probable that in every region, and even in every epoch in the same region, one or more of the processes mentioned above took place.

Although they are still deeply held, hypotheses involving a direct, single influence have recently been losing adherents. Within a few years we have gone from the concept of a "Mother Culture" to that of many "Sister Cultures." For example, Christine Niederberger has pointed out that radiocarbon dates do not support the early existence of the Olmecs at a single cultural site. On the contrary, beginning in the thirteenth century B.C. there was a synchronous emergence of Olmec symbolic and stylistic manifestations. This is apparent in places far from the Gulf Coast, where works with an artistic quality far surpassing that of simple provincial copies were made from local raw materials. Based on such evidence, Niederberger proposed that around 1200 B.C., as a result of a general process of economic osmosis, the first pan-Mesoamerican culture was born, with the so-called Olmec style as its most tangible evidence. The process involved a simultaneous cultural maturation of numerous ethnic groups inhabiting a vast and geographically diverse territory.

If what Niederberger proposes was true, the societies of the Gulf Area—strictly defined as the Olmecs—because of their degree of socio-economic development might be considered the most advanced example of the culture that characterized the Middle Preclassic period. During this period chiefdoms with different levels of development proliferated, though all of them had a high degree of political centralization, a hierarchical social organization, an appreciable level of technical and artistic specialization, and a complex ceremonialism.

CHAPTER THREE

The Mesoamerican Classic Period

A GENERAL VIEW OF THE CLASSIC PERIOD

The term "Classic," the basis of the most-used nomenclature of the Mesoamerican periods, is implicitly loaded with aesthetic judgment. It designates an era of great splendor, when the arts, particularly in urbanism and architecture, peaked in Mesoamerica simultaneously with an unexcelled affluence among the elites, commercial prosperity, the unquestioned power of rulers, and the great evolution of the calendar, writing, and sky observation. The Classic period begins in A.D. 200, but its roots can be found much earlier—about 400 B.C.—when population growth; a greater concentration of population; an increasing division of labor with its concomitant specialization; the production of goods destined for regional and interregional exchange; and greater stratification of villages, regional centers, and protourban capitals occurred. Many scholars call this glorious end of the Preclassic period the Protoclassic, because many of the social, economic, and political processes fundamental to the Classic period developed then. These included the deepening of class differences, the development of interchange networks, the appearance of ruling lineages, and the beginnings of complex systems of arithmetic, calendrics, and writing. At this time massive architecture developed in some of the planned urban centers, notably Kaminaljuyú and Izapa in the middle of the Southeast, El Mirador and Uaxactún in the Petén, San José Mogote and Monte Albán in Oaxaca, Tres Zapotes in the Gulf, and Cuicuilco and Teotihuacan in Central Mexico.

This process reached its greatest heights during the Classic period, with the most crucial change the polarization between cities and rural areas. The capital cities became so large that they were incapable of feeding themselves. The rural areas became the source of sustenance, while the cities became the great concentrators and distributors of wealth. The tranformation in this period was stimulated by abundant harvests; adequate channels for the flow of resources from society's periphery to its center, large-scale specialized manufacture of goods destined for commerce; the integration of regional production centers; reliable interregional trade, the control of mercantile networks; and the existence of complex administrative structures capable of starting and organizing production, directing and protecting commerce, and redistributing the goods that flowed into the capitals.

Urban centers that controlled key regions with developed agricultural techniques and abundant complementary resources, particularly those from lakes and rivers, had an advantage. For the greatest development of cities, however, control over strategic natural resources was needed. This was the case for Teotihuacan, which ran nearby obsidian mines and was able to produce enormous quantities of volcanic glass tools in its many specialized workshops. In addition to being centers for the production and distribution of manufactured goods, cities were the settings for political decisions that were crucial for society and the stages for the principal religious activities.

One of the most difficult challenges for archaeologists of the Classic has been the identification of the agricultural techniques that fed the cities. Researchers have proposed a wide utilization of orchards, cultivated terraces, flood and canal irrigation, dams, and chinampas as well as other techniques allowing intensive production. Raised fields, terraced hillsides, fields enclosed by stone walls, and small raised orchards have all been the subjects of intense study in the Maya area. It has been proposed that well irrigation and high-water-table agriculture were used in the Oaxaca Valley. According to researchers, the springs in the Teotihuacan Valley led into canals and there was an inland zone that was usable for chinampa cultivation. We now know, however, that most of the Teotihuacan and Oaxacan fields depended on rainfall and at the same time deny that simple slash-and-burn (swidden) maize cultivation would have been sufficient to sustain a city.

It is possible for archaeologists to understand the technology of the Classic, but social, political, and cultural aspects remain obscure. Despite the remarkable recent advances in Maya epigraphy, the kinds of messages contained in the hieroglyphic texts are too limited to provide answers to the many questions of historians. Among them are questions dealing with social and political organization at the time. If we have trouble understanding what the basic Maya social units were, how their governments were organized, and what relationships existed between different cities, one can imagine our ignorance in regards to Teotihuacan, which did not have writing as the Maya did. Which ethnic groups dominated the city? What languages did they speak? How were the neighborhoods organized? What kind of government did the city have? Were the people ruled by royal lineages? In the absence of multifarious texts we have to await technical and methodological advances in archaeology, physical anthropology, and iconography in order to answer these basic questions with any certainty.

Despite these limitations, however, we can clearly see that there were two different branches of practice, of social and political concepts, in the traditions of the Classic. This separation in traditions, which began in the Late Preclassic, can be clearly seen in differing systems of calendrical reckoning and different levels of complexity in the recording of thought. The first branch (including Teotihuacan) retained relatively simpler systems of calendrical reckoning based on the combination of a 365-day agricultural-religious cycle and a 260-day divinatory cycle. The systems of the other branch (particularly the Mayas) were much more complicated. This branch's calendar, in addition to the two-cycle combination, used a 360-day historical-divinatory cycle as well as a Long Count Initial Day Calendar, requiring extremely complex calculations.

In recording thought, the first branch tried to depict mental representations while the second branch depicted verbal expressions. In the first branch a symbol (ideogram or figurative symbol) represented an idea, while in the second branch a symbol (logogram or verbal symbol) represented words, which, in turn, represented ideas. A logogram could be semantic or phonetic. The three-step process caused the second branch to follow some linguistic rules, including rules of syntactic order.

As is usually the case in systems of recording thought, neither the first nor the second branch is absolute and each has some mixed characteristics. In the area of numeration, numbers in the first branch did not have positional values; however, the second branch, which used place-value notation, invented the equivalent of "zero" or "place taken."

The second branch, then, took a giant step forward during the Classic, as can be seen in Maya advances in writing and computation of time. This divergence was apparently due to differences in the social and political institutions of the two branches. It is interesting to note that the most powerful polity of the Classic, Teotihuacan, did not use writing, numbers, or a calendar as the Mayas did. Given the extent of the interactions between the Mayas and Teotihuacan during the Early Classic, the absence of these complex systems in Central Mexico can only be explained by the existence of social and governmental arrangements that did not need them. This assertion, to which we will return in subsequent chapters, is based on studies that have emphasized the political and propaganda value of Maya calendrical and writing systems.

Another difference between the cultures of Central Mexico and those of the Southeast during the Classic was the relative level of warfare. Neither Teotihuacan nor the Mayas were peaceful people, but the latest research shows that the Mayas lived in an atmosphere that might almost be called one of endemic warfare. Nothing that extreme has yet been found in Teotihuacan. Nevertheless, even Maya warfare during the Classic did not reach the level of pronounced militarism that prevailed during the Postclassic.

In general the most important cohesive factor during the Classic was long-distance trade. When the great capitals joined to exchange goods, they also facilitated cultural interaction as never before. Commercial efficiency was made possible by an extremely organized network that was begun, developed, and controlled by Teotihuacan until the middle of the seventh century. After Teotihuacan collapsed, the network became fragmented and other cities assumed control of trade, but the original network was never resurrected.

Cities were the most spectacular manifestations of the Classic. Teotihuacan is unique, with its orthogonal plan and regularly spaced streets. Monte Albán rises majestically, dominating the width of the valley, its terraces going down the slopes from its Great Plaza. The Maya cities—

a constellation in the jungle—generally follow the contours of the land but always maintain the harmony of their architectural complexes, including plazas, temples, palaces, and ball courts. In all areas of Mesoamerica, cities were built following cosmic models and the movements of astronomical bodies on the horizon. Urbanization was complex and advanced, and care was taken with details. Building began with massive administrative and ceremonial architectural centers, followed by extensive, sometimes extremely compact residential zones. City builders also managed the storage and distribution of water, providing storm drains and removal of wastes. Roads and aqueducts were profusely decorated, with continuous iconographic messages carved into sculptures in the round, mosaics, smooth polished and painted stucco surfaces, and sumptuous murals. All of these helped to make each city a prototype of power, religion, and knowledge.

Cities were production centers for the prestige goods worn by local elites and interchanged throughout the superarea. Their workshops produced carved semiprecious stones, feather headdresses, fine cotton garments, and shell jewelry in addition to luxury ceramics of the most varied shapes, decorations, and functions. The workshops also produced enormous quantities of utilitarian goods made primarily of clay and of stones such as obsidian and flint. These objects were usually made in standard sizes and shapes, and some were mass-produced with molds.

Many of the characteristics of religion that developed in the Classic endured until the Spanish conquest. Much of the Mesoamerican pantheon crystallized during this period; personified deities were depicted in Classic paintings and sculptures with attributes and costumes that allow us to identify them on the basis of the iconography of subsequent periods. Gods associated with rain, fire, earth, and the progression of time became extremely important and were used to justify the power of the rulers. It is probable that, from the beginning of the Classic, priests monopolized knowledge about the course of time, the will of the gods, mathematics, astrology, history, art, and even—some scholars have proposed—trade and politics. They used all their knowledge to benefit the powerful, who clearly enlisted the priesthood as a useful adjunct.

Conventionally, the Classic is dated between A.D. 200 and 650/900, but the limits vary considerably when we look at different cultural areas; the period spanned 200–650/750 in Central Mexico and 292–810/909 in the Southeast, for example. The difference in starting dates is simply due to an earlier or later start in beginning urbanization. However, the reasons for the large disparity in ending dates for the Classic—indicated by the dates when the great cities declined—are more complex. The cities fell one by one over a period of at least 150 years for reasons that are still unclear, precluding generalizations about the temporal subdivisions. Experts on the Southeast distinguish the Early from the Late Classic on the basis of the presence of Teotihuacan in the area in the former and its absence in the latter. Additionally, the most vigorous cultural push of the Mayas took place in the Early Classic. In the Late Classic a sufficient flowering of the Mayas took place that many scholars consider this period to be the apotheosis of Mesoamerican civilization. Some periodizations attempting to compare the later dates of the Maya area with those of Central Mexico name the period from A.D. 650 to 900 the Terminal Classic. We will return to this topic in the chapters dealing with the end of the Classic and the Epiclassic.

Among all the Classic capitals none had the physical, urban, and political dimensions of Teotihuacan. So disproportionate was the size of Teotihuacan compared to the next greatest centers that one could say there was a case of megacephaly in Central Mexico. It is estimated that the city reached 125,000 inhabitants, and perhaps even 200,000. These are very high numbers not only for Mesoamerica but for anywhere in the world at that time. In the Oaxaca area, on the other hand, there was a proliferation of cities, particularly in the Valley of Oaxaca and in the Mixteca Alta and Baja regions. An interesting hierarchy of urban centers developed in the Oaxaca Valley based on the size and importance of the centers in the regional system. Monte Albán, which maintained a strong relationship with Teotihuacan, sat at the apex of its region.

Things were very different in West Mexico. With the exception of Guerrero, the area was extremely isolated from the rest of Mesoamerica. In a strict sense this area never reached an urban phase, making a distinction between the Preclassic and the Classic in West Mexico vague. This relative evolutionary backwardness led to the appearance of many local cultures in the West. Although these cultures were relatively independent of each other, they shared a considerable aesthetic development in ceramics.

The dates of the Classic encompass practically all of the existence of the northern area. The area's difficult ecological conditions resulted in a late agricultural settlement, possibly by outposts from the neighboring societies of the West, the Center, and the Gulf at the dawn of the Christian Era. The groups brought advanced techniques to the North that allowed these lands to be cultivated somewhat more successfully. A thousand years later, the farmers abandoned North Mesoamerica. Although the area as a whole could be characterized as a territory shared by sedentary societies, societies with a mixed economy, and hunter-gatherers, different processes occurred in its three zones. The central zone could not sustain much development. In the eastern zone, because of cinnabar mines, centers established in the rocky foothills of the mining region flourished. In the western zone the Chalchihuites culture, whose northernmost extensions reached Durango, flourished.

The Gulf differed from the North in keeping close relationships with the rest of Mesoamerica, particularly Teotihuacan. Nevertheless, despite the exquisite art objects produced in this area during the Classic, only three important urban centers are presently known. Two of them, El Tajín and Cerro de las Mesas, were independent, and the other, Matacapan, was an enclave of Teotihuacan.

Finally, during the Classic multiple city-states arose in the Southeast. These city-states were the cradle of the greatest artistic splendor of Mesoamerica and the places where the calendar, numeration, and writing achieved a unique complexity.

CENTRAL MEXICO IN THE CLASSIC

Teotihuacan was the quintessential Mesoamerican city. Nevertheless, its greatness and hegemony were preordained centuries before it became an urban area. As we discussed above, in the late Preclassic two cities, Cuicuilco and Teotihuacan, ruled the Basin of Mexico. Between 100 B.C. and A.D. 150 Cuicuilco lost its place as the major population center in the area, while Teotihuacan doubled its population. Some time later, at the dawn of the Christian Era and perhaps due to the eruptions of Xitle, 75 percent of the population of the Basin moved to the Teotihuacan Valley. We must ask why such a concentration of humanity

occurred in such a small area and why the most famous city of the
Classic flourished precisely there.

The 505-square-kilometer Teotihuacan Valley is less than 6.5 percent
of the total surface of the Basin of Mexico. It is rich in alluvial land and
benefits from various sources of water, among them the San Juan, San
Lorenzo, and Huixulco Rivers as well as numerous permanent springs.
Furthermore, in prehispanic times Lake Texcoco extended as far as the
fertile plains of Acolman.

Besides agriculture, Teotihuacan had obsidian, the most economically important mineral of the time, and manufactured a variety of
obsidian utensils that reached all the corners of Mesoamerica. Gray-
streaked obsidian was obtained from Mount Olivares, near Otumba;
green obsidian was extracted from a small volcano west of Tulancingo
and from the exceptionally rich mines of the Sierra de las Navajas near
Pachuca. The region was also the source of an excellent clay for pottery
making and of basalt, slate, *tezontle* (a porous volcanic rock used in construction), andesite, and sandstone.

There were two other factors that facilitated Teotihuacan's urban
development. First, its valley lay on a privileged position across the most
direct trade route between the Gulf of Mexico and the Basin of Mexico.
Second, it contained numerous artificial caves—former quarries of
basalt and *tezontle*— that became sacred, making the region a prestigious shrine. At the end of the Preclassic, the Pyramid of the Sun was
erected on top of one of these underground caves. This man-made
cavity consists of a one-hundred-meter-long access tunnel and a four-
part chamber representing the Underworld.

Thanks to the studies of Rene Millon, William T. Sanders, and
George L. Cowgill, we know the historical sequence of the metropolis
and its rural surroundings from its beginning to its end. By the first
Classic Phase, Miccaotli (A.D. 150–250), Teotihuacan could be considered
a true city. It did not expand in area but rather in density and complexity. This was a time of flowering and of commercial expansion. In fact,
there is evidence that Teotihuacan's obsidian reached Altún Ha in
Belize. The construction of the north-south axis, later called the Avenue
of the Dead (*Miccaotli*) by the Mexicas, dates to this time. The Ciudadela,
the Temple of Quetzalcoatl, and possibly the Temple of Agriculture and
the Viking Group were also built during this period.

The population of Teotihuacan increased during the following phase, Tlamimilolpa (A.D. 250–400). The Moon Plaza, the Temple of Feathered Conches, and the Great Compound in front of the Ciudadela were built at this time. Most of the apartment complexes also date from this period. The best evidence for the cosmopolitan character of the city is the establishment of an Oaxaca barrio, reflecting the strong Teotihuacan presence in the Valley of Oaxaca, particularly at Monte Albán. But Teotihuacan reached much further, to Kaminaljuyú in the Guatemalan Highlands. Another evidence of the extent of foreign relationships is the artistic influence that the city received from the Gulf Coast. Beginning with the Tlamimilolpa Phase, the luxury ceramic called Thin Orange by archaeologists, was exported together with obsidian, which was always a key component of Teotihuacan's trade. The origin of these ceramics is still debatable. We know that the clay mines and manufacturing site were in the southern part of the modern state of Puebla, but Teotihuacan was indisputably the distributor to all of Mesoamerica.

The phase of maximum splendor was Xolalpan (A.D. 400–550). The population averaged 125,000 inhabitants but possibly reached 200,000. According to Millon, by A.D. 600 Teotihuacan was the sixth most populous city in the world. Despite this, the city shrank in area by greatly concentrating its population, affecting the configuration of the apartment compounds.

The last phase of Classic Teotihuacan was Metepec (A.D. 550–650). The population diminished to 85,000 during this period. There is evidence that the center of the city was looted and burned, and it is calculated that at least 147 buildings were damaged by fire. Despite having by then lost its Mesoamerican hegemony, Teotihuacan's size still made it an important center in the Central Plateau. With its 30,000 inhabitants, it would retain this importance for almost two more centuries (Xometla and Oxtotícpac Phases, post-650).

As we have mentioned, during the Classic, radical changes took place in settlement patterns in the Basin of Mexico in connection with the rise of an urban/rural dichotomy. During the period of A.D. 300–650, an extremely high percentage of the 230,000 inhabitants of the Basin lived in Teotihuacan. The remaining population was distributed among 9 regional centers, 17 large villages, 77 small villages, and 149 hamlets.

Two of the most interesting questions of this urban/rural relationship concern the reason why the people aggregated and the source of their food. Among several global explanations is the one proposed by Sanders, who linked the increase in population and the dramatic changes in settlement pattern and political organization in the Classic to the development of hydraulic agriculture. According to Sanders, Teotihuacan reclaimed land from the swampy sources of the San Juan River by building chinampas devoted to intensive cultivation. In addition the people cultivated numerous large fields with permanent irrigation from the many springs in the Valley. This is an intriguing hypothesis, but other investigators doubt that it is possible to prove on the basis of archaeological remains that these agricultural techniques were actually employed in such remote times.

Nevertheless, most of the crops were rain fed. Scholars believe that Teotihuacan practiced swidden agriculture, in which the land is fertilized by cutting and burning the ground cover. This technique allows crops to be planted two or three years in a row, followed by an equal period of rest that allows the land to regain its nutrients. These scholars are convinced that Teotihuacan farmers, like modern peasants, built terraces on moderate sloping hills with walls made from rocks and agave plants. The existence of flood irrigation, achieved by guiding water in ravines with small dams, has also been suggested. On the other hand, Sanders proposed that the alluvial lands around the city were not cultivated by farmers but rather by two-thirds of the city dwellers—an unusual case, but one that is found elsewhere. These cultivators would have been individuals also engaged in other activities, primarily handicrafts. Even so, there would have been a sizable farming population in the suburbs of Teotihuacan.

A diet based on maize, beans, squash, and chile was supplemented with many other cultigens as well as by foods obtained through gathering, hunting, and fishing. Animal protein came primarily from rabbits, deer, and domesticated dogs, with a smaller proportion coming from turkeys, geese, quails, armadillos, squirrels, and lizards. Nearby Lake Texcoco and the rivers feeding it provided Teotihuacan with birds, including migratory ones, as well as fish, frogs, turtles and an infinity of insects and their eggs, which were scooped from the water. The lake was also a source of salt.

Despite the incredible volume of food it produced, Teotihuacan's prosperity was due to its handicrafts. As we stated above, the city depended to a large extent on the export of manufactured goods, primarily objects made from obsidian. Numerous specialized workshops for making prismatic blades, knives, and projectile points were found almost everywhere in the city. Besides obsidian, artisans in Teotihuacan worked minerals such as basalt, andesite, slate, flint, and sandstone. All sorts of goods such as scrapers, rasps, points, mortars, polishers, crushers, door hinges, and stone-facing slabs were made. Teotihuacan is also famous for its polished stone objects, particularly its greenstone masks.

Ceramics were also important, the clays coming from different places in the Valley, and—because of their volcanic origin—after firing producing the black, cream, pinkish, grayish, and brown colors characteristic of Teotihuacan ceramics. There was also specialization in the making of ceramics, with some potters concentrating on the production of wares for the domestic market. An interesting example is a workshop found in Tlajinga, where bowls and amphoras of the type called San Martín Orange were made in ovens dug into the hardpan subsoil (*tepetate*). Other potters produced ritual objects such as theater-type censers, which were made next to the Ciudadela. Teotihuacan ceramics took many forms and were richly decorated. Mass production commonly required the use of molds as well as the technique of coil pottery. There was a proliferation of human figurines with large flat heads, totally or partially bald and wearing large headdresses. Containers were also made with in the characteristic shapes that would spread the Teotihuacan style throughout Mesoamerica, including cylindrical tripod vases (*cajetes*) with extremely thin walls and "merlon-shaped" supports. Often, the ceramic vessels were adorned with a complicated geometric symbolism as well as natural figures.

About A.D. 600 Teotihuacan exhibited an amazing regularity based on the two orthogonal axes that ordered its urban space. The Avenue of the Dead, the main axis, ran north to south, terminating at the Moon Plaza. The other axis, five kilometers long, ran east to west, following the modified bed of the San Juan River that passed along the north side of the Ciudadela and the Great Compound. These axes divided the city into four quadrants, causing the image of the city to correspond to that of the earth, whose sacred symbol was a great flower with four petals. At the same time, the axes were the basis for a grid that created large blocks, many of them sixty meters on a side. The streets were straight and lay over the potable water system and the network of sewers and drains that emptied into the San Juan River.

Architecture at Teotihuacan followed a rigid plan in which symmetry and the rhythmic repetition of elements affirmed that the earthly city was a replica of the divine archetype. The predominant style was the *talud/tablero* combination, a sloping lower section (talus) combined with an overhanging rectangular vertical panel (entablature) with a protruding border. This combination was repeated almost endlessly, with superimposed talud/tablero units that made solid-looking buildings of several tiers and great plasticity. This arrangement, characteristic of Teotihuacan's architecture, was widely diffused during the Classic. Rather than being monotonous, these modules were varied due to both the play of light and shadow and the brightly painted colors on their stuccoed surfaces. The horizontal skyline was broken by vertical stone plaques of a symbolic and ornamental character that crowned the buildings. Teotihuacan's public architecture was matched by its equally monumental geometric-style sculpture, characterized by prismatic monoliths with images of gods and animals usually associated with water and fertility.

A bird's-eye view of the city reveals a succession of closed spaces devoted to work and private life and of large open spaces devoted to the public activities of religion, commerce, recreation, and government. The Avenue of the Dead, more than three kilometers long and forty-five meters wide with a slope of about thirty meters, spanned by staggered terraces, is the spinal column of the city. The urban center is dominated by two cyclopean temples. The Pyramid of the Moon rises at the northernmost end of the Avenue, its plaza forming the most beautiful ceremonial architectural space in the city. Not far south of it, alongside the Avenue of the Dead, looms the Pyramid of the Sun, the biggest structure of the site. This enormous mass, perhaps dedicated to the cult of an aquatic deity, retains its primitive character because most of its taludes were never modernized by the addition of tableros.

Following the downslope of the Avenue of the Dead, one crosses a bridge over the bed of the San Juan River and arrives at the two largest open spaces in the city. The Ciudadela, which—despite its name—did not have a defensive function, lies to the east. It is square in shape, four hundred meters on a side, bordered by a platform with stairs and topped with small temples. Two dwelling complexes at its northeast and southeast quadrants were probably inhabited by the supreme rulers or high-ranking priests. A red pyramid with four superimposed platforms lies at the rear of the precinct. Thanks to archaeological excavations, the original decor of the principal facade of the Temple of Quetzalcoatl, which was partially covered and protected by the red pyramid, is now visible. By A.D. 500 this temple was hidden from the inhabitants of Teotihuacan. Undoubtedly the most sumptuous architectural structure built in the long history of Teotihuacan, its four facades were totally covered by monoliths that repeatedly portrayed the sinuous body of the Feathered Serpent, bearing a headdress. For a long time this image was mistakenly thought to be the face of Tlaloc. Today, we know that the temple as a whole refers to a myth about the creation of time and its chief protagonist, the Feathered Serpent—the patron of rulers. To the west, on the other side of the Avenue, is the Great Compound, which some archaeologists have suggested was either the marketplace or the administrative center of the city. One of the most interesting architectural groupings in Teotihuacan is the so-called Three Temple Complex. Each one of these complexes includes three temples placed, according to tradition, on the north, west, and east sides of a rectangular plaza to emphasize the importance of the central space, which was probably used for collective worship by the residents of the barrio.

Interspersed between these wide public spaces were the dwellings of the citizens of Teotihuacan. These varied from simple one-family huts to intricate apartment complexes housing between twenty and one hundred individuals. So far, more than two thousand such complexes have been found, varying in quality depending on the status and economic level of their dwellers. All, however, were large rectangles (often sixty by sixty meters), bordered by tall, smooth walls. It would have been difficult for passersby to know what went on within the dwellings, because they had no windows. Usually there were only one or two entryways. The interiors consisted of numerous rooms placed around small patios, with porticoes built to admit light, capture rainwater, and allow ventilation. The rooms were connected by labyrinthine passageways. The compounds appear to have been subdivided into family apartments, each of which had areas for preparing and consuming food, sleeping and resting, storing food and raw materials, worship and burials, and waste disposal. There were also areas associated with religious rituals that were shared by all the families. These common areas were large patios, with altars occasionally provided with pyramidal temples. Some places also had areas used for raising domestic animals. All the complexes had a single story and were covered with flat roofs.

It is assumed that the planning and construction of each apartment compound were done at one time and that, over time, the compounds were remodeled, primarily by expanding the number of rooms within them. Studies by physical anthropologists indicate that while in some complexes males were genetically related, female skeletons were not related. This has been interpreted as the result of exogamy and virilocality (a newlywed couple living in the groom's family residence) within a lineage structure.

The inhabitants of these compounds can be described by analyzing their archaeological remains. Studies of their funerary practices, the objects they produced and used, and their mural paintings indicate that a barrio unit was made up of two or more complexes based on its inhabitants' ethnicity, kinship, profession, and worship. It is possible that the units were organized like those that, many years later, were called *calpultin* in Nahuatl. The best-known examples of this kind of unit were those in the Oaxaca Barrio of Tlailotlacan, those of the Merchant Barrio of San Francisco Mazapan, and those of the high-ranking military lineages in Amanalco Barrio (Techinantitla and Tlacuilapaxco). There is no doubt that Teotihuacan was a multiethnic society, spatially divided in apartment compounds that facilitated social cohesion of the ethnic groups as well as retention of their particular culture and language. Furthermore, as Millon has suggested, this kind of organization simplified central administration, the obtaining of tributes, recruitment of labor for collective works, and control by the state.

It seems fitting at this point to ask who the predominant ethnic group in Teotihuacan was and whether its members held power legitimately. Over several decades, many different peoples—such as the Otomis, Nahuas, Totonacs, Mazatecs, and Popolucas—have been proposed as the principal inhabitants of the city, but so far, the evidence for none of these is convincing. We do not even know the name of the city, which the Nahuas in the Postclassic called "the Place of Deification," alluding to their myth about the creation of the sun and moon.

Another very interesting and controversial question concerns the type of political organization capable of uniting the heterogenous components of Teotihuacan's society. In contrast with the political units of the Classic Mayas, which were composed of relatively uniform groups and integrated on the basis of a ruling lineage, Teotihuacan must have exercised a type of territorial rule over its population. That is to say, Teotihuacan could not have developed its government on the traditional basis of kinship; rather, a ruling elite would have been placed over all the lineages of the city. This could have been one of the many lineages that eventually rose to dominate the others, or a joint group composed of members from each one of these groups. Whatever group constituted the elite, their power must have been that of representatives of a territorial god whose powers included those of the lineage deities.

A hypothesis of power based on territoriality allows us to answer one of the great enigmas of Mesoamerican history: why, despite its being the most powerful city of its time, Teotihuacan never fully developed writing, the calendar, mathematics, astronomy, or an individualized representation of its rulers to the level achieved by its Maya contemporaries. As we will see, scholars have tied such developments to an ideological strengthening of lineage rulership, which Teotihuacan did not need. Its many images alluding to power do not exalt individuality and have relatively few traces of writing or calendrics.

The iconography of Teotihuacan's elites—particularly the representations of individuals as gods distributing the fruits of agriculture—was the basis, several decades ago, for proposing the existence of a hegemonic priestly class that had a political role and redistributed economic goods. This somewhat idyllic view of a theocratic state assumed the absence of military coercion and of human sacrifice. Recent archaeological investigations reveal a very different picture composed of armed rulers, gods, and mythological animals as well as many symbolic references to sacrifice and the sacrificed victims themselves, buried underneath important temple structures. Nevertheless, as Esther Pasztory points out, in contrast with peoples such as the Olmecs, Mayas, Mixtecs, and Mexicas, the culture of Teotihuacan did not depict warriors with conquered victims at their feet or held by their hair. Pasztory points out that the art of the city did not exalt war or conquest but rather the offering of hearts in their most abstract sense. This leads us to suppose that the sacrificial victims were both citizens of Teotihuacan and war captives.

Although it is sometimes difficult to distinguish between symbols of war and symbols of fertility, imagery associated with war and sacrifice never matched the overwhelming presence of aquatic and fire deities throughout Teotihuacan. Aquatic deities are associated with the concept of divine gifts, because the gods or, in some cases, simply their hands generate streams of water inside of which foods flow. On the other hand, fire deities are related to the dry season and transformation. The most important deities of Teotihuacan's pantheon were the storm god, fire god, water goddess, earth goddess, feathered serpent, and the god covered with human skin, who, later in the Postclassic, would be called Xipe Totec.

Because of the enormous importance of Teotihuacan, almost every archaeological investigation of the Classic in Central Mexico has focused on this city and its neighboring settlements. We know comparatively little about the history of contemporaneous societies in other valleys in Central Mexico, but we can assuredly say that they lived in Teotihuacan's shadow, which hindered their fully autonomous development. The power of Teotihuacan is clear in the northern and western parts of the Basin of Mexico as well as in the two corridors that lead toward the Gulf of Mexico and toward Tehuacán and Oaxaca through the Puebla-Tlaxcala Valley. The Tenanyécac Culture, which developed in the middle of the Puebla-Tlaxcala Valley A.D. 100–600, lost a number of settlements and became markedly more rural. In the southern part of the Valley, the city of Cholula—whose pyramid shows Teotihuacan's architectural influence—flourished during the Classic. The characteristic talud/tablero facades lie on top of the original construction of the temple, and figures that have been identified as strange insects with bodies in profile and full-front faces, are painted on them. Other paintings on the facade of a palace adjoining this pyramid, also dating to the Classic, are a series of full-figure individuals who are drinking from large bowls leading to their name, "the drunkards."

In the northwest of the Basin of Mexico, in the valley where, in the Postclassic, the city of Tula would rise, the settlements of Chingú and

Villagrán developed within Teotihuacan's sphere of influence. Apparently, on the basis of extensive irrigation systems and the exploitation
of limestone deposits, both climaxed A.D. 200–400. Chingú was larger
than two km² and, like Teotihuacan, was laid out orthogonally and had
dwelling complexes, as well as a plaza similar to the Ciudadela. It is possible that only the ruling elite came from Teotihuacan, because the
domestic pottery of Chingú did not come from that metropolis. Similarly, in the Amatzinac Valley, the eastern part of the Morelos Valley,
Teotihuacan's presence in this eastern part of the Morelos Valley can
be seen particularly in its ceramics.

From the Early Classic to the Epiclassic, the large center of Cantona
grew in the Basin of the Oriental, on the border between Central Mexico
and the Gulf of Mexico. Its prosperity was due to its agricultural production, the exploitation of obsidian mines at Oyameles in the Pico de
Orizaba, and its location on important routes between the Highlands
and the Coast. The city was built on a sloping basaltic flow, its monumental edifices scattered on a rough terrain without the planning characteristic of the other settlements of the Highlands. Although it is not
the case in every one of the twenty-four ball courts in the city, Cantona
typically has an unusual architectural grouping of a pyramid, a ball
court, and one or two plazas. Numerous streets and avenues link the
dwelling units. Some three thousand of these dwellings, characterized
by patios enclosed by stone walls, have been identified. Cantona used a
building technique in which volcanic rocks were piled on top of each
other without the use of mortar or stucco, resulting in bare facings.

OAXACA IN THE CLASSIC

Monte Albán was a city by the Late Preclassic, urbanism spreading
throughout most of Oaxaca in the several subsequent centuries.
Capitals with large, clearly stratified populations spread through the
length and breadth of this area. Most of them were exceptionally
centralized settlements, with temples, palaces, ball courts, and other
huge buildings as well as stone monuments with well-developed writing
in their centers. They were true cities, concentrating the political and
religious power of vast territories that were occupied by localities ranked
according to their relative importance.

Roughly speaking, the period of generalized urbanism and maximum splendor in this area occurred from A.D. 250 to 800/900—that is, during the entire Mesoamerican Classic. The best-known archaeological zones of Oaxaca are the Mixteca Alta (Las Flores Phase) and the Valley of Oaxaca (Monte Albán Phases IIIA and IIIB–IV). There are also considerable data for cities in other parts of the area. For example, important increases during the Classic have been found and studied in places such as Cerro de las Minas and Tequixtepec in the Mixteca Baja (Ñuiñe Phase), Huauhtla and Eloxochitlan in the Mazatec Sierra, Rio Viejo and Rio Grande on the coast, San Juan Luvina and Ayotzintepec in the Chinantla, Quiotepec in the Cañada, and La Ladrillera in the Isthmus.

A considerable increase in the number and size of settlements took place in the intermontane valleys of the Mixteca Alta. One of the most impressive examples of this phenomenon is the Nochixtlan Valley, where only 35 sites have been found in the Preclassic, compared to 113 in the Classic. Contrasting with the contemporaneous situation in the Valley of Oaxaca, a hegemonic capital never existed in the Mixteca Alta. Instead, many relatively small, comparably mature urban centers developed, doubtless competing among each other for dominion of the Mixteca Alta Valley. This helps to explain why many of these settlements were built in high places.

Research on settlement patterns in Nochixtlan has uncovered considerable variety in the configuration, location, function, and size of Classic Mixtec sites. There is a full gradation in size, the smallest settlements varying between 100 and 500 m² in area, followed by places such as Topiltepec that occupy between 500 and 700 m² and those that reach 1 km² such as Cerro Jazmín, and culminating in the famous city of Yucuñudahui, which measures 2 km². Yucuñaudahui replaced Yucuita, the Preclassic capital of the valley, and became one of the principal cities of the Mixteca Alta. The city was built on a great height, approximately 400 meters above the valley, and had a complicated urban plan in which the main plazas, palaces, and religious buildings were distributed along a linear L pattern. Especially worth mentioning are its ball court, its bas-relief sculptures, and Tomb 1, which resembles those in Monte Albán, consisting of a cross-shaped antechamber and a square chamber 3.5 meters on each side.

Clearly, the greatest urbanization in the area occurred in the Oaxaca Valley, the Zapotec cradle of one of the most imposing cities of Mesoamerica. After A.D. 250 several new centers comparable to the Classic capitals of the Mixteca developed, in addition to hamlets, villages, and towns that occupied the three lobes of the valley. Some of these centers are Loma de la Montura, Huijazoo, Zaachila, Jalieza, Macuilxochitl, Lambityeco, Yagul, and Mitla, all these sites belonging to the second or third rank in the regional hierarchy, with a population estimated at between five hundred and three thousand inhabitants. The approximately one thousand hierarchically different sites in the valley were clearly and indisputably under the control of Monte Albán. As we have discussed, Monte Albán had held dominion over the region since the late Preclassic, when it conquered San José Mogote.

From the top of a hill located exactly at the intersection of the valley's three lobes (Etla, Tlacolula, and Zimatlán), Monte Albán dominated a fertile agricultural province that was also rich in sources of water, lime, pottery clay, salt, and flint. During its maximum expansion in Phase IIIB, the city covered about 6.5 km^2, occupying the hills of Monte Albán, Atzompa, El Gallo, and Monte Albán Chico. Its population, conservatively estimated, was between fifteen thousand and thirty thousand. Monte Albán differed from other Mesoamerican cities in that it lacked large avenues and streets organizing urban space. Instead, the city was ordered by the Great Plaza and Atzompa, the two ceremonial and administrative districts of the city, which were surrounded by dwelling terraces.

According to Kent V. Flannery, the best evidence for the political, economic, and religious supremacy of Monte Albán in the Oaxaca Valley is the richness and monumental size of its temples and palaces. The Great Plaza, built four hundred meters above the valley floor, was the nerve center of the city. This wide space (270 by 125 m) had been leveled and stuccoed since the Monte Albán II Phase, but most of the buildings that we admire today date from Phase IIIB. The great civic and religious ceremonies, during which up to fifteen thousand people gathered, took place at the Main Plaza. The architectural complex is composed of numerous stucco-covered, painted stone buildings. Their facades are adorned with talud/tableros of the typical Zapotec style known as "doble escapulario" (double scapulary), characterized by superimposed horizontal moldings ending with downward vertical strips.

At the southern end of the Great Plaza is the South Platform, the largest pyramid of the site and the foundation for an important temple. The building as a whole is more than 25 meters high. The main Ball Court; Temples II, P, and Q; and two large palaces are on the eastern side. Two temple-palace-patio complexes called System IV and System M, as well as the palace called Building L, are opposite. The North Platform, an imposing mound with limited access having a portico and a sunken patio, closes the Plaza on the north. Because of its configuration, the North Platform would have been the ideal location for the residence of the supreme ruler of Monte Albán. Finally, the strange Building J (mentioned in the Preclassic chapter) and buildings G, H, and I, a group of typical Zapotec two-room chapels, are located in the center of the Plaza.

According to Richard E. Blanton, the city of Monte Albán was divided into fifteen large barrios, which may have corresponded to an equal number of lineages or corporate groups with their own economic activities. Complexes of two to four mounds placed around patios can still be seen in the center of these barrios. Because of these specific characteristics, it is not out of the question to propose that these spaces were originally consecrated to the worship of the patron deity of the barrio and that other spaces were the luxurious dwellings of high-ranking families. The dwelling terraces where most of the population lived surround these interesting complexes, which lie in ruins today. More than two hundred obvious dwelling terraces have been identified so far. The smallest terraces are 10 meters long and 5 meters wide, and the largest ones are 300 meters long and 100 meters wide.

Even though the size and quality of the dwellings varied enormously depending on the wealth of the residents, all of them followed the same pattern, a group of freestanding rooms facing a rectangular patio. It is estimated that 96–98 percent of the inhabitants of Monte Albán lived in small- or medium-sized houses with an area, including roofed and open spaces, of 312 m² on average. The smaller houses had cane or wattle-and-daub walls, and their burial areas were simple pits or pits bordered with flagstones. Middle-level houses were more solid, built with adobe walls, with several flagstone-bordered graves and, usually, a tomb with offerings and decorations, indicating that the families that lived here were of higher rank.

The 2–4 percent of the remaining population lived in the fifty-seven spacious mansions in the city. It is possible that these stone-walled, stucco-floored houses were reserved for hereditary nobles. Based on their size (an average of 2,473 m², including roofed and open space) and the many rooms available in each one, it has been proposed that large families with many servants lived there. They are exactly the type of residences in which Alfonso Caso and Ignacio Bernal found the most spectacular tombs of the site. Tombs 103, 104, and 105, found in terraces north of the Great Plaza, are particularly famous. They are very likely royal tombs, because their walls are covered with paintings of deities and lineage ancestors and the glyph called "Jaws of the Sky," which, according to Joyce Marcus, was used in later periods to denote royal ancestry.

These tombs, which were dug into the bedrock, are cross-shaped, with a principal chamber, a forechamber, a beautifully carved entry, and a stair to the surface. The tombs were roofed with large slabs, enabling them to withstand the enormous weight of the temples and palaces that were later erected over them. Generally, the tombs housed the remains of one or two individuals, although some containing multiple burials have been excavated. Many of the skeletons were disarticulated, which implies that they were moved during successive burials, in some cases for ritual purposes.

All the dignitaries at Monte Albán were buried with rich offerings composed of adornments made from shell, greenstone, mica, obsidian, and travertine (*tecali*), as well as crude hard-stone figurines. However, the objects most commonly found in the tombs—which are uniquely Zapotec—are grayish ceramic urns. Contrary to what one might suppose, these most beautiful pieces do not contain funerary remains. Generally, they are empty or contain a few greenstone beads, shells, animal bones, or obsidian knives. These urns are famous for their elaborate shapes, full of iconographic information, rather than for their contents. Each is a cylindrical vase completely covered on one side by a full-body anthropomorphic figure. There is a surprising diversity among the urns, the figures varying widely in position, sex, headdress, mask, calendric glyphs, and objects carried in their hands. On the basis of these multiple attributes, the images have been identified as ancestors; priests or rulers dressed as deities; or the gods of rain, of maize, of fire, of death, and so forth.

Besides the royal tombs, one of the most impressive aspects of Monte Albán is the profusion of glyphs carved on stelae, slabs, doorposts, and lintels. There are so many that it appears that, during the Classic, only Southeast Mesoamerica exceeded the Valley of Oaxaca in the number of monuments with inscriptions. The sculptures, going back to Monte Albán Phase I, are the best examples of Zapotec writing. Thanks to studies by Caso and, more recently, by Javier Urcid, we know that there are more then one hundred different glyphs. Like the epi-Olmec and the Maya systems, the Zapotec is a mixed system. It is basically logographic; that is to say, each glyph represents a word. In this system some glyphs have phonetic value, following the principle of homophony (the rebus principle), and some are syllabic. The principal glyphs are complemented by determinatives that indicate the grammatical categories of the words. There are also calendric glyphs that specify dates or name persons according to the day on which they were born or baptized.

Although the Zapotec inscriptions are short, they have a clear linear order that reveals their syntax. As a result of detailed study of the texts, basic grammatical components such as subject, verb, and object as well as locatives and time markers have been found. Inscriptions are never isolated but are generally accompanied by images of men and women identified by name glyphs. These images are usually part of historical scenes such as conquests, births, and royal weddings. For example, it is common to find images of rulers sitting on thrones, holding scepters symbolizing their power. There are also repeated images of dignitaries, perhaps from distant cities, as well as prisoners with their hands tied behind their backs.

The Classic history of Monte Albán is usually divided into two phases. The first, Monte Albán IIIA (A.D. 250–600), is characterized by close relations between the Oaxaca Valley and Central Mexico. As we shall see, these ties were very different from those that Teotihuacan established with places such as Kaminaljuyú or Matacapan. Despite the unequal sizes of the capital in the Basin of Mexico and Monte Albán (Monte Albán had a third of the area and a quarter of the population of Teotihuacan), the Zapotec capital was powerful enough to resist any expansionist attempt by Teotihuacan. In fact, both archaeology and iconographic representations point to possible peaceful contacts between the two cities.

An in-depth comparison of Teotihuacan and Monte Albán shows enormous differences between the two in urban planning, the use of space, regional settlement patterns, and the importance of writing. This suggests that the influence of Central Mexico on Monte Albán is less than many authors have proposed, apparently limited to architecture and craft production, primarily ceramics.

Monte Albán Phase IIIB–IV, also called Xoo, A.D. 600–800/900, corresponds to the maximum splendor of the site and to a diminishing of contacts with the Basin of Mexico due to the collapse of Teotihuacan. This flowering did not last long. The still unexplained dissolution of the centralized power that Monte Albán had exercised for centuries occurred between A.D. 750 and 800/900. Although the hills where the city was located were never abandoned, its population and its hegemonic influence diminished at the end of Phase IIIB–IV. Flannery and Marcus have highlighted two symptomatic events that occurred at this time. On the one hand, old centers of the Oaxaca Valley such as Zaachila, Jalieza, Mitla, and Cuilapan acquired unusual power in the region, although not as great as the power Monte Albán held in the past. On the other hand, large public monuments with military themes were no longer erected and were replaced by small genealogical registers that emphasized royal marriages, foreshadowing the enormous importance that matrimonial alliances would have in the intricate politics of these newer times.

WEST MESOAMERICA IN THE CLASSIC

While states flourished and cities proliferated in most of Mesoamerica, the social organizations called chiefdoms by anthropologists persisted in West Mexico. It is clear that there was a gradual increase in social and political complexity in the West between the fourth century B.C. and the seventh century A.D., but it was not sufficient to make possible a clear distinction between the Preclassic and the Classic. Also, during the Classic there were few relationships between West Mexico and the rest of Mesoamerica.

The exception to this was Guerrero, as there was a clear artistic influence from Central Mexico throughout course of the Balsas River and its tributaries. River settlements with pyramids up to thirty meters high, plazas, and ball courts characterize the Guerrero Tradition. Vessels with a compound silhouette, vases, plates, pots that are neckless or have a short neck, and tecomates predominate in Guerrero ceramics. The pieces are monochromatic orange, red, buff, or black, with a shiny finish and incised geometric decoration. However, the predominant craft at Guerrero was the carving of hard greenish or gray stones. This industry, which goes back to the Preclassic, is generically called Mezcala and includes different styles. Just as in the past an Olmec-looking style had existed along with local varieties, during the Classic pieces with clear Teotihuacan inspiration were made, in addition to the schematic styles characteristic of the region. As most of the known pieces have been looted from sites, we know little about the life of those who made them. La Organera and El Mirador are among the few Guerrero sites where Mezcala figurines have been found in an archaeological context.

A second group in this region are the Bajío Cultures, heirs of Chupícuaro, which are found in Guanajuato and the north of Michoacán. The principal vestiges left at their sites are terraces, platforms, and buildings with columns made of mud and stone. The Bajío dwellers made ceramics during the Classic, mostly tripod cajetes and vessels with basketlike handles. The most recognizable decoration is a polished polychrome with geometric decor; pseudocloisonné was used as well.

Further north are the sites of the Shaft Tomb Tradition, in a crescent moon extending from the southern half of Colima across Jalisco to western Nayarit. This tradition, which began in the Preclassic and lasted to the sixth century A.D., is named for its peculiar burial practices. As we discussed earlier, the graves were dug with a vertical shaft into the subsoil, opening into one or several chambers. Like tombs in Colombia and Ecuador, most of these tombs are separate from the residential areas, a funerary practice that is common in the West but rare in the rest of Mesoamerica. During the Classic, these shafts were as deep as sixteen meters. The multiplicity of chambers suggests that the tombs were used for families or lineages for some time. Offerings of ceramics and jewelry were customarily deposited next to the bodies. Sometimes, these offerings are so finely made or of such remote origin that they signify the high rank of the deceased. The ceramics include figurines, vessels, and miniature scale-models of everyday and family scenes, providing excellent ethnographic evidence about festive practices and building styles. The ceramics provide information about houses with one or more rooms, some raised on platforms with terraces and vestibules. Each room had its own four-sided roof and decorated walls, platforms, and covers. It is important to note that archaeological investigations of tombs have not resulted in information in proportion to their impor- tance, because the tombs have been systematically looted.

This tradition's ceramics are found beyond the area of the tombs, varying considerably from one region to another. So far, three large groups corresponding to the territories of the states of Colima, Nayarit, and Jalisco have been identified. Colima ceramics are characterized by beautiful, realistic hollow figures of humans, animals, and plants. They are generally well-polished monochrome red, black, or brown containers with spouts made by shaping, appliqué, and incision. The pieces shaped like humans, dogs, parrots, and squashes are well known. Tripod pitchers, often with effigy legs, predominate in the Comala Phase. In Jalisco, on the other hand, most pieces are anthropomorphic, although there are some boxes and ceramic bottle gourds. These combine the modeling technique with red-on-cream or red-on-buff colors in the Ameca type and with white-on-red in the so-called "lamb face" anthropomorphic figurines. The human figures, characterized by long faces and prominent noses, are shown singly or in groups, frequently engaged in everyday activities. Nayarit sculptures are not much modeled, the facial characteristics, garments, and adornments being shown by paint. Red, black, orange, and buff colors as well as negative decoration has been used. The figurines are not containers and, like those from Jalisco, primarily represent humans alone or in groups, although there are a few animals and squashes. Anthropomorphic figures are characterized by widely separated eyes and profuse adornments on each figure, mostly nose rings and multiple earrings.

Excavations by Phil Weigand in the Ameca Valley in Jalisco showed unusual population concentrations. Numerous settlements with different sizes and functions distributed around centers with large public buildings were found in a relatively small area. The latter, which disprove allegations that there was no monumental architecture in the West, show a hierarchical structure corresponding to a more developed political organization than has been attributed to the area in this period.

These architectural complexes, commonly called *guachimontones,* are unique to the West and can be as big as 125 meters in diameter. A guachimontón is a round central platform with additional levels up to 17 meters high. The platform is surrounded by a ring-shaped patio, and the patio, in turn, is surrounded by a ring-shaped banquette. There are between eight and sixteen evenly distributed platforms on the banquette. When the sites flourished, their inhabitants also built numerous ball courts.

Teuchitlan, where the most spectacular guachimontones are to be found, provides the name for a tradition that began in the Arenal Phase of the Preclassic (350 B.C. to A.D. 200) but reached is apogee during the Classic in the Ahualulco Phase (A.D. 200–400) and Teuchitlan I (A.D. 400–700) (see plan 4). Weigand found the peculiar guachimontón architecture widely distributed from the southeast of Nayarit to the northwest of Jalisco and even extending into Zacatecas through the Bolaños-Mezquitic Canyon.

NORTH MESOAMERICA IN THE CLASSIC

In the first century A.D. Mesoamerica expanded as never before, particularly to the north along the wide periphery that had been the domain of hunter-gatherers for millennia. The northern boundary that resulted from this expansion paralleled the boundary of Mesoamerica in the sixteenth century, but lay 250 kilometers further north. According to Pedro Armillas, this boundary began at the mouth of the Pánuco River in Tamaulipas and went up the Tamesi River, including the Tamaulipas Sierra and the Ocampo area (still in Tamaulipas). It continued through the settlements of Guadalcázar, Peñasco, and San Juan Sin Agua in San Luis Potosí, then proceeded through Ojo de Agua and Atotonilco in Zacatecas and Antonio Amaro, Zape, and Loma San Gabriel in Durango. It ended approximately at the mouth of the Mayo River in Sonora.

A considerable number of archaeological sites show that village life first arose in this vast expanse between A.D. 1 and 100. Nevertheless, archaeologists are still looking for clues to explain where these farmers came from. We still do not have conclusive evidence for a long native process of plant domestication by local groups, for diffusion due to prolonged contact between nomads and sedentary groups, or for colonization by farmers coming from South or West Mexico. Currently,

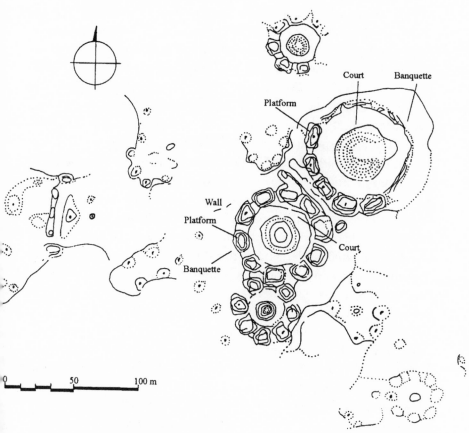

Plan 4. Teuchitlán Archaeological Zone, Jalisco. West Mesoamerica Area, Classic period. (Based on P. C. Weigand)

scholars lean toward the theory of colonization by waves of immigrants from centers as diverse as Capacha, El Opeño, and Chupícuaro in the West; Zacatenco, Tlatilco, and Cuicuilco in the Basin of Mexico; and various locations on the Gulf Coast. J. Charles Kelley argues for gradual migrations. Pedro Armillas, Beatriz Braniff, Marie-Areti Hers, and others disagree, feeling that the intrusion by farmers could have been sudden, perhaps due to demographic pressures or the onset of heavier rainfall, making sedentary life possible in an area characterized by its aridity.

All we can certainly say is that by the first century A.D. there was a very dynamic North Mesoamerican area that lasted until the tenth century.

Broadly speaking, this area resembles the letter U, including a sector that crossed the Central Plateau from east to west, with two extensions that extended north along the humid slopes of the Sierra Madre Oriental and the Sierra Madre Occidental. This shape divides the area into three zones.

The first zone is the central region, referred to in the archaeological literature as the Tunal Grande, which includes the contiguous territories of the modern states of Guanajuato, San Luis Potosí, Zacatecas, Aguascalientes, and Jalisco. To date, more than twenty important sites have been identified in the Tunal Grande, most of which flourished between A.D. 600 and 900. Studies of sites such as Electra in the state of San Luis Potosí show that the societies of the Tunal Grande never achieved a level of development comparable to that in the rest of Mesoamerica. The small settlements in this zone lacked sizable public buildings and were composed of houses built on platforms that enclosed buried patios, a type of architectural compound similar to that found in the dwellings of the Chalchihuites Culture.

The second zone, the eastern branch, can be subdivided into the region south of Tamaulipas and the culturally similar regions of Río Verde in San Luis Potosí and the Sierra Gorda in Querétaro. We know that villages predominated during the Classic in southern Tamaulipas. Well-known sites such as Balcón de Montezuma and San Antonio Nogalar are characterized by an irregular arrangement of tens of low, circular limestone platforms. Each platform was the base of a modest cylindrical hut, perhaps with a conical roof made from perishable materials. The village of Balcón de Montezuma, excavated by Jesús Nárez, had more than 80 such platforms and was located at the top of a hill with almost impregnable slopes. In contrast, San Antonio Nogalar was a larger settlement located in a valley, consisting of about 160 platforms, two truncated cone temples, and a ball court. Recognizable among the materials found in these two villages were ceramic vessels and pipes reflecting intensive relations with societies both in the Huasteca and in the Mississippi Basin. According to studies by Richard S. MacNeish and Guy Stresser-Péan, southern Tamaulipas seems to have peaked during the first five centuries A.D., although it may have been occupied until the Postcassic.

The Río Verde and Sierra Gorda regions had a parallel cultural development, due not only to their relative proximity to each other but also to their similarities as suppliers of cinnabar, a reddish mercury ore prized in all of Mesoamerica for its ritual uses, primarily in funerals. An initial period, characterized by an egalitarian sedentary life-style and a constant influx of people, ideas, and products from Central Veracruz, the Pánuco Region, Teotihuacan, and perhaps the Mississippi Basin, took place in the Río Verde Basin from 250 B.C. to A.D. 500. From A.D. 500 to 1000 the region flourished, with a growing population and greater autonomy. A clear process of hierarchization of settlements reflects a gradual loss of social equality in the Río Verde region. According to Dominique Michelet, in Río Verde Phase B there were tens of hamlets, a few villages, and a ruling center called RV.120, with 231 buildings scattered over 25 hectares. Apparently, RV.120, from its position in the southern part of the region, channeled the ceramics produced to the San Luis plateau and the cinnabar mined in Guadalcázar and processed in RV.13 to Teotihuacan and El Tajín.

Sierra Gorda, a region occupied during the Classic by complex societies devoted primarily to agriculture and mining, is located in the modern state of Querétaro. Its main centers, Ranas (see plan 5) and Toluquilla, built on high, rocky hills surrounded by deep chasms, are famous today for their pyramidal platforms and their ball courts paved with limestone slabs in a characteristic linear distribution determined by the topography. Besides local objects, objects from the Central Plateau and the Gulf Coast have been exhumed from the ruins of Ranas and Toluquilla. Apparently, these imports were obtained in exchange for raw materials such as fluorite, calcite, and, above all, cinnabar. To evaluate the importance of cinnabar mining in Sierra Gorda, it suffices to mention that there are between two and three thousand cinnabar-mine entrances, including those in El Soyatal, that date from between the first and fifth centuries A.D.

The western branch is the best known of the three northern zones, because the spectacular Chalchihuites Culture developed there. This branch runs for six hundred kilometers along the Sierra Madre Occidental territories of Durango, Zacatecas, and Jalisco. During the first three centuries A.D. practically all the inhabitants of the river valleys and spurs of the Sierra lived in small farming communities. According to some scholars, the regional settlement pattern at that time resulted from two basic factors: the proximity of water sources and terrain that facilitated

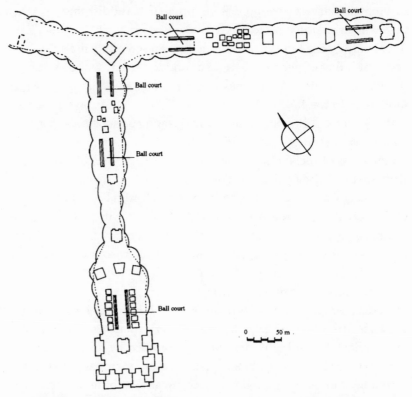

Plan 5. Ranas Archaeological Zone, Querétaro. North Mesoamerica Area, Classic period. (Based on P. Primer)

military defenses against raids by nomads or by their neighbors. At that time villages were simple groups of single-family architectural units, each of which had a small central patio with an altar and was bordered by a rectangular platform. This, in turn, was the foundation for other stone veneer platforms supporting adobe or wattle-and-daub houses. The uniformity of housing units and of all the excavated mortuary offerings suggests a relative sociopolitical equality and the absence of privileged groups.

However, significant changes took place in the peasant societies of the Chalchihuites Culture between A.D. 300 and 500. It is probable that during this period the first intensive cultivation, on enormous artificial terraces irrigated by canals, began. Apparently, a veritable population explosion occurred and social complexity suddenly grew. Evidence of these changes can be seen in the clear alteration in the area's regional settlement pattern and in its architecture. Farming villages multiplied, and some of them grew disproportionately. The Malpaso Valley, for example, saw the development of La Quemada, a large 17-hectare hegemonic center connected by a complex road network to its satellite settlements (almost all smaller than 0.6 hectare). Primary housing units added small pyramids and elaborate altars to their basic pattern, while hypostyle rooms, semiroofed gigantic spaces at least 400 m² in area, were built in capitals such as Alta Vista.

All these changes preceded a long flowering between A.D. 500 and 900. We can say that in the sixth century, societies of the Chalchihuites Culture—although not at the level of complexity of other Mesoamerican societies—had completely abandoned their prior social equality and uniformity. The emergent elite enjoyed the benefits of agricultural tribute, control of commerce, and the production of export goods. A large percentage of the farming labor force, previously engaged solely in agriculture, was employed, at least seasonally, in building monumental buildings, defensive works, road systems, and cultivation terraces. Collective labor was also used for mining. The extraction of minerals such as ocher, hematite, and turquoise, used to make sumptuary goods, must have yielded great benefits to emergent elite groups in places such as Alta Vista, El Chapín, and Pedregoso. Mining was based largely on the demand for scarce raw materials by the major cities of Mesoamerica. This dependency became so intense that this economic element of the Chalchihuites Culture may have existed merely as a subsidiary aspect of the Teotihuacan economic complex.

Another area in which the local elites were possibly favored was that of long-distance trade. In addition to being an important mining center, Alta Vista was a port of trade in a continental route that connected Teotihuacan with Paquimé and Chaco Canyon. Hawks bells, copper mirrors and bells, tropical animals, precious feathers, cotton mantles and clothing, and turquoise and amber jewels could have been moved along a commercial route with the regional centers of the Chalchihuites Culture as their intermediate stops. In fact, scholars such as Kelley and Weigand have proposed that Alta Vista might have been a true colony ruled by Teotihuacan warriors, merchants, and astronomers, an elite whose principal mission was to provide exotic materials to the metropolis. This hypothesis, although suggestive, is not supported by enough evidence to outweigh the numerous indications of a purely local elite.

A distinctive aspect of Chalchihuites Culture is the relative absence of structures such as temples and pyramids used exclusively for public rituals. Perhaps the reason for this is that the rulers legitimated their power through their military rather than their religious roles. Nevertheless, archaeologists have found traces of important ritual practices such as the ball game, human sacrifice, cannibalism, and the collecting of trophy heads in the area. At El Huistle archaeologists discovered that decapitated crania were exhibited on wooden racks known by the Nahuatl name of *tzompantli*. The most impressive religious items found were two-headed serpents and what is probably a prototype of a *chac-mool* (a reclining figure holding an offering plate).

According to Hers, we can divide the western branch into four cultural regions with their own characteristics within the dominant Chalchihuites Culture. The southernmost region includes the Juchipila and El Teúl Valleys, while Las Ventanas is the best-known site. Las Ventanas is an unusual settlement because it consists of adobe houses erected in a natural opening of a sheer cliff, resembling the Mogollon and Anasazi pueblos.

The Bolaños-Mezquitic River Basin differs considerably from the other regions of the western branch because, for centuries, the river allowed the local societies to establish strong links with the cultures of West Mexico, particularly the Teuchitlan Culture. These connections can be seen most clearly in the circular platforms and patios in places such as El Totoate and shaft tombs such as those in Valparaíso.

Somewhat to the northeast, a region extends from the Malpaso Valley to the high Súchil that contains the biggest centers of the North: La Quemada and Alta Vista. La Quemada occupies several terraces on the top of an elongated hill protected by a wall and inaccessible cliffs. Without a doubt its stone constructions—among which are a hypostyle room measuring thirty by forty meters, a ball court, and numerous elite housing modules—are some of the most spectacular structures to be found in the Mesoamerican North.

The fourth and last region, which extends from the Guadiana Valley to the southern borders of the state of Chihuahua, may represent a late expansion of the Chalchihuites Culture. Typical sites of the region are Weicker, Zape, and Schroeder. The latter contains a large pyramid, a ball court, and numerous masonry platforms that supported houses made from perishable materials.

Based on new datings of sites, it is thought that the Chalchihuites Culture began to decline in the ninth century, at which time some sites were abandoned. From this data, Hers has proposed that the Nonoalcas, together with the groups that left this area, jointly initiated the Toltec Culture. Hers bases this proposal on the presence in the north, five hundred years before Tula, of pseudocloisonné ceramics, copper and turquoise objects, *tzompantli*, hypostyle rooms, and a sculpture she considers a forerunner of the *chac mool.*

THE GULF IN THE CLASSIC

During the Classic, the Gulf Area maintained close relationships—either as an exporter of valuable materials, as a corridor for commerce, or as the location of enclaves—with the rest of Mesoamerica, predominantly with Teotihuacan. The Central Mexican presence in the Eastern Lowlands is reflected in various ways. An outstanding example of an iconographic loan, a superb ceramic piece unequaled in Teotihuacan, is an image of the old god of fire with a large brazier on his head in La Mixtequilla. As was the case in the Basin of Mexico, ceramic anthropomorphic figurines with articulated extremities were manufactured in the Gulf Area. Likewise, the architectural talud/tablero style spread in the east (although in local versions), and foreign pieces are found among the ceramic remains, attesting to the important interchange between the two areas.

We must emphasize, however, that Central Mexican influences in the Gulf Area impinged on established societies that had been there for centuries and had deep cultural roots in the area. Thus, despite a Teotihuacan presence, these peoples retained the strong idiosyncracies of their millennial tradition. An example of this in the Classic is the Mixtequilla Tradition, which includes numerous sites scattered in the lower basins of the Papaloapan, Blanco, and Jamapan Rivers. An outstanding site in this tradition is Cerro de las Mesas, which might be the heir of the epi-Olmecs who inhabited the region in remote times. The sculptural style of their stelae not only evokes these origins (particularly La Mojarra) but also reveals the ties they had in the distant past with groups on the Pacific Coasts of Chiapas and Guatemala, particularly with Izapa. Stelae from Cerro de las Mesas retained the canonical shape of a personage portrayed in profile with one foot forward, richly arrayed with a helmet in the shape of a fantastic, grotesque mask and accompanied by dates in the Long Count. The calendrical inscriptions of the site are the northernmost examples of this system, and date to A.D. 468 and 533. Nearby, south of Cerro de las Mesas, is Matacapan, which, because of its many Teotihuacan-like characteristics, is quite atypical for the area.

The most important sites in the Gulf Area can be grouped into two large regions: to the south, Central Veracruz, from the Papaloapan River Basin to the Cazones River Basin; to the north, the Huasteca, up to the Pánuco River Basin. With the exceptions of El Tajín and Matacapan, the settlements of Central Veracruz do not show the significant qualitative changes associated with the transition from the Preclassic to the Classic. In sites such as Cerro de las Mesas, Las Higueras, El Zapotal, Remojadas, Nopiloa, and Dicha Tuerta we continue to see the spatial arrangements and building techniques characteristic of the Preclassic, even though the dimensions are larger at these sites. Ceremonial centers built from mud, adobe, and rounded stones, the larger buildings having pyramidal bases with one or more sections, are common. Wattle-and-daub chapels must have been erected on these bases. The floors of the most important buildings are often burned earth. The walls of some buildings are covered with smoothed clay or thin layers of stucco.

The Classic in Central Veracruz is characterized by its production of objects of great artistic quality, all apparently related to religious aspects of the culture. In La Mixtequilla, sites such as Los Cerros, Apachital, Dicha Tuerta, Nopiloa, Remojadas, and Tlalixcoyan produced hollow ceramic figurines of infants that, because of their happy appearance, have been called "smiling-faces." All of them have cranial deformations and many have dental mutilations as well. They have strange haircuts or headdresses with raised designs on the flat frontal plane representing monkeys, herons catching fish, frets, curls, braids, the symbol for movement, or elaborate iconographic complexes. Approximately life-size clay statues, many of which were images of gods with realistic and serious expressions contrasting with those of the "smiling faces," were also produced in La Mixtequilla. For example, an unbaked clay skeleton representing the god of death was excavated in El Zapotal. Impressive ceramic images called *cihuateteo* (women deified because they died in their first childbirth), were found next to it. Other pieces particular to this region are zoomorphic figurines (jaguars, dogs, alligators) that have been called toys because they have wheels, although there is no evidence to date that they were intended to be toys. These interesting objects, found in burials, have prompted serious questions, as the mechanical use of wheels is rare in Mesoamerica. Because there are no technological antecedents leading to objects with such limited practical uses, some people claim that the wheels are a unique and accidental contribution from some Old World vessel.

An unusual group of sculptures, the yoke-palmate stone-votive ax (*yugo-palma-hacha*) complex—possibly funerary religious objects associated with the ball game—is found in Central Veracruz. The stone yugos and palmas portray items of protective gear, made from leather and wood in real life, that were used while playing the ball game. The yugos are generally horseshoe shaped, although some are completely closed. The palmas are treelike objects with an unusual protrusion at the front of the base. The votive axes are so named because of their resemblance to an actual tool. It has been proposed that they represent the heads of those decapitated in ritual games, which ended with the death of one of the contenders. Such sculptures began to appear in the Preclassic, but the most elaborate ones were made in the Late Classic. The finely carved decorations include human figures, animals, and the interlaced scrolls with raised edges that are characteristic of Classic Veracruz.

Only twenty-nine kilometers apart, El Tajín and Santa Luisa are located in a rainy tropical jungle at the extreme north of Veracruz. Both were exceptionally active builders and expanded their boundaries, principally by exploiting three bountiful alluvial plains: Espinal, San Pablo, and Gutiérrez Zamora. It was long thought that the Totonacs were responsible for El Tajín's splendor. Today, however, more prevalent theories propose that the city has always been the product of the people who have inhabited the region since the Preclassic. These groups likely belonged linguistically to the *Inic* group of the Maya family and spoke

Huastec. El Tajín developed rapidly and, surpassing Santa Luisa, became the major power in the Tecolutla and Cazones Basins. We know that its relationship with Teotihuacan was extensive, but we do not know the exact nature of that relationship. By A.D. 600 El Tajín had achieved sufficient economic and cultural power to become the political hub of Central and North Veracruz. Perhaps this is the date of the construction of the Arroyo Group. As we shall see, the city attained its maximum splendor later, during the Epiclassic period.

Many of the cultural wares that we have named as characteristic of Classic Central Veracruz circulated through the principal exchange routes of Mesoamerica. Thus, wheeled miniatures reached places such as Tula and Quelepa in El Salvador, while yugos, palmas, and hachas were imported by inhabitants of regions as distant as Central America and the Sierra Gorda in Querétaro.

The Huasteca also has archaeological traces worth mentioning. This part of the Gulf region includes an area extending from north of El Tajín to the Pánuco River Basin and, from the Coast, inland to the Sierra Madre Oriental. During the Classic its population was relatively scattered, with the larger concentrations in the lower Pánuco Basin. Almost all the settlements were small, and even the larger ones, which had public buildings around plazas, were unplanned. A predominant architectural pattern in the Huasteca region consists of round or rectangular buildings with rounded corners. These can be seen in sites such as Tamtzán in the state of Tamaulipas and Huaxcamá, Tancahuitz, Cuatlamayán, and Tampozoque in San Luis Potosí. In Tamtzán the platforms are covered with stone, and in Huaxcamá they are covered with stucco that still retains traces of alfresco paintings. In this site the stairs, which do not have balustrades, rise considerably due to the shallowness of the thread of the steps relative to the riser. At the end of the Classic El Tajín's architectural style may have influenced styles in San Luis Potosí with the introduction of the talud/tablero unit, but El Tajín apparently did not transmit its mania for building ball courts. On the other hand, in the Hidalgo sector of the Huasteca tombs have been found inside conical structures or pyramids.

For most of the Classic, sculpture in the Huasteca utilized an iconography that did not clearly distinguish between deities on the basis of particular costumes or emblems. Thus, male fertility deities are identified only by their erect penis, while female fertility deities differ only by their prominent hips and breasts or by their posture with their hands on their abdomen. This changed at the end of the Classic when, in both stone and shell sculptures, deities appear that can be clearly identified by their attributes as can those in Central Mexico. This is one more proof of the increasing ties of the Huasteca with Teotihuacan and El Tajín, corresponding to the simultaneous weakening of ties with North Mesoamerica and particularly with Río Verde.

SOUTHEAST MESOAMERICA IN THE CLASSIC

Investigations of the Mayas in the last few years have been exceptional not only in their number, but also in the differences in their focus, the advances they have achieved, and the impetus they have provided for academic interchanges both among Maya scholars and in the wider Mesoamerican context. The value of such productive and globally valuable scientific research is clear; nevertheless, we must attempt the overwhelming task of selecting a few themes and providing a panoramic view of the Mayas in this chapter.

Recent scientific research on the Mayas has fundamentally transformed our concepts about them. Scholars such as Joyce Marcus, Jeremy Sabloff, and Linda Schele, reviewing the latest research, emphasize that the idealized vision of the Mayas as a peaceful people governed by priests and devoted to astronomy and the philosophy of time, who almost never practiced human sacrifice, has been totally abandoned. For decades, renowned scholars such as Sylvanus G. Morley and J. Eric S. Thompson popularized a hypothetical scenario in which such sites as Tikal, Palenque, and Copan were merely ceremonial centers where the peasant population met on feast or market days. For many years this vision limited methods of analysis, distorted our view of the history of the Mayas, and inhibited comparisons with their contemporaries. They were touted as the creators of a unique civilization. Today this idea of a monolithic, unique, and isolated world is crumbling, opening new research perspectives and returning a human face to the Mayas.

The Southeast Mesoamerican area was clearly Maya (see map 14). It included all the peoples of that tradition, and only a few of its inhabitants were not culturally or linguistically Maya. The area can be divided

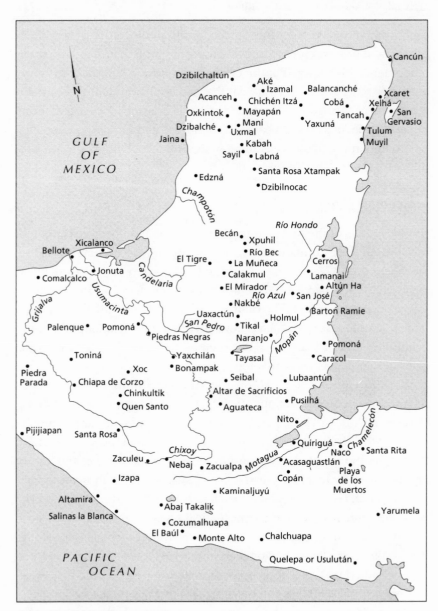

Map 14. The Maya territory.

roughly into three geographic and culturally contrasting parts. The southern region includes Chiapas, Guatemala, El Salvador, Honduras, Nicaragua, and Costa Rica—a belt that runs from the confluence of the mountains of North Chiapas to the Gulf of Nicoya. This is the area where non-Maya people mingled with the Mayas. Most of the region consists of highlands (more than 1,200 meters above sea level) that are cool or cold, a rough terrain with isolated valleys and important lacustrine basins. In the area of the Pacific, however, the altitude drops dramatically, forming a long coastal region with a torrid climate and rich alluvial soils.

The central region extends from the Gulf of Mexico to the Caribbean. It consists of hot, humid, dense, tall jungle lowlands and abounds with lakes, swamps, and rivers with wide meanders. The center is the Petén, the region of greatest development of Classic tradition. To the west is the Usumacinta Basin, which flows, with the Grijalva River, into the exuberant Tabasco region. The eastern area is the Belize River Basin; the southern region is the Pasión River Basin; and the rich Motagua region, surrounded by mountains, lies to the southeast.

The northern region corresponds to slightly more than the northern half of the Yucatán Peninsula. It is also composed of lowlands, but with a much lower rainfall than that of the central region, and is covered by a low forest growing on a thin layer of soil. The peninsula consists of a huge flat limestone slab, its monotony broken only by small northwestern mountains, and there are almost no surface rivers. The ancient inhabitants obtained water from *chultunes* (bottle-shaped excavated pits) or *cenotes* (natural openings that allowed access from the surface to subterranean currents). Culturally, the region is divided into the region of Campeche to the west; the Rio Bec region to the south, bordering the Petén; the Chenes region in the center; immediately to its northwest the hilly Puuc region, whose traditions and styles extended to the northern plains; and the East Coast region.

To the envy of students of other areas of Mesoamerica, the Maya Classic period has been dated with impressive precision because its dates are based on stone monuments with calendric inscriptions in the Maya Long Count. According to this absolute dating method, the Classic began in A.D. 292, ended in 909, and was divided into the Early and Late Classic by a hiatus in the recording of dates. This apparent precision is moot today, however, because we have recognized the gradual pace of historical change. Thus, some Maya specialists use round numbers to date the Early Classic from approximately A.D. 250 to 600 and the Late Classic from 600 to 900. The division at A.D. 600 is not artificial, because it is based on two fundamental milestones: the cessation for a time of the political-religious practice of erecting stelae and lintels, and the notable difference in the archaeological remains in each of these two periods.

Broadly speaking, the Early Classic is characterized by the influence of Teotihuacan and by an unusual impetus of the most characteristic Maya cultural elements. The Late Classic, which lacked influence from Central Mexico, was a period of considerable population growth, with large urban centers and the greatest economic, political, and cultural development of the Classic period. The end of the Classic is marked by a collapse that led to the decline of numerous Maya capitals. As we shall see, recent research reveals that this process of decline was not as uniform as had been thought. When the main power centers in the central region fell, the power centers in the North flourished; furthermore, there was no marked difference between warfare in the Classic and the Postclassic.

Following this general survey, we will review the historical process of the area in somewhat greater detail. We have noted that there was an unquestionable—though not completely understood—influence from Teotihuacan, there are various kinds of evidence of direct contact with the Central Mexican metropolis during the Early Classic: a copying of the architectural style of Teotihuacan, the cylindrical shape of some funerary pits, the presence of exchanged sumptuary objects and locally made copies of them, and inscriptions on public monuments, as well as the results of strontium analysis of human bones. In their totality these indicators point to intrusions of people from Teotihuacan who imposed foreign symbols, ideology, and tastes in the Maya area. Nevertheless, such intrusions do not appear to be imperialistic advances by Teotihuacan into the Southeast (with the exception of Kaminaljuyú, according to some authors). The most credible hypothesis is that foreigners who were separate from and politically independent of Teotihuacan became Maya rulers by marrying local noble Maya women. As time went by, newer generations assimilated the local culture, but they also kept the tradition of their outside origin as an important ideological element.

In the southern region these three and one-half centuries are marked by the fate of Kaminaljuyú, an ancient and prosperous commercial center that followed the architectural canon of Teotihuacan in its ceremonial buildings. Between A.D. 450 and 500, two large pyramidal temples with the characteristic Teotihuacan talud/tablero were built and expanded in the Guatemalan city of Kaminaljuyú. Important dignitaries were buried at the base of these buildings, along with Teotihuacan-style objects such as tripod vases (some imported from Central Mexico, some locally made). Hypotheses concerning the possible presence of Teotihuacan natives in the Guatemalan city vary considerably. Some archaeologists even propose that it was conquered and converted into a Central Mexican enclave.

Teotihuacan's influence is also evident in the central region but, there too, there is no clear evidence for one particular interpretation. For example, the typical Teotihuacan talud/tableros were copied in the powerful Tikal, and the rulers of this Maya city, Nun Yax Ayin (Curl Snout) and Siyah Chan K'awil (Stormy Sky), were pictured with Teotihuacan-style regalia and symbols. Nun Yax Ayin is dressed and armed in the style of Central Mexico. At precisely this time Tzakol 3 ceramics appeared in the Petén. Just as Teotihuacan's green obsidians have been found in Tikal, there are pieces of Tikal's Tzakol ceramics in Teotihuacan. Copán and Uaxactún are other cities in the Petén influenced by that distant civilization, and Yaxhá is laid out in a strange mixture of the irregularity characteristic of Maya cities and the typical arrangement of Teotihuacan streets.

At the same time, the population of the central region increased notably and cultural traits considered characteristic of the Classic Maya—that is, the stele/altar combination narrating the most significant events of the rulers, the so-called Maya arch and the vault it produces, complex writing, and the exceptionally beautiful polychrome ceramics—spread generally throughout the region. Large, populous cities with tall temples and sumptuous stucco-covered limestone palaces enclosing wide plazas were built. The bulk of the population lived in extensive irregular areas surrounding the urban nucleus.

During the Early Classic the architecture and ceramics of the northern region followed the patterns of the central region. One of the many examples of this is a carved stone lintel dating to the fifth century that was found in Oxkintok. But there were other influences in the northern region than the Central Maya model: in Acanceh, in the Puuc region, a Teotihuacan-style talud/tablero platform with stucco zoomorphic figures was found next to a platform with stairs just like the stairs in the Petén.

The Late Classic has been defined as the prototypical florescence of the Southeast area; however, the southern, central, and northern regions did not develop to the same degree or in the same way. In the southern region, the Guatemala Valley, a demographic and building climax occurred about A.D. 800 or 900 after the influence of Teotihuacan decreased. The Pacific Coast of Guatemala, in the Late Classic, was the setting for a very different non-Maya tradition—the Pipil. These Nahuatl speakers lived in the prime cacao-growing area of Cotzumalhuapa and built several sites there, including El Baúl. The carving of yugos and hachas in this region, as well as the representations in stone of rituals associated with the ball game, seem to tie this region to the traditions of the Gulf Coast. The sculptures show an obsession with death, decapitation, the worship of celestial deities, and the cacao plant.

Some cities in the central region do not seem to have undergone a violent transition between the Early and Late Classic. In contrast, in some important sites in the Petén and the Usumacinta Basin, not only was the erection of carved stone stelae temporarily suspended, but there was also a systematic destruction of public monuments that might be attributable to civil warfare. After a long period of instability, the cultural push renewed and the population grew vertiginously, perhaps due to a vigorous economy and the expansion of trade networks. At that time hundreds of cities and towns were built, containing the most sumptuous stone monuments and buildings in Maya history. Tikal and Calakmul were the most powerful capitals of the Petén. Palenque and Yaxchilán were the strongest to the west, and Copán, with its nearby jade mines, to the southeast. Each of these great cities exercised a fluctuating dominion, through force or through matrimonial alliances, over the surrounding cities and towns. After three centuries of growth the central region collapsed, irreversibly affecting its culture and power.

One of the most serious questions faced by Maya experts is how a population as large as that proposed for the Late Classic was fed, particularly in a tropical jungle environment. The first answer suggested was that people were fed by means of a swidden agriculture system, but when population density approaches 320 people per km^2, intensive agriculture is required. The calculated population of Tikal was 600 inhabitants per km^2, which forced the Mayas to reduce swidden agriculture's fallow period, to use intensive farming techniques, and to diversify crops, particularly tubers and vegetables. This required not only the use of terraces but also the recovery of swampland, the building of canals, and the use of *bajos* (depressions in the terrain) in times of drought to store water by covering the bottom with clay to prevent water loss.

Modern survey techniques, including those involving artificial satellites, produced a great stir among scholars when they revealed the traces of veritable networks of canals in the jungle. Subsequent investigations showed not only that these works were not prehispanic but that they were postcolonial or even nineteenth-century constructions, and that they had proliferated as a means of extracting precious woods from the jungle. As a side effect of this study, groups of raised fields were also discovered. In the Candelaria River basin, seed and pollen analysis confirms the intensive use of these raised fields to grow maize. Over a long period of time, excessive agricultural production degraded the soils. For example, we know that the inhabitants of Copán cut down the trees in their valley excessively, and the analysis of lake sediments in the Petén show the erosion and salt increase due to agricultural abuse.

Our knowledge of the internal organization of Maya society is rather limited. Extrapolating what we know about the Postclassic, we can suppose that the inhabitants of the central region in the Late Classic could be roughly divided into nobles and commoners. Evidently, there were numerous social levels within each of these two large categories, as reflected in the various levels of wealth and comfort found in the dwelling units of Tikal. Based on archaeological evidence, it can also be inferred that these were extended families with two or more married couples and that the various segments were distributed over several chambers surrounding a common patio.

In the central region, political power was distributed over a still undetermined number of cities that dominated their smaller surrounding populations and had shifting relationships of war and alliance among themselves. Marcus, referring to the Lowlands, notes that the number of capitals calculated by archaeologists varies from ten to one hundred.

Thus, there was nothing resembling an empire but rather a constellation of city-states that formed networks of military, social, political, economic, and ritual subordination.

The structure of power must have been extremely complicated. Noble families performed diverse functions, which were inherited by strict rules of succession. Because the principal ruler was a semidivine figure, hieroglyphic inscriptions and images centered primarily on him and his consort, thus blurring the power possessed by an entire privileged social group. Legitimacy of power derived from the relationship between a deity and a human group through a sacred link—the ruler. This semidivine being was required to belong to the lineage that was closest to the patron deity. It is thought that matrilineage was particularly important in the succession, which explains the iconographic female hierarchy. Dynastic history was a mirror image, a human recapitulation of the divine adventures of the people's patron in the other world. This parallelism had to be reflected in a concordance between the movements of the heavenly bodies and the precise calendrics registered in stelae and tablets. The dynastic link to the supernatural had to be periodically renewed, which led to the great bloodlettings of the ruler and his consort. Sculptures show them in the act of self-sacrificing by piercing their tongues and passing thick cords through the wounds (see fig. 6). This sacrifice, possibly aided by a psychotropic drug, produced ecstasy, the ensuing mystical encounter with the first ancestor renewing the pact with the ruling order. The importance of a lineage-based organization resulted in dynasties that remained in power for centuries. The rulers of Tikal referred to their third-century founder, Yax Moch Xoc, while those of Copán spoke of K'inich Yax K'uk' Mo', who began a dynasty that lasted from the beginnings of the fifth century to 820.

Despite the beliefs of those who idealized the Maya world, war was not a sporadic event in their culture. Physical anthropologists have found evidence of massive sacrifices and mutilations. Sculptures and pictographs show battles and acts of cruelty towards the vanquished. Written texts speak of confrontations, conquests, victories, and rulers exalted by these events, and archaeologists find moats and parapets circling Becán and between Tikal and its neighbor, Uaxactún.

During the Classic, trade linked the Maya cities and a good part of Mesoamerica as well. It is difficult to estimate the volume of perishable

Fig. 6. Lintel 24, Yaxchilán, Chiapas, depicting Shield Jaguar and Lady Xoc auto-sacrificing. Southeast Mesoamerica Area, Classic period.

goods, but durable goods, particularly sumptuary goods, allow us to reconstruct trade routes. Apart from land routes, rivers such as the Grijalva, Usumacinta, Candelaria, Champotón, Hondo, Nuevo, and Motagua functioned as aquatic highways. It is possible that coastal navigation was as important in the Classic as we know it to have been in the Postclassic.

As much as possible, secondary cities followed the model of the great capitals, the most impressive of which was Tikal. It is calculated that in the Classic period Tikal had a population of ten thousand in the urban center, with an area of sixteen km², but if the surroundings were counted, the population would have been thirty-nine thousand, with an additional ten thousand nearby. Like the other Maya cities, Tikal has a layout very different from Teotihuacan's orthogonal design. Even though the Maya cities followed cosmological canons, their arrangements seem anarchic at first sight. Cities were structured on the basis of an administrative ceremonial center composed of several plazas, surrounded by temples and palace groups. These architectural centers were often linked by avenues. Residential complexes were often organized according to a decreasing level of wealth until they faded into the vague boundary of the jungle.

Houses were built atop rectangular stone or earth platforms to avoid flooding during the rainy season. Depending on the geographic location, water was provided during the dry season utilizing chultunes, cenotes, aqueducts (for example, the aqueduct from the Otulum River at Palenque), or old quarry pits (as was done at Tikal). Some cities were joined by *sacbeoob*—wide, flat, straight limestone roads. Cobá had sixteen of these, including the longest one known, a one-hundred-kilometer road to Yaxuná. Whether these roads, which required an enormous human effort to construct, were built for trade, political, or only ritual purposes is still a matter of debate.

Plazas, pyramidal temples, palaces, ball courts, and monumental arches were notable features of ceremonial and administrative centers. Sometimes the centers were built on heights in order to form acropolises, as was the case at Copán, Yaxchilán, and Piedras Negras. The general effect was that of an overelaborate luxury, in which limestone from most of the area, green trachyte from Copán, sandstone from Quiriguá, and brick from Comacalco were profusely carved or covered with layers of molded and painted stucco. Images of humans, deities, and animals; calendric glyphs; complete texts; and mythological scenes were depicted on tablets, tableros, lintels, and jambs. Chapels sat atop tall temple pyramids (sixty-five meters in the case of Temple IV in Tikal) and were topped with roof combs. Palaces were sumptuous one-story buildings erected on platforms with stairs and composed of galleries of small rooms with frequent interior patios. Obviously, not every building called a palace today was used as a residence. Some of them are too small and uncomfortable to have been permanent dwellings. These are thought to be priestly cells, rooms used for administrative or ritual ceremonies, or sites of mystical rituals.

The so-called Maya arch, the vault it produces, and the stele/altar complex are basic components of Maya Classic architecture. The terms "arch" and "vault" are not really accurate. The "arch" in buildings is formed by two inclined columns or pillars in which the stones approach each other at the top until they join and close the intervening space. Because neither the "arch" nor the "vault" distribute the forces or the pressures onto their supports, these had to be built close to each other. In the case of roofed rooms, thick walls were needed in order to support the weight of the roof, considerably reducing the interior space. Although the architecture of the central and northern Maya zones has unmistakable characteristics, the styles of the two are different enough that political regions have been proposed on the basis of these differences. Distinct styles include those of Petén, Usumacinta, Motagua, Río Bec, Chenes, and Puuc. The Petén style, found in places such as Tikal, Uaxactún, Yaxhá, and Naranjo, involves a profusion of formidably tall temple pyramids with steep stairs. The building platforms have massive "apron" moldings that wrap around corners. The enclosures are small, the walls are thick, and the tall, massive roof combs are made possible by the thickness of the walls supporting them. Influences from the Petén extend south to the Pasión River Basin, as seen in sites such as Seibal and Altar de Sacrificios, and east to the Usumacinta Basin, where Yaxchilán, Piedras Negras, Bonampak, and Palenque are to be found. However, buildings in this region have significant variations from those in the Petén. They have open porticos and larger rooms, less massive walls, and hollow roof combs that lessen the burden on supporting walls and diminish the wind resistance of the roof combs. In the Motagua region the cities of Copán and Quirigúa are characterized by their finely carved stone ashlars, their grotesque masks of the Witz Monster (mountain god) at the corners of the buildings, and the gorgeous overdecorated, finely carved sculptures associated with them. The most characteristic feature of the Río Bec style, found in the south of the Yucatan peninsula, is the building of massive towers imitating stepped pyramids with chapels on their tops. In reality these are just decorative elements; the entrances to the temples are false fronts, and the steps of the staircases are too narrow to be climbed. This style appears at Río Bec itself and at Xpuhil and Becán (see plan 6). In the center of the peninsula, in the Chenes region, sites such as Dzibilnocac, Hochob, and Santa Rosa Xtampak cover the entire surfaces of the facades of their monumental buildings with a profuse mixture of grotesque masks with tremendous jaws that are themselves doors to the interior. Near Chenes is the Puuc region, with its unique architecture that uses a rich decor of carved stone veneers composed of small drums, beaded moldings, and mosaics in the shapes of frets and helices. This style is characteristic of Uxmal, Kabah, Sayil, Labná, and Oxkintok, but it extended beyond the Puuc region to the north-central part of the peninsula up to Chichén Itzá.

The stele/altar complex was a characteristic of the central as well as the northern Maya region. A stele is a vertical monument, generally a slab, embedded in the ground and carved with an image of a king and inscriptions commemorating him, the stele representing the cosmic tree. An altar is a short, wide, usually cylindrical horizontal stone placed in front of the stele. Sometimes it portrays a mythical animal—usually an earth monster. A stele is the quintessential historical indicator during the time of Maya splendor. A concept that was the confluence of many other cultural elements underlies its creation: beliefs, knowledge, artistic practices, and manifestations referring to power come together in the stele. The indisputable advances in the use of numbers, writing, the computation of time, and knowledge of celestial bodies as a whole were a response to the intellectual obsession of the elites, who based the legitimacy of rulers on a cosmic regularity that seemed to influence even the will of the gods.

In effect, maximum regularity had to be found in time. It was believed that there were invisible gods in time who traveled in the world using paths that were rigidly established by the exactitude of a geometric

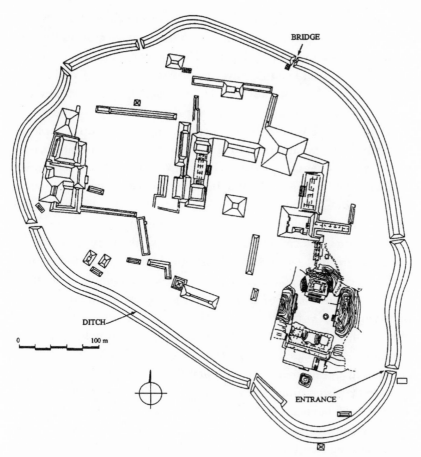

Plan 6. Becán Archaeological Zone, Campeche. Southeast Mesoamerica
Area, Classic period. (Based on P. Primer)

cosmos. Each time-god—each destiny—had a personality and a way of
acting upon different living things. In turn, the geographic location of
the god's appearance and his burden followed a strict sequence.
Through these sequences, the lives of rulers and of the government
itself were tied to historic and cosmic cycles. Events were interpreted as
the fulfillment of cyclic movements, and humans could know these
cycles by means of mathematics and astronomy. The perpetuation of
power depended on a cyclical passing of the baton. Panels in Palenque
show Lord Chan Bahlum, in the other world, receiving rulership from
his deceased father. The alternation of life and death as a chain of

succession was one of the chief preoccupations of the nobility. Stories of the myth, which confirmed the mechanism of succession through death, are shown in pictures. The polychrome vases found in the tombs of nobles often bear beautiful mythological scenes (see fig. 7) that have been interpreted by specialists such as Michael D. Coe, based on texts that were written centuries later in the *Popol Vuh*. Among the myth's characters are the twins, Hunahpú and Xbalanqué, faithful copies of their fathers. Their fathers, Hun Hunahpú and Vucub Hunahpú, were the first twins. They accepted a challenge from the Lords of the Underworld and died in the encounter, but the new pair of twins, Hunahpú and Xbalanqué, were engendered from their remains. The vases show scenes of this inheritance brought about by death.

Sacred wars determined by the cycle of Venus were also cyclical. Armies confronted each other to honor the Morning Star, and captives were sacrificed to the gods to ratify the periodical fulfillment of destinies.

The use of numbers to understand the nature of time required a particular way of writing numbers. The system was one of place value, with only three symbols (the dot, bar, and shell), although these could have quite complicated variants (faces and even full bodies of gods). Mesoamerican numbers were vigesimal (based on the number 20). At the lowest register, units were represented by dots and each 5 units by a bar. Thus, 3 bars and 4 dots represented the number 19, the maximum possible for that level. To write the number 20, one had to pass to the second register, that of the 20s, in which a dot represented 20. In this register, again, the maximum was 3 bars and 4 dots ($19 \times 20 = 380$). In the third register, the 400 level, a dot represented 400. Successive registers increased by multiples of 20. This kind of notation would have been impossible without a way to show registers that were occupied but empty. That is, there was a need for a symbol to fill the function of zero, which was most commonly symbolized by a shell. For example, if the unit register had 2 bars and 2 dots, a shell in the 20s register, and 3 dots in the 400s register, the number would be read as $(12 \times 1) + (0 \times 20) + (3 \times 400) = 1,212$. Two peculiarities of the system must be pointed out: first, it only handled whole numbers; second, in dealing with time it used the year, or *tun*, of 360 days as the unit in the third register. As a result, in time calculations the maximum unit in the second register is 17 because the number 18, corresponding to 18 20-day months, func-

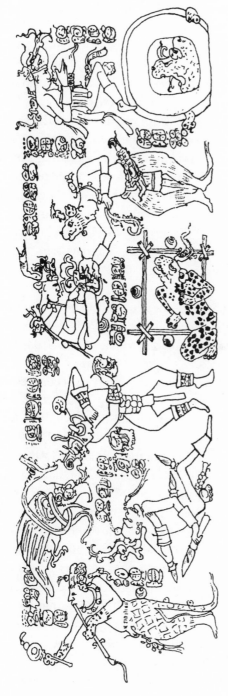

Fig. 7. A ritual dance scene on a Maya vase. Southeast Mesoamerica Area, Classic period.

tions as a dot in the third register; that is, a dot in the third register is 360, not 400.

Using this system, the Mayas were able to handle gigantic numbers, which were indispensable for linking both the historical present and the most remote mythical dates in dynastic lines. Further, the positional system allowed numerous calendrical cycles of very different sizes to be combined in various series. Without illustrating the principal series in detail, we would like to describe the combinations of three important cycles. The first is the agricultural cycle, including the main religious festivities, which consisted of 365 days, with 18 20-day months plus 5 complementary days (*haab* or common year). The second is the ritual cycle of 260 days, produced by the combination of 20 signs and 13 numbers (called *tzolkín* today). The third is the historical cycle of 360 days (tun), its 5 smallest units being the day (*kin*), the 20-day month (*uinal*), the 18-month year (*tun*), the 20-year unit (*katún*), and 20 20-year units (*baktún*).

The first combination of these was calculated, as in the rest of Meso-america, by using the "calendar wheel." On the calendar wheel the haab and the tzolkín were combined in a cycle of 18,980 days, corresponding to 52 365-day years and 73 260-day periods. The calendar wheel, together with the tun count, were used in a second combination that began with a very old event, which is why it was called the Long Count. The remote milestone corresponded to a day in which three dates of the three cycles had coincided, that is, the date 13.0.0.0.0 (baktún 13, katún 0, tun 0, uinal 0, kin 0) of the tun count, 4 Ahau (4-Lord) of the tzolkín count and the 8th day of the month *Cumkú* of the haab count. Following the Goodman-Martínez-Thompson correlation with the Julian calendar (the Gregorian calendar was not used until colonial times), calendric specialists correlate the day 13.0.0.0.0 4-Ahau 8-Cumkú with August 13, 3114 B.C. The Mayas used the Long Count to give full meaning to their present.

Other counts verified the regularity of the cosmos. Their calendric combinations were complemented by wheels that ascribed influence on the surface of the earth sequentially to different groups of deities (such as the 9 Lords of Night), with lunar and venusian cycles (according to some authors those of other planets as well), and with the eclipse tables. All of these were synchronized without the use of fractions. To achieve this, the Mayas determined celestial orbits with the naked eye and no more help than the alignments of their buildings with significant points on the horizon or crossed sticks that let them see movements of the celestial bodies.

Calendrical records were inextricably tied to written records. Because of their complexity, the written records resisted interpretation. Their decipherment has accelerated in the last fifty years through an academic debate that has produced spectacular moments both in its advances and in its confrontations. Among the numerous participants in the debate, key names are those of J. Eric S. Thompson, Yuri Knorosov, Heinrich Berlin, Tatiana Proskouriakoff, Floyd G. Lounsbury, Peter Mathews, Linda Schele, and David Stuart. As a result, a large percentage of the symbols have been interpreted to a greater or lesser degree. The writing system is basically logographic—its symbols represent words, and these follow the syntactic sequence of a discourse. It is also a mixed system, because it has semantic elements (for example, a symbol that usually represents a noun or a verb) as well as phonetic elements. The latter, usually syllabic, are consonant-vowel (CV) units that combine according to well-established rules. For example, a monosyllabic word with the formula consonant-vowel-consonant (CVC) such as *cuch* = "load", "destiny", "role or task" is written with two syllables, CV + CV (*cu* + *chu*) but it is pronounced CV (*cu* + *ch*) because the final vowel is omitted. Phonetic and semantic elements combined into rectangular cartouches are ordered syntactically into columns. The columns are usually read from left to right and from the top down, in pairs—that is, using two columns side by side to read the two cartouches on the same line. Morley and Thompson thought that Maya writing was used only for religious, calendrical, and astronomic topics, avoiding commonplace and political themes. Berlin and Proskouriakoff disagreed with this and produced evidence of their views that moved the investigation forward considerably. We now know that these texts supported dynastic histories and that they constituted one of the great propagandistic and mythical supports for the ideology of power. Furthermore, more prosaic uses are beginning to appear; for example, a vessel may have written on it the kind of drink—such as chocolate—for which it was intended. We expect that progress in the decipherment of Classic Maya writing will continue to transform the ideas we have about these people.

TEOTIHUACAN AND THE CLASSIC

This general description of the Classic shows that in this period of growth the great regional differences that started in the Late Preclassic were accentuated. Each region developed forms of expression so specific and rich that Mesoamerica became a vivid mosaic. Nevertheless, the different traditions continued to be part of the same cultural current, based on a shared history and strengthened by complex webs of interrelationships. Just as in the Middle Preclassic, in the first seven centuries of this era a cohesive force and a dominant tradition existed whose presence left a deep imprint on almost all the territory of Mesoamerica: that of Teotihuacan. Teotihuacan, like the Olmec culture, left its imprint on each locality and each epoch in a specific way. Fortunately, the quantity and quality of the information on the cohesive forces produced by Teotihuacan allow us to distinguish the differences in its influence in detail.

Everything seems to indicate that there was a common denominator—the advancement of trade—in all the expansions of Teotihuacan's influence. The dominion of the Central Mexican metropolis was based not on military might but rather on its inclusion of its contemporaries in a vast exchange system. For centuries, Teotihuacan produced and exported manufactured pottery and green obsidian objects, and its inhabitants took these goods to the most remote regions. This commercial interchange not only affected the specialized manufactures of the peoples involved, but their cultural and political life as well.

Teotihuacan's influence was not uniform over all of Mesoamerica. Apparently, the city directly controlled a wide territory that surrounded it, which provided its sustenance and the raw material for its industries. Along trade routes, its presence materialized in broad corridors strengthened by settlements of many different types. These corridors tied the metropolis to influential nuclei, including colonies, enclaves, exchange ports, and capitals that formed part of the trade network or, simply, allies. This sort of trade network required an army strong enough to protect the free flow of goods and, probably, to discourage prospective rivals. This should not be confused with the kind of armies required by expansionist states whose might is based on conquest and tribute. In the case of Teotihuacan, there is no doubt that a strong army and an ideology with militaristic leanings existed. However, the iconography in

Teotihuacan as well as in Tikal and Monte Albán seems to show that the size of its army seldom exceeded its needs as a protector of trade. Gods and humans were shown armed, but never in battle or subjugating the conquered.

This interpretation can be contrasted with archaeological data and hypotheses that try to explain the influence of Teotihuacan in the five areas—the North, the East, the Gulf, Oaxaca, and Southeast Mesoamerica— in a different way. The North exhibits two patterns, one in the eastern branch and the other in the western branch and central region. Phil C. Weigand and J. Charles Kelley think that the western branch contained colonies governed by bureaucrats from Teotihuacan. From this perspective, centers such as Alta Vista were subsidiaries to Teotihuacan's economic structure. Groups of warriors, merchants, and astronomers would have come to these regions in order to organize the exploitation of minerals such as turquoise, hematite, flint, and ocher that were destined for the manufacture of sumptuary goods. At the same time, these centers would have functioned as exchange ports, tying Teotihuacan to Paquimé and Chaco Canyon. Thus, Alta Vista would have been a market in which exotic products such as copper hawk bells and mirrors, turquoise jewelry, tropical animals, cotton clothing and blankets, and multi-colored feathers could have been found. Despite the attractiveness of this proposal, there is not enough evidence for the presence of a colonizing elite from the Basin of Mexico. Other than the explosion in mining and the plausible role of the northern sites, there is no evidence of a cultural incursion. First, the architecture of the main centers and the villages is purely local in styles and techniques. Further, funerary customs in this area were different from those of Teotihuacan, nor are there evidences of elite ritual distinctions; apart from differences in wealth, the burials of commoners and nobles are the same. The only elements attributable to Teotihuacan's tradition are pseudocloisonné ceramics and the circles of pecked circles and crosses associated with astronomical activities found in Alta Vista, which is located on the Tropic of Cancer.

There are more products from Teotihuacan in the other two branches of the northern area, particularly anthropomorphic figurines and Thin Orange ceramic vessels. However, they are not the majority of the imported goods, which also argues against these settlements' being direct colonies of Teotihuacan. The northern part of Querétaro is interesting in this context, as there was an intense exploitation of cinnabar—a mercury ore used primarily for ritual purposes—in that area during the Classic. Nevertheless, the presence of Teotihuacan ceramic and Gulf Coast stone artifacts is not enough to prove that Teotihuacan controlled those mining activities. In summary, although North Mesoamerica could have belonged to a trading network run by Teotihuacan, there is no clear evidence of its direct presence.

Teotihuacan had more influence on West Mesoamerica than on North Mesoamerica. Some Teotihuacan objects that probably arrived by trade have been found in Colima and Nayarit. The strongest Teotihuacan influence can be seen in specific areas of Guerrero, Jalisco, and Michoacán. For example, Teotihuacan was particularly interested in specific sites in the Balsas Basin because of the abundance of semiprecious stones, particularly green ones prized in making masks, in that region. Teotihuacan's influence is most evident in the Michoacán sites of Tingambato, Tres Cerritos, and Otero and the Jalisco sites of El Ixtépete and El Grillo. All of these sites have monumental architecture with talud/tablero facades in Teotihuacan style. This is particularly interesting in Tingambato, where this innovation occurred about A.D. 600. Nevertheless, detailed studies have shown that the building techniques at Tingambato were very different from those in Central Mexico. In the case of ceramics found in funerary offerings at Tingambato, although they are also in the style of Teotihuacan, they are made from local materials. From this evidence we can conclude that—whether the dominant ethnic group at sites such as Tingambato was from Teotihuacan or not—the architecture and ceramics were copies made by the local population.

In the Gulf Area the most interesting site with Central Mexican influence, without a doubt, is Matacapan, which lies at the crossing of exchange routes. The site's location is favored both by the fertility of the land and by its abundant mineral resources, including salt, cinnabar, volcanic stones, and—above all—kaolin, which enabled Matacapan to become an important source of fine paste pottery. A large portion of the ceramics recovered in archaeological excavations are containers and figurines imitating Teotihuacan style. Conversely, the most abundant foreign ceramic in Teotihuacan seems to come from Matacapan.

This suggests that, during the Late Tlamimilolpa and Early Xolalpan Phases in Teotihuacan, people belonging to the Teotihuacan tradition lived in Matacapan. One hypothesis claims that the Veracruz site was a true enclave of Teotihuacan. This is based on the fact that a large part of the remains of the daily life of the inhabitants of Matacapan shows that their practices and customs were identical to those of the inhabitants of the great capital in Central Mexico. These remains include ceremonial and domestic goods, burials under the floors (as in the metropolis), and at least one large pyramid with talud/tablero. The reciprocal relationship of Teotihuacan with the Gulf can be seen in the remains of possible Veracruz residents in the metropolis. Evelyn Childs Rattray has shown that in the northeast part of the city between A.D. 200 and 500, adjacent to a typically Teotihuacan dwelling complex, there were numerous structures with round platforms and access ramps that are thought to have been used for storage. Foreign ceramics are unusually abundant at this site, coming predominantly from southern Veracruz and from the Maya area. The funerary practices as well as the ceramics found in the tombs of these people were foreign.

One of the most fruitful relationships between Teotihuacan and societies located away from the High Plateau was that with Monte Albán. Everything points to the relationship's being intense as well as peaceful, but probably limited to areas of trade and diplomacy and, perhaps, to political matrimonial ties. The long-lasting relationship between the two metropolises was expressed in various ways. As we saw, there was at least one barrio of Zapotec dwellers in Teotihuacan. Even though its inhabitants were well integrated into the life of the city from A.D. 300 on, they preserved their ancestral tradition for generations. Although this dwelling complex was built in Teotihuacan style and its inhabitants used objects from this tradition, they recreated typical Monte Albán funerary customs, pottery, and inscriptions. As Marcus Winter has noted, the inhabitants of the barrio called Tlailotlacan furnished the Valley of Oaxaca with green obsidian, which was suggested by the abundance of obsidian from the Sierra de las Navajas in Oaxacan territory during Monte Albán Phases IIIA and IIIB–IV. Besides these obsidian objects, abundant ceramics of Teotihuacan origin as well as local imitations of *candeleros* (candlesticks), *florero* vases, Tlaloc jars, and cylindrical vases were also found, showing the preference of Zapotecan nobles for foreign styles. Nevertheless, the most interesting evidence of this long term relationship can be seen in five stone monuments. Four of the monuments were embedded in the corners of the South Platform of the Main Plaza of Monte Albán. The same scene, a high-ranking Teotihuacan delegation visiting the ruler of Monte Albán, is depicted in all four. Two of the eight figures wear tasseled Teotihuacan headdresses, indicating their high rank. The peaceful nature of their mission is clearly shown by the complete absence of weapons, and by the fact that they carry a bag of copal (a ritual object) and some gifts. The fifth monument, which is known as the Lápida de Bazán, comes from Mound X. A more detailed scene, possibly representing a meeting between a functionary from Teotihuacan and a ruler from Monte Albán, is depicted on it. None of the protagonists have weapons, although some of the delegates from Teotihuacan have helmets and military ornaments.

There is no doubt that the most important relationships established by Teotihuacan were those it had with the Southeast area. However, the exact nature of these relationships is still controversial. Three principal foci can be identified: the Guatemalan Highlands at Kaminaljuyú, the Motagua Valley at Copán, and a region in the Petén centered in Tikal. Kaminaljuyú had long been an important exchange center. As we have said, Teotihuacan's influence during approximately fifty years there is shown primarily by the building of temples with talud/tablero facades. Typical cylindrical vases with covers, vases with the image of the rain god, florero vases, Thin Orange ceramics, and green obsidian were also found at Kaminaljuyú. This led to the theory that Kaminaljuyú was made an enclave of Teotihuacan because Teotihuacan was attracted by the possibility of controlling the production and interchange of obsidian from Chayal and cacao from the Pacific region from this center. It is claimed that Teotihuacan's influence might have extended from Kaminaljuyú to the Maya Lowlands. This influence can be seen both in ceramic shapes and architecture there and in the possible insertion of Central Mexican nobility into the ruling dynasty at Tikal. However, there are other theories based on the idea that the architecture at Kaminaljuyú is not really Teotihuacan's but only a copy made using local techniques. Imported Teotihuacan ceramics and obsidian objects are outnumbered by local imitations, and are not found even in elite domestic contexts. This implies that scarce imported objects were prestigious and their use was limited to religious ceremonies and funerary offerings. According to these interpretations of the data, influences could have come directly from Teotihuacan or by way of Matacapan. From this perspective, Kaminaljuyú would have been neither an enclave of Teotihuacan nor a military outpost but rather a port of trade whose elite had great regard for the prestigious Teotihuacan tradition. This view is strengthened by the fact that there are no traces of warfare in the Guatemala Valley at that time. As we mentioned earlier, a third hypothesis is that Teotihuacan people who were not connected to the metropolis installed themselves as rulers in Kaminaljuyú and were fused into the Maya aristocracy and culture.

Teotihuacan's influence in Tikal dates to the fourth and fifth centuries A.D. However, the nature of this relationship is disputed. It can be seen in large buildings of talud/tablero style located in the Mundo Perdido compound; in a ball-court marker similar to the one found at La Ventilla, Teotihuacan; in several elite funerary offerings; and in the problematic Deposit 50, which is a cylindrical tomb dug in Teotihuacan style, containing a tripod cylindrical vase with incised sides. The vase shows a scene in which a Maya personage in a talud/tablero temple greets a group composed of four armed soldiers and two Teotihuacan dignitaries with tasseled headdresses who are carrying covered cylindrical vases as gifts. However, the most valuable information comes from Tikal's Stelae 4, 31, and 32 and Yaxhá's Stele 11. All four show persons with indisputable Teotihuacan dress and symbols: tasseled headdresses, the attributes of Tlaloc, and typical Central Mexican weapons (darts and spear throwers). The most complex scene, on Stele 31, depicts the ruler Siyah Chan K'awil (Stormy Sky), flanked by two images of his father, Nun Yax Ayin (Curl Snout), in a peaceful pose but armed and dressed in Teotihuacan style. Lengthy debates have resulted in quite different interpretations of this stele. One of the most popular interpretations posits that Nun Yax Ayin was a descendant of the ruling family of Tikal. His attire meant that the Maya elite had special regard for Teotihuacan's regalia, considering them to be prestige symbols. This special regard derived from Teotihuacan's great economic power and fame and from the extensive commercial interchanges between the Mayas and the inhabitants of Central Mexico. However, according to a recent interpretation of this image and of several epigraphic texts by David Stuart, a man called Siyah K'ak' (Smoking Frog) came to Tikal in

A.D. 378. This, coincidentally, was the year that the ruler Jaguar Paw died. Apparently, Siyah K'ak' then became the regent of the young Nun Yax Ayin, who began a new dynasty. There is some doubt as to the ethnicity of this ruler, because his father's name, Atlatl Cauac (Spear Thrower Owl), is the same as an important Teotihuacan military emblem. Based on this fact, Stuart holds that there clearly was an intrusion of people from Central Mexico into Tikal's rulership.

Work done by William Fash, Barbara Fash, and David Stuart reveals Copán as an interesting example of the impact of Teotihuacan on Southeast Mesoamerica. Numerous objects made in Central Mexico have been recovered in Copán in contexts dating to the beginning of the fifth century. Some of these are Thin Orange ceramic vessels, pyrite mirrors with slate backs, and items made with green Pachuca obsidian. The objects were primarily found in public buildings and elite tombs, particularly in a structure called Yax. The largest amount of green obsidian found so far in any site outside the Basin of Mexico was discovered in this building's fill. Another important building, known as Hunal, was built in talud/tablero style and was adorned with Teotihuacan-style murals. A tomb attributed to K'inich Yax K'uk' Mo, the founder of Copan's dynasty, is inside this building. Strontium analysis of the skeleton of the deceased indicates that he was not a native of the Copán Valley. On the other hand, analysis of the skeleton of his presumed wife shows the same chemical composition as that of the area's inhabitants.

Conditions changed completely in the Late Classic. Despite Teotihuacan's decline and the disappearance of its direct influence on the Southeast, Teotihuacan's symbolism was retained in cities such as Copán, Piedras Negras, Yaxchilán, Palenque, and Dos Pilas. While there were many of these symbols in Copán, they were a late Maya embellishment than an authentic reflection of Central Mexico. Thus, what had been an accurate copy of Teotihuacan style and fashion in the Early Classic became an omnipresent evocation of a former link in the Late Classic. The Maya rulers continued to refer to the old and prestigious affiliation with Teotihuacan, but emphasized warlike motifs such as rectangular shields, spear throwers, and headdresses; year glyphs; and reptilian figures. This militaristic symbolism has been interpreted as the ideological medium that the rulers used to maintain their authority at a time of increasing warfare.

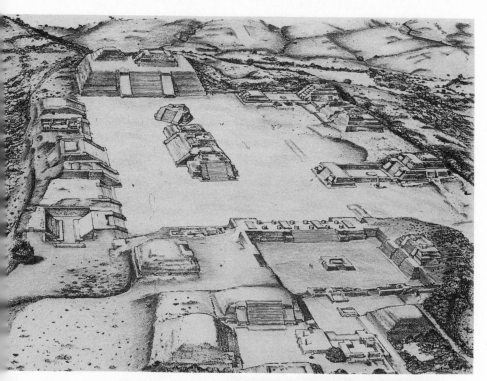

Perspective of the Great Plaza of Monte Albán, Oaxaca. Oaxaca Area, Classic period. (Illustration by Beatriz Saldaña. Redrawn from Paul Gendrop © *Arqueología* Mexicana, INAH)

Urn with deity wearing a jaguar headdress, Oaxaca. Oaxaca Area, Classic period. (Courtesy of Salvador Guilliem)

Genealogic tombstone from a tomb near Cuilapan, Oaxaca. Oaxaca Area. Classic period. (Courtesy of Salvador Guilliem)

Ñuiñé polychrome urn representing the old god. Cerro de las Minas, Oaxaca. Oaxaca Area, Classic period. (Courtesy of Salvador Guilliem)

Bas-relief representing the god of death. Tomb 1, Zaachila, Oaxaca.
Oaxaca Area, Classic period. (Courtesy of Salvador Guilliem)

Mounds called "guachimontones," Teuchitlán, Jalisco. West Mesoamerica Area, Classic period. (Photograph: Ignacio Guevara © *Arqueología Mexicana*, INAH)

Squash-shaped ceramic vessel with anthropomorphic supports, Colima. West Mesoamerica Area, Classic period. (Photograph: Ignacio Guevara © *Arqueología Mexicana*, INAH)

Mezcala-style anthropomorphic statuettes found in Tenochtitlan, Distrito Federal. West Meso-america Area, Classic period. (Courtesy of Salvador Guilliem)

Talus walls of the defensive system of La Quemada, Zacatecas. North Meso-america Area, Classic period. (Photograph: Ignacio Guevara © *Arqueología Mexicana*, INAH)

Mural fragment at Las Higueras, Veracruz. Gulf Area, Classic period.
(Photograph Carlos Blanco © *Arqueología Mexicana,* INAH)

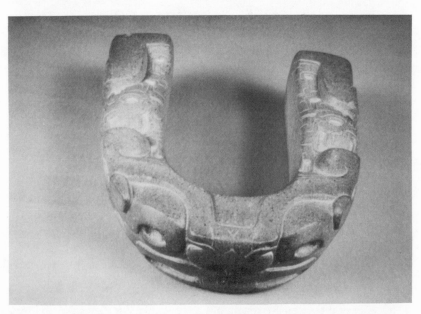

"Yugo"-type stone sculpture, Veracruz. Gulf Area, Classic period. (Photograph:
André Cabrioler © *Arqueología Mexicana,* INAH)

Representation of a Maya ruler on a stele, Copán, Honduras. Southeast Mesoamerica Area, Classic period. (Photograph: Leonardo López Luján)

Panel with image of a ruler of Palenque, Chiapas. Southeast Mesoamerica Area, Classic period. (Photograph: Carlos Blanco © *Arqueología Mexicana*, INAH)

CHAPTER FOUR

The Mesoamerican Epiclassic Period

THE FALL OF THE CLASSIC PERIOD

One of the most significant transformations in Mesoamerican history occurred between A.D. 650 and 750: Teotihuacan lost the political and economic supremacy it had held for five long centuries. The renowned Classic metropolis fell so precipitously that it is calculated its population declined from 125,000 to 30,000 inhabitants in 150 years. There is much evidence that the buildings in the central zone were ritually burned and destroyed during the final Metepec Phase. Simultaneously, its enormous commercial and military influence began to diminish beyond the confines of the Basin of Mexico.

Because Teotihuacan's influence had been so strong during its time of splendor, it is not unexpected that its collapse reverberated in most of Mesoamerica. The breakup of Teotihuacan's network was followed by 200 years in which the great Classic capitals fell and the ephemeral power centers of the Epiclassic rose. With the fall of famous sites such as La Quemada, Monte Albán, Palenque, and Tikal, a significant period of sociopolitical disintegration foreshadowed a new epoch. A number of archaeological markers clearly distinguish this period, which runs from the seventh to the ninth century. Broadly speaking, a clear break from the refined cultural traditions of the Classic occurred. Furthermore, many Mesoamerican capitals lost at least half of their population, and some were simply abandoned. Simultaneously, the peasant populations that had fed the urban masses emigrated to new territories.

For example, William T. Sanders and his coworkers estimate that after the burning of Teotihuacan's center the city lost about 95,000 people and the population of the rest of the Basin of Mexico shrank to 75,000. These numbers show that the decrease was not just a relocation of people from the city to nearby areas within the Basin. Another indicator was the appearance, about A.D. 650, of Coyotlatelco ceramics, which belong to a very different culture than that of the Metepec Phase.

As Alfonso Caso and Ignacio Bernal have pointed out, Monte Albán's hegemony over its region ended at the end of Phase IIIB. Its population dropped considerably, and the remaining inhabitants occupied the southern part of the hill. The Great Plaza would never be refurbished, and no more public buildings with military themes would be built there.

Charles D. Trombold found that in northern Mesoamerica the inhabitants of the Malpaso Valley at first clustered in the most fertile and better-watered zones; following an excessive growth in population density in these areas, however, people migrated in various directions—to the north, to the northwest, and, above all, to Central Mexico. La Quemada was abandoned in A.D. 850 and Mesoamerica's border shrank 250 kilometers southward, leaving the area to hunting-gathering bands.

The process was even more apparent in the Southeast. The ruling elites of many capitals seem to have disappeared completely between A.D. 810 and 909. The principal administrative structures and palaces were completely abandoned. Temples were no longer built, and nobles were no longer buried in the temples along with polychrome vases and jade jewelry. Stelae carved with dynastic texts and dates in the Long Count were no longer erected. This did not simply represent the cessation of a ritual or an artistic expression; the erection of stelae was one of the formal bases of dynastic power, as a stele validated and confirmed the kinship between the king and his divine ancestor. To all these changes we can add the sudden appearance of fine orange and fine gray ceramics, indicating the arrival of new groups from the plains of Tabasco.

Such strong evidences of change along the length and breadth of Mesoamerica are proof of an indisputable collapse. The difficulty lies in finding plausible explanations for what we can see archaeologically. Many scholars have tried to explain the collapse, although most of the explanations have focused on a site, a zone, or at most a particular area.

There are two main hypotheses concerning the destruction of Teotihuacan. One, proposed by scholars such as Wigberto Jiménez Moreno, compare the decline of this civilization to that of Rome. That is, an assumed decadence of an idyllic theocratic state encouraged an invasion of the Chichimecs—barbarian and warlike peoples from the north—who put an end to the glorious history of the city. The scholars also acknowledge the possibility that Mixtec or Huastec groups invaded the city. However, the proposal made by René Millon and Enrique Nalda, that the collapse was caused by Teotihuacan's inhabitants themselves, is more convincing. There is archaeological evidence of a new militaristic tone during the Metepec Phase. In this period there was a proliferation of paintings dealing with war and personalized portraits emphasizing the prestige of the rulers. We can add to this some evidence of a possible fortification of Teotihuacan, though this evidence is debatable. The bolstering of power of the military and the rulers was perhaps a response to a growing discontent of the peasants, who had to cope with the growing demands of the elite, or to a struggle between different factions within the nobility. Regardless of the agent—Chichimec invasion or internal revolt—the systematic burning of the city clearly signifies that the perpetrators intended to erase all traces of the ruling group.

On the other hand, some scholars have proposed that Teotihuacan collapsed due to a (very questionable) exhaustion of the soil and overexploitation of nearby forests. Others argue that the collapse was a direct consequence of competition with emergent centers such as El Tajín, Cacaxtla, and Xochicalco. According to Jaime Litvak King, Xochicalco was the driving force of a domain with the sole purpose of filtering traffic in tropical goods (cacao, feathers, greenstones, and cotton) from the Balsas Depression and northeastern Guerrero to the Basin of Mexico. According to Litvak King, Xochicalco, together with Cholula, El Tajín, and Tula, caused Teotihuacan's fall in the seventh century by destroying the economic basis of the city's power—that is, by stopping the flow of goods from its trade routes.

It is now clear that the disintegration of Monte Albán's power was an extremely gradual process. As we pointed out earlier, there had been a sudden increase in population during the Monte Albán IIIB Phase, and peasant villages had multiplied in the Oaxaca Valley as never before. Some scholars suggest that the trigger for the collapse was an overpopulation of the arable lands in the Valley and the competition for basic resources that ensued. Others suggest that the real cause for the fall was the weakening of Teotihuacan's might. The absence of Teotihuacan eliminated Monte Albán's role as the guarantor of regional security and resulted in a gradual relocation of its citizens to new centers such as Lambityeco and Zaachila.

Various explanations are offered for the decline of the northern area and the radical shrinking of the border. One group of archaeologists agrees with Kelley, who argued that Alta Vista's reason for existence vanished with the fall of Teotihuacan. When the Central Mexican metropolis collapsed, there was no longer a need for this northern colony to function as a mining center, a supplier of exotic goods, and an exchange site for the route to Chaco Canyon. A second group of archaeologists agrees with Armillas, who proposed that a terrible deterioration of climactic conditions made even minimal farming impossible and led to an abandonment of Alta Vista and La Quemada and a massive migration of peasants southward.

The majority of hypotheses concern the central Maya area. By 1973 there were so many different hypotheses regarding the "mysterious" collapse of the Mayas that Richard E. Adams and Jeremy A. Sabloff independently published attempts at classifying them. Both classifications reveal a variety of traditional explanations, most of which were unicausal. Perhaps the most important group of scholars favored internal causes. Among these, some scholars, assuming that the Mayas practiced swidden agriculture, held that the collapse was directly caused by soil exhaustion. According to this view, the increasing need for food forced farmers to shorten the fallow periods of the cornfields. The result was an inevitable loss of fertility and the proliferation of savannah ecosystems. Other scholars argued that explanations must be sought in demography. They proposed either an excessive growth in population that made it impossible to sustain the system employing simple technology, or a large decrease in male births that led to the self-destruction of the society.

This group also included proponents of natural phenomena, which today we know were localized, sporadic, or nonexistent as causes of the collapse. These causes included hurricanes, earthquakes, climactic deterioration, epidemics, and insect plagues. Finally, the more suggestive proposals argued for sociopolitical internal causes such as constant warfare between city-states and peasant revolts against despotic rulers. The latter proposal emphasized the unrest of the lower classes due to the constantly increasing demands of the Maya elite.

The second group of proposals emphasized the enormous importance of relationships with the rest of Mesoamerica throughout Maya history. For this reason, some authors give priority to external economic and sociopolitical causes of the collapse. One of the most popular proposals is that of an invasion by Putún Maya groups or groups from Central Mexico.

Even though many of the hypotheses we have mentioned are supported by credible evidence, there is a tendency today to discard them because of their simplistic nature. In their place, explanatory models have been constructed whose complexity more closely fits the new body of data regarding the Mayas. Thus, the general breakup of societies of the Classic can no longer be attributed to a single cause. Even though we do not yet know the definite "trigger" for the collapse, newer hypotheses emphasize a combination of factors.

One of the best of these complex models is the one developed some time ago by Gordon R. Willey and Dimitri B. Shimkin. To summarize their ideas, the culmination of cultures in the Classic had produced an unusual growth of population and a multitude of competing centers. This dual phenomenon led to substantial internal and external pressures. Among the internal pressures was an excessive agricultural exploitation of the jungle as a response to an ever-increasing demand for food. At this time the already large differences between nobles and commoners widened further. While the elites grew ever more powerful, peasants daily confronted enormous demands for tribute even though they were malnourished and afflicted by contagious diseases. All these factors caused a decrease in agricultural production and a competition between centers for maximal control of resources. One of the most important external pressures was the destabilizing effect of the intrusion of groups of traders from the coastal plains of Tabasco. Thus, lacking a technological solution, the economic and demographic bases of a system involving about five million people irrevocably weakened. The process ended with the collapse of the system, a decline in population, and the rise of simpler political organizations.

According to the latest advances in Maya archaeology, as summarized by Marcus, the Maya collapse should not be seen as a monolithic event. Three possible versions of the collapse can be reconstructed, each occuring in a different region. The data from the region of Lamanai, Nohmul, and La Milpa indicate that there was not a general collapse; although some important centers were abandoned, other centers in the region continued to exist. By contrast, according to some scholars, the Copán Valley shows a general, though very slow, collapse between A.D. 800 and 1250. Finally, research in the Petexbatún region reveals a climate of extreme violence, leading to a sudden and general collapse of all the power centers in the region.

A GENERAL VIEW OF THE EPICLASSIC

After the collapse of the Classic, a short period intervened that has been called the Epiclassic (as well as the Late Classic, Terminal Classic, Proto-Postclassic, and First Phase of the Second Intermediate period). At most the Epiclassic runs from A.D. 650/800 to 900/1000. The principal indicators of this era were social mobility, a reorganization of settlements, changes in spheres of cultural interaction, political instability, and changes in religious doctrines. Like many other scholars, we believe that the bases of the Postclassic were established in the Epiclassic.

The Central Highlands, the Gulf Coast, the Yucatán Peninsula, and probably the modern territories of Chiapas and Guatemala were linked in a fashion that we do not yet understand. In the Epiclassic, Mesoamerica became a massive crucible in which culturally and ethnically different peoples came into contact and fused. Peasants, freed from centralizing yokes, shunned their birthplaces and settled in more productive nearby lands. Artisans, who specialized in making sumptuary goods, traveled much further in search of elites who could sponsor their activities. To these movements we can add those of merchants, warriors, priests, and rulers, all of whom belonged to ethnic groups that played a decisive role in Mesoamerican history. A few of these ethnic groups were the Olmeca-Xicalancas, the Itzás, and the Nonoalcas. We should also mention the continuous migratory incursions of the northern nomads and seminomads, warlike peoples who would forge new life-styles with the Mesoamericans.

As a consequence of the withering away of the old reservoirs of power, vigorous new centers rose up, although none of them achieved anything like the hegemony achieved by Tikal, Monte Albán, or Teotihuacan. After the seventh century Mesoamerica was politically balkanized. Although it is true that the so-called City of the Gods remained supreme in the Basin of Mexico until A.D. 950, vital expansionist societies rose and fell on the other side of the mountains. The Epiclassic saw the culmination of places such as Cacaxtla, Xochicalco, Teotenango, El Tajín, Zaachila, Jalieza, Lambityeco, Uxmal, Kabah, and Sayil. These regional centers created a situation of competition and low-level integration, but—amid a climate of uncertainty—they searched in vain for political superiority. The relative duration of each of them depended on its success in the struggle for scarce resources, specialized production, and trade routes as well as its ability to develop statelike controls.

In this context there was an unusual growth in military forces. This is not to deny that there was constant warfare during the Classic, but during the Epi-Classic political instability resulted in the permeation of the military through all aspects of society. Many of the cities were located in places chosen for their strategic location and were built on the basis of rigorous defensive design. Walls, moats, palisades, bastions, and fortresses were indispensable elements for the survival of any city during this period. At the same time iconographic images alluding to warfare proliferated as never before in Central Mexico. In fact the importance of the new states can be confirmed by the richness of their public buildings, replete with symbols of sacrifice and death, battle scenes, and human figures with the emblems and symbols of power.

This was also a period characterized by proliferating multiethnic settlements, extremely diverse marriage alliances, and confederations of two or more political entities. The wealth of cultural contacts is expressed in public art through eclectic styles that depict real or fictitious relationships with propagandistic intent. Hypostyle architecture spread, allowing the construction of large interior spaces; so, too, did the use of the *tzompantli* ("skull rack").

Southeast Mesoamerica merits particular mention. As we have seen, the political disintegration of the Maya capitals of the central zone began sixty years after the fall of Teotihuacan and ended at the beginning of the tenth century. This temporal shift in Central Mexico has led most Maya scholars to avoid using the term Epiclassic to refer to this period, calling it the Late or the Terminal Classic instead.

It is interesting to note that, precisely in the ninth century, the Río Pasión region was reborn for a period of only one hundred years. This ephemeral rebirth was directly connected with the arrival in the region of supposedly Putún Maya groups. Their fine paste ceramics, found at Altar de Sacrificios and Seibal, without a doubt were made in the Tabasco Lowlands. After their intrusion the invaders were depicted with Maya trappings and symbols of power, as if they had usurped the throne of the local rulers. But they also carry strange emblems and symbols of gods not worshipped in the region. For example, one of the personages carries a mask with a long bird beak like that of the wind god, an avatar of Quetzalcoatl. It is possible that the ongoing cultural decay made the intrusion of these foreigners possible.

According to Willey, a massive exodus northward must have taken place in the same century. He argues that non-Maya groups would have guided the local population to the then-flourishing capitals of the Yucatán Peninsula. Sabloff has a more radical proposal—that the Classic Maya civilization did not collapse but, rather, moved to the North. According to Sabloff, the final decadence of the central zone coincided with the flourishing of the northern zone. He feels that this explains the similarities in tools, agricultural techniques, urban planning, and religious beliefs of the two areas. For Sabloff the Río Bec, Chenes, East Coast, and Puuc regions were extensions and cultural heirs of the Petén. Puuc societies developed A.D. 800–1000, most prominently at Uxmal, Kabah, Sayil, and Labná. Interestingly, Puuc and Toltec styles appear together in Chichén Itzá around A.D. 900. Thanks to numerous radiocarbon dates, today no one questions the overlap of both styles and of the Cehpech and Sotuta ceramic phases there. The old idea that one phase followed the other and that the southern and northern architectural groups in Chichén Itzá were not contemporaneous has been abandoned. As we will see, Chichén Itzá was simply one more of the crucibles of this era in which several cultural traditions fused.

CENTRAL MEXICO IN THE EPICLASSIC

The history of Central Mexico is particularly interesting during the Epiclassic (A.D. 650/800–900/1000). After Teotihuacan got weaker, the valleys adjacent to the Basin of Mexico became fertile ground for an explosive growth of belligerent centers, notably the cities of Cacaxtla, Xochicalco, and Teotenango, which were located, respectively, in the Puebla-Tlaxcala, Morelos, and Toluca Valleys. Like other Epiclassic capitals, these three cities developed rapidly. The cities were built on heights that dominated large areas, they had complex military defense systems, and they included different ethnic groups, which were perhaps united into a single political unit.

Another distinctive aspect of Cacaxtla, Xochicalco, and Teotenango is their art, which we could term eclectic. In contrast with their writing system, the roots of which extend to the incipient Teotihuacan tradition, the artistic traditions of these three centers are the result of impressive cultural amalgams. Obviously, the eclecticism of the Epiclassic can be interpreted in many ways—as the result of massive migrations, matrimonial alliances, the presence of foreign intellectuals, the political alliance of different ethnic groups, conquests, extensive trade relationships, or rulers interested in presenting a cosmopolitan image. Nevertheless, despite the fact that many elements of this art have recognizably foreign origins, we know that the inhabitants of Central Mexico adapted these elements, combined them, and incorporated them into new symbolic contexts.

We would like to emphasize that this new era of contacts in many different directions was only possible because of the destruction of a system that focused entirely on Teotihuacan. It is also important to remember that it was the omnipresent influence of the city, not the city itself. Teotihuacan continued to be the most important city in the Basin and even in Central Mexico between A.D. 650 and 950 (the Xometla and Oxtoticpac Phases). If William T. Sanders's as well as Richard A. Diehl's estimates are correct, the city was thirteen km² in area at this time, with a population of thirty thousand. Tikal may have been the only larger contemporaneous city.

Rather than focusing on the relative influence of Teotihuacan during the Epiclassic, the current debate centers on whether (1) its inhabitants at that time were the descendants of the occupants of Teotihuacan in the Metepec Phase; (2) some of them had come from other groups, presumably from the north; or (3) they had been completely replaced by people from the societies that made the famous Coyotlatelco ceramics. The source of these ceramics, used to date the Epiclassic occupation in the Teotihuacan Valley as well as many other regions in Central Mexico, is the subject of debate. The ceramics belong to an ancient pottery tradition that used red decoration on a buff background. The predominant motifs of Coyotlatelco pottery are crosses, dots, and frets. Most experts tend to put the source of this style in the north—somewhere in the present states of Querétaro, Guanajuato, San Luis Potosí, or Zacatecas—only a few leaning toward the Basin of Mexico, particularly Teotihuacan, as the source. However, this is a difficult stance to defend, as Metepec Phase and Coyotlatelco ceramics are diametrically opposed.

Meanwhile, northwest of Teotihuacan, Tula was taking the first steps in building its immense reputation. Robert H. Cobean and Alba Guadalupe Mastache hypothesize that Coyotlatelco groups from the north settled in this area during the Prado Phase (A.D. 700–800), with Magoni as their principal center. Because of these new migrations, the area became a veritable ethnic and cultural crucible during the Corral Phase (A.D. 800–900). Tula Chico, the largest settlement in this phase, covered between three and five km².

On the opposite side of Teotihuacan, beyond the Sierra Nevada, was Cacaxtla, the ruling center in the Puebla-Tlaxcala Valley during the Epiclassic. Cacaxtla was located on a massif bordered by the Zahuapan and Atoyac Rivers, dominating well-irrigated fertile lands. It is possible that Cacaxtla was established around A.D. 600 by the Olmec-Xicalancas, a Nahua-oriented group affiliated with the Popoloca-Mixtecs, who came from the coast of Tabasco. According to some hypotheses, the Olmec-Xicalancas ruled the valley until A.D. 900, when they were defeated by Chichimec-Poyauhtecas or Toltec-Chichimecs and expelled to the south toward the Zacatlán Sierra. According to other interpretations, the Olmec-Xicalancas stayed at Cacaxtla between A.D. 500 and 900 and in Cholula between A.D. 800 and 1100, after which they were banished permanently from the valley.

Cacaxtla's plan is a 1,700-by-800-meter rectangle, adjusted for topographic irregularities. In prehispanic times the city was practically impregnable, because of an impressive defensive system consisting of a wall, numerous glacis, and nine moats. The main entrance, facing west, was protected by a watchtower. The major areas that were cultivated lie in the lower part of the site. Next to them, on a higher level, are dwelling terraces and the La Mesita glacis. Finally, in the highest area, 120 meters above the valley floor, rise the palaces and the larger temples: the Plaza of the Three Pyramids, Los Cerritos, and the Great Platform. Ten stepped platforms must be climbed in order to reach this architectural group. The Great Platform was the nerve center of Cacaxtla. It is an enormous pyramidal platform (200 x 110 x 25 meters) on which the most important religious and residential areas were built. Among these are the Palace, composed of a porticoed patio and several rooms; the Patio of the Altars; and the North Plaza. However, Cacaxtla's fame in modern times is due to Diana López de Molina's 1975 discovery of its impressive mural paintings. What is truly surprising about these murals is that they harmoniously combine the Maya custom of drawing human figures in a naturalistic manner and the glyphic tradition born in Teotihuacan and crystallized in Central Mexico during the Epiclassic.

The Battle Mural, a nearly 26-meter-long fresco painted on two taluds of Building B about A.D. 650, depicts a violent armed confrontation between two clearly differentiated ethnic groups. The victors have grayish-brown skin, aquiline noses, and unmodified skulls. They wear jaguar skins and carry round shields, obsidian knives, spears, and spear throwers. The losers have been identified as Mayas on the basis of their reddish skin, their profiles, and their cranial deformations. With the exception of their two leaders, the losers all lie on the ground wounded, terribly mutilated, or dead. Contrasting with their opponents, they are all naked and wear only feathers, pectorals, earspools, and other jade jewels. Their leaders stand proudly unarmed and wearing rich bird costumes.

The murals of Building A were painted one hundred years later. Marta Foncerrada de Molina interpreted their theme as an exaltation of war—a fundamental bargain that humans make with the gods, who in turn assure humans fertility of the earth, a heroic rank, and supernatural authority. Two scenes with red background stand out on the principal walls of the building, reminding us, as Michel Graulich points out, of the obsession with duality in Mesoamerican religion. The south wall depicts a figure who is clearly Maya, wearing a bird helmet and costume and standing on top of a feathered serpent. He holds a large ceremonial scepter topped by a serpent head, the latter with a protruding tongue shaped like a flint knife. Significantly, the glyph 13-Feather, associated with the thirteen upper heavens and with masculinity, transparency, and dryness, accompanies this Bird-Man. The north wall depicts a man wearing a jaguar costume and helmet. He is standing on top of a serpent with jaguar skin and holding a bundle of darts with drops of water falling from its end. Like the other figure, Jaguar-Man is accompanied by a glyph, in this case 9-Reptile Eye, which is associated with the earth, femininity, darkness, and wetness. The equally interesting jamb panels of Building A show two figures on a blue background who may also be complementary: a Jaguar-Man pouring water out of a Tlaloc-decorated vessel and a Maya man holding a snail from which a little red-haired man, perhaps the sun, emerges.

These murals, as well as those found more recently in the Red Temple and other buildings on the Great Platform, are the raw material and source for all suppositions about the origin of the Olmec-Xicalancas. It is not clear whether the artists were independent Mayas under contract to the rulers of the site or Olmec-Xicalancas, a people immersed simultaneously in Maya and Central Mexican cultures. What is certain is that their eclectic style refers to an era of intense intercultural relationships and city-states that included different ethnic groups in their midst.

Cholula is a few kilometers south of Cacaxtla. Florencia Müller, on the basis of a limited number of stratigraphic cuts, claims somewhat bluntly that the center of this site was uninhabited between A.D. 800 and 900. Nevertheless, as Sanders, Diehl, and McCafferty say, there seems to be enough evidence to contradict this. Müller herself points to local production of ceramics during the Cholula IV (A.D. 700–800) and Cholulteca I (800–900) Phases. She also points out that there are sherds in the first phase that show relationships to objects from Teotihuacan, the Mixteca, the Gulf of Mexico, and the Maya area. In the second phase there are also Xochicalco-like ceramics. To this evidence we can add that of three monuments found in Plaza G, located at the southern corner of the Great Pyramid, or Tlachihualtepetl. These are Altars 1, 2, and 3, huge slabs with carved relief volutes in mature El Tajín style, dated after A.D. 700.

Xochicalco, the Epiclassic capital of the Morelos Valley, had an existence as brief as it was intense. Between A.D. 650 and 900 (Phase G) the villages that had occupied seven hills next to the Tembembe River merged to become this cosmopolitan city. According to Kenneth G. Hirth and Ann Cyphers Guillén, Xochicalco was probably the result of a federation of the elites of settlements in West Morelos, the federation being formed in an attempt to consolidate regional political control after the fall of Teotihuacan. The creation of this kind of federation would explain the accelerated and "unnatural" population growth in a valley with little agricultural potential. Also, the cooperation of all the ethnic groups that had joined together would explain the brief time in which all the enormous public and elite buildings of the city were built. Nevertheless, Xochicalco's explosive growth was followed by a violent destruction of the city's center and an exodus of its inhabitants. This decisive event is recorded in the evidences of fire seen in the principal buildings of the site and in the sudden shrinkage of the settlement after A.D. 900, when it contracted from four km² to less than twelve hectares.

During Xochicalco's time of splendor, most building activities took place on Cerro Xochicalco, a prominence measuring 1,200 by 800 meters and rising 130 meters above the valley floor. During this time an architectural remodeling took place that involved leveling considerable portions of the hilltop. The most important buildings, such as the Temple of the Feathered Serpents, the Main Ball Court, the Acropolis, and Structures A, C, D, and E, were built there. In the middle and lower sections large residential terraces, small groups of domestic platforms, and defensive works such as bastions, glacis, moats, walls, and ramparts were built. The city also had a complex net of ramps and walkways that joined the sectors of the city and roads that communicated to other sites in the valley.

Cerro Xochicalco, the heart of the city, had three large lobes oriented to the south, north, and west. Like El Tajín, the settlement on Cerro Xochicalco was divided into two large sections: a complex of low plazas open to the public and an acropolis with limited access. Thus, the plazas and buildings associated with commerce, massive assemblies, ball games, public religion, and the large, popular festivals are located on the south and west lobes of the hill. The north lobe, at a higher elevation, was exclusively for the elite. The residences of the highest dignitaries of the state, two small ball courts without stands, and the main buildings for private religious ceremonies—among which the Temple of the Feathered

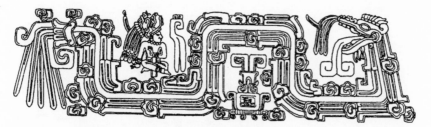

Fig. 8. Relief on the Temple of the Feathered Serpents, Xochicalco, Morelos. Central Mexico Area, Epiclassic period.

Serpents stands out—are located there. The Temple is the most beautiful, famous, and studied structure in Xochicalco. Its facades are huge relief-carved friezes, perfectly fitted without mortar and covered by a thin layer of painted stucco. The undulating bodies of two feathered serpents with feather crests and forked tongues, decorated with shell cross sections, extend on each of the four sides of the talus (see fig. 8). In the spaces left free by the undulations are carved the dates of 9-Reptile Eye, anthropomorphic figures seated Maya style, images of Lord 2-Movement, and what may be calendrical corrections. Higher, on the tableros, a row of seated characters are depicted in profile. They all have a fleshless mandible before them, which seems to bite a circle with an incised cross inside it. Above both recurrent elements are found glyphs that vary from one square to another, and which may be the names of rulers in the Xochicalco dynasty or the toponyms for tributary towns or for the members of a federation.

Finally, we come to Teotenango, a city on the southeast end of the Toluca Valley. The dating of this center is problematic, because it is not based on radiocarbon dates like those we have for Cacaxtla and Xochicalco. According to Piña Chan, Phases 2 Earth (A.D. 750–900) and 3 Wind (900–1162) are characterized by the presence of Coyotlatelco pottery, although pottery in the second phase differs by having a decoration with "influences of Mazapa pottery." On the basis of this decoration, Piña Chan assumes that the most splendid phase, 3 Wind, is later than A.D. 900. In our opinion the city plan (see plan 7), the architectural style, and the proportions of the ball court as well as the iconography and the writing system of its monuments are very similar to those of Cacaxtla and Xochicalco, suggesting that they are contemporaneous. Unfortunately, we do not have a radiocarbon date for this project.

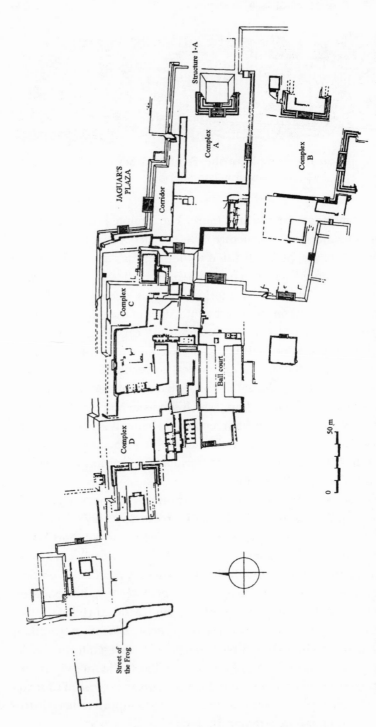

Plan 7. Teotenango Archaeological Zone, Estado de México. Central Mexico Area, Epiclassic period. (Based on R. Piña Chan)

Teotenango was built atop Tetépetl Hill, a long mesa that is from 70 to 250 meters high and is close to springs and thick conifer forests. The site clearly had defensive purpose because, in addition to being protected by the steep flanks of the hill, it had glacis, moats, ramparts, and defensive walls. Apparently, Frog Street was one of the principal passages connecting the villages at the bottom of the valley with the top. The settlement, during Phase 3 Wind, occupied 1.65 km², mainly on the eastern part of the hill. The North Complex, the largest group of buildings, includes several artificial platforms on which are built large sunken plazas, pyramidal temples, a ball court, and elite residences. Some of the most important sculptures of the site are the Teotenango Stele, the Triangular Section Tablet, and a natural outcrop showing a sitting jaguar devouring a heart, with the date 2 Rabbit on the top.

THE GULF IN THE EPICLASSIC

The fertile tropical lands of the Gulf Area were a propitious environment for the development of societies that excelled in agriculture, craftsmanship, art, and commerce. The products of these societies—such as vanilla, cotton, fine ceramics, multicolored cloth, exotic bird feathers, and the skins of wild animals—were greatly appreciated by their Southeast, Oaxacan, and Central Mexican neighbors. Apparently, Matacapan controlled much of the flow of trade during the Classic. However, after Teotihuacan's fall Matacapan's power faded, being replaced by El Tajín, a capital that, thanks to its commercial development, attained a splendor that is still impressive.

The ruins of El Tajín, which remained buried in the jungle for centuries, still hold fast many of its great secrets. The intense investigations carried out there during the last few years have produced a respectable amount of archaeological material, the analysis of which is revealing important data that illuminate many of the mysteries still surrounding the city. As one would expect, the research is in a creative phase during which many previously held ideas are being questioned and many hypotheses are being entertained. Among these are theories concerning the age of the site, as it seems that its splendor and decadence occurred later than previously estimated. Jürgen Kurt Brüggemann, who carried out the last excavation, has extended the dates, proposing that

El Tajín flourished between the eighth and twelfth centuries and was abandoned after a century of decay. Others argue that the apogee occurred between A.D. 900 and 1100, after which El Tajín was intentionally destroyed. Jeffrey K. Wilkerson attributes the destruction of the city to an incursion by diverse foreign ethnic groups. This would have led to the abandonment of many of the sites in the region, their population taking refuge in fortified mountain sites.

Another point of debate is the place that the Totonacs had in the history of the city. Wilkerson thinks that the destruction and abandonment of El Tajín preceded the arrival of the Totonacs. In contrast Lorenzo Ochoa feels that the stylistic change seen in the final phase of the city could have been due to the Totonacs, which would place them in the region in the eighth or ninth century. According to this idea, the Totonacs, after becoming integrated into a multiethnic society, adopted the architectural elements of El Tajín, using them later in the spurs of the Sierra Norte of Puebla, in places such as Yohualinchan.

In any case the city's peak corresponds to the time when Teotihuacan's control of commerce in the Gulf Area ended. It is probable that El Tajín took over the obsidian distribution network, as is suggested by the architecture of the rich obsidian sources in Central Veracruz, Zaragoza, and Oyameles. El Tajín, closely tied to Teotihuacan during the Classic, was its successor in Veracruz when the old city lost its power. Sculptures in the Epiclassic depict El Tajín as a militaristic power. 13 Rabbit, a ruler shown in several reliefs, is pictured triumphant over cruelly treated defeated enemies.

During its peak the city covered 196 hectares and perhaps had fifteen to twenty thousand inhabitants distributed among five barrios (see plan 8). It was necessary to adapt the city's layout to difficult conditions, primarily due to the uneven terrain and copious rainfall in the area. The architects of El Tajín dealt with the torrential rains by using complex drainage systems, subterranean canals, and storage tanks. The city had a low and flat center, a large hill to the north, two smaller heights to the east and west, and a wide perimeter. The southern half of the city center had buildings surrounding the so-called Grupo del Arroyo, which included the largest plaza in the city. It is believed that the majority of the population gathered there to celebrate festivals or participate in commercial activities. The other half of the center was the city's main

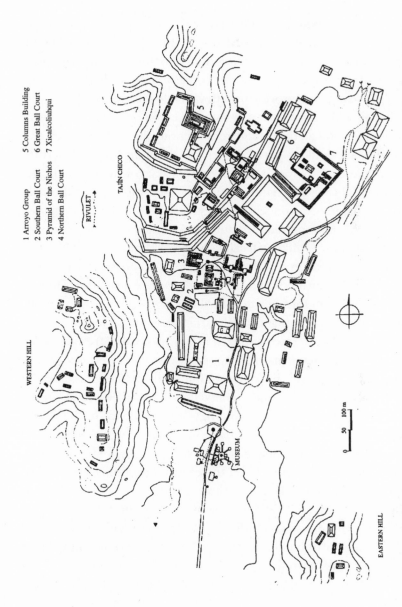

1 Arroyo Group
2 Southern Ball Court
3 Pyramid of the Nichos
4 Northern Ball Court

5 Columns Building
6 Great Ball Court
7 Xicalcoliuhqui

RIVULET

WESTERN HILL

TAJÍN CHICO

EASTERN HILL

MUSEUM

0 50 100 m

Plan 8. El Tajín Archaeological Zone, Veracruz. The Gulf Area, Epiclassic period. (Based on S. J. K. Wilkerson) religious and sporting area. At its center rose El Tajín's most beautiful monument, the Pyramid of the Niches. Many temples, plazas, and an exceptional number of ball courts (seventeen counted so far) surround it.

Three of the ball courts have carved bas-reliefs on their walls. The images in these panels provide us with valuable information about religious beliefs at the time, generally showing ceremonies associated with the ball game. Human beings and gods—among them Quetzalcoatl and rain and death deities—partake in rituals of killing and self-sacrifice involving piercing the penis. On the upper part of some tablets, the unfolding of a celestial character into two seems to refer to the well-known Mesoamerican concept of celestial duality. It should be added that one of the most unusual structures in Mesoamerica is in the center of Tajín: a gigantic fretlike wall called Xicalcoliuhqui.

From the northern end of the center, one climbs to the different artificial levels of the northern hill, known today as El Tajín Chico. This hill had been leveled to form terraces for building plazas and sumptuous buildings, mostly palaces and lavish structures for religious uses. The retaining walls of the terraces, which had large decorative frets and stairs for access, gave the city a majestic aspect because they resembled *taludes* (sloping walls) of gigantic buildings. El Tajín Chico was a restricted area, perhaps only accessible to the nobility. It was the highest level, and—judging by the splendor of its buildings—the residence of the ruling lineage. An outstanding example is the Building of the Columns, filled with reliefs of scenes from the life of 13 Rabbit. Finally, we would like to mention the buildings erected on the east and west hills, which were relatively separate from the rest of the city.

The architecture at El Tajín is some of the most interesting in Mesoamerica, not only due to the oddity and the proportions of its elements but also because of its building methods. The site was painted in brilliant colors, predominantly red but including a few blue buildings. The flat mortar roofs of the buildings were constructed from gravel, sand, and lime made by burning seashells. Other roofs were heavy massive slabs made of mortar and wood, which supported an upper story. Some scholars claim that the Maya false arch was also used at El Tajín Chico.

The most striking architectural elements of El Tajín are, without a doubt, the niches, the frets, and the high, narrow flying cornices. The niches, with their extremely varied shapes and structural as well as decorative functions, were made from precisely fitted slabs with almost no mortar so that they would support their own weight. The outstanding example is the Pyramid of the Niches, which repeats this element 365 times along the four sides of its seven levels—a clear allusion to the solar year. El Tajín also has stairs flanked by wide balustrades that are finished with a niche and a cornice. The balustrades of the Pyramid of the Niches are further decorated with strips of stepped frets (*xicalcoli-uhqui*) made from fitted prismatic stones. Huge columns, made from tambours carved with scenes of ritual and noble life, are also found in El Tajín. Another motif found throughout the city, which surely has a deep religious significance, is an interlaced scroll. This element, which is rooted in the art of the Classic Veracruz societies, diffused in the Epiclassic, being found from El Tajín to the capitals of Central Mexico.

CHAPTER FIVE

The Mesoamerican Postclassic Period

A GENERAL VIEW OF THE POSTCLASSIC

About twenty years ago, the Classic and Postclassic periods were sharply differentiated. The former was thought of as a cultural climax, a period of peace, and the latter as a period of war and political instability. Metaphorically speaking, if the Classic was peopled by bees, the Postclassic was inhabited by hive-destroying termites. In this idealized scenario Classic rulers were priests devoted to philosophical speculations, keeping the calendar, and observation of the heavens, whereas the rulers in the Postclassic were brave warriors obsessed by the obligation to provide the gods with the blood of their enemies. This view, promoted primarily by Maya scholars, began to be replaced a few years ago by scenarios that make the inhabitants of the Classic seem more human. Decipherments of hieroglyphic texts, archaeology, iconographic studies, and physical anthropology continue to provide data about the warlike characteristics of city-states in the Classic period, the human sacrifice practiced by their inhabitants, and the expansionist ambitions of their rulers.

We still perceive differences between the two periods, but they are less clear now—particularly when we consider that the principal characteristic of the Postclassic was militarism. The expansion of military capabilities and other defining elements of the Postclassic such as great population mobility, political instability, cultural diffusion, and hegemonic expansions began, even if modestly, during the transitional period of the Epiclassic. However, there is a clear difference in the amount of information available for the Classic and Postclassic. When we study the Postclassic, in addition to archaeology and physical anthropology we have documents in native languages, in Spanish, and, to a lesser extent, in Latin. This allows us to know the latter part of the Postclassic to a greater degree than is possible for earlier periods.

The collapse of the great Classic capitals upset political arrangements, fragmented trade networks, and created power vacuums. As we have discussed, new centers restored and controlled trade routes—at least regionally—but strong competition between them led to an increase in warfare and thus to greater political instability. This climate of uncertainty may have been a factor in the movements of large numbers of people, some displaced by war, some looking for territories better suited to their purposes, and some clearly intent on conquest. An important component of this series of migrations was the inflow of groups from the North. Armillas has hypothesized that climatic conditions became completely intolerable to farmers in the northern area of Mesoamerica, forcing numerous migrations to more benign areas. The climate worsened so much that by A.D. 1000 the area was devoid of farmers and left to hunter-gatherers. It is logical that this contraction of the border had enormous repercussions on neighboring areas, which—lacking strong political centers or sufficient power to counter the massive flow from the North—suffered from enormous demographic pressure.

These migrants were primarily failed farmers, but hunter-gatherers were also included in the human flood. They were collectively referred to by the generic term Chichimecs, though properly applies only to hunter-gatherers. When they arrived at more propitious lands in Central Mexico, the nomads and farmers assimilated more complex lifeways while, at the same time, infusing a new militaristic vigor into the societies receiving them. According to historical documents, they soon became integrated into the political life of the various regions, and in some cases even managed to take control. Their military prowess was an important component of their success. The bow and arrow, deftly handled by the newcomers, was the Chichimec symbol par excellence.

In the new political restructuring, particularly that in which northern peoples were involved, power centers were no longer satisfied with economic domination through control of trade but also sought conquests that would produce a constant stream of tribute to the new capitals. In such an environment aggressions, rivalries, and wars of resistance soon arose. This climate fostered the development of militaristic ideologies, which proclaimed a new supra-ethnic regional order and justified the use of force when weaker towns were not convinced of the benefits they would reap by incorporation into the sphere of influence of the powerful.

Visual representations, as well as documents in the sixteenth century, refer to orders of professional warriors often attired as fierce animals (eagles, jaguars, coyotes), who formed their own religious cults. Military units often served as mercenaries or bodyguards, a military career being prestigious and the ideal vehicle for social mobility. Frequently, this militaristic ideology was joined to the cult of the Feathered Serpent. Rulers of the new regimes thought they carried his divine fire within them, and we find rulers named Quetzalcoatl in Central Mexico, Kukulcan in the north of the Yucatán Peninsula, and Gucumatz in the Guatemalan Highlands. Later in this chapter, we will discuss the ways in which myths about Quetzalcoatl and the image of his celestial capital, Tollan, were used to explain and justify the new political order. Other myths functioned similarly, among them the Myth of the Fifth Sun, which made wars of conquest sacred, impelling warriors to capture enemies destined for the sacrificial stone. At this point we would like to emphasize that although ritual human sacrifice had been practiced for a very long time in Mesoamerica, its use was greatly expanded during the Postclassic by peoples who based their expansionist aspirations on its practice.

The need for sites located on heights and defended by moats and ramparts, which multiplied in the Epiclassic, was even greater during the Postclassic. Mexico-Tenochtitlan and Mexico-Tlatelolco achieved strategic advantage through their island location, Tulum through its sheer cliffs, and K'umarcaaj and Iximché through their ravines, steep slopes, walls, and parapets.

Artistic and cultural expressions of the Classic and Postclassic were also noticeably different. Sculpture, particularly religious sculpture, lost its exuberance and became rigidly conventional, martial, and stark. In some regions, Central Mexico among them, figurative art became less delicate and architecture was impoverished. A simple comparison of Teotihuacan and Tula clearly illustrates this change. The Maya area must be excluded from these generalizations because, as the cities in the central zone declined, a renaissance occurred in the northern zone that can be seen in the exceptional architectural technique of the Puuc. However, it is also important to remember that Southeast Mesoamerica, which was the acme of writing and calendrics during the Classic, simplified both systems to such an extent during the Postclassic that the Long Count was no longer used.

The message transmitted in visual arts of the Postclassic was clearly warlike. Depictions of human sacrifice proliferated at this time, and images of animals—mammals or birds of prey—devouring hearts were carved on temple walls. The racks of trophy skulls, or *tzompantli* in Nahuatl, were copied on the facades of religious buildings. Sculptures of armed warriors as columns, telamons, altars, or standard bearers were parts of religious buildings, and their relief-carved, stuccoed profiles paraded along friezes and banquettes. All these elements were consistent with an effervescent era that exalted the merit of force, everything tending to justify the expansion of the new powers.

The Postclassic extends from A.D. 900/1000 until the Spanish conquest in the sixteenth century. It is usually divided into two periods: the Early Postclassic (900/1000–1200) and the Late Postclassic (1200–1521). The boundary between the two periods is based on important political events, coinciding with the fall of Tula in the Central Plateau in 1150 and the conquest of Chichén Itzá in the Yucatán Peninsula about 1250. Central Mexico, for several reasons, is the prototype of Mesoamerica's Postclassic. First, the area was invaded by numerous groups of farmers and hunter-gatherers displaced by the contraction of the Northern Frontier who irreversibly changed the culture and political life of the local societies. This surely led to societal models that were multiethnic and bellicose. In addition, the most important symbols of militaristic ideology in the Postclassic came from Central Mexico and diffused from there, first by means of the Toltecs and their followers and later via the Mexicas, the latter ruling in a way never seen before in Mesoamerica.

The modern emphasis upon Central Mexico in the Postclassic is based on historiography as well as history. To an extent unequaled anywhere else in Mesoamerica and of priceless value, the written sources describe political events, customs, traditions, literature, beliefs, and other diverse themes in the public and private life of the Mexicas and their neighbors, particularly Texcoco and Tlaxcala. This emphasis on the Mexicas and their language, Nahuatl, occurred because the Mexicas functioned as Europe's gateway to Mesoamerica. Because they were the most powerful indigenous people at the beginning of the sixteenth century, the Mexicas bore the brunt of the invasion and the administrative and political center of New Spain was established in their capital. There, using the Latin alphabet, the Spaniards wrote down descriptions of the traditions of the conquered, relying on the Mexicas as their principal source of information about the Indian past.

Using political events in the Basin of Mexico, we can divide the Postclassic period in Central Mexico into three parts: (1) the Toltec, extending from the occupation of Tula Grande until its fall (900–1150); (2) the Chichimec, beginning at the end of the twelfth century with the arrival of Xolotl's people; and (3) the Mexica, extending from the formation of the Triple Alliance in the first half of the fifteenth century until 1521, when Tenochtitlan fell to the Spanish.

Two basic processes distinguished the Postclassic in Oaxaca. The first was the movement of populations that produced both wars and power centers occupied, by common agreement, by two or more ethnic groups. The principal locale for these groups was the Oaxaca Valley, although the process later became general, complicating the area's linguistic and ethnic mosaic. The second process was directly connected to the attempt of the Mixtec ruler 8 Deer Jaguar Claw to put together a vast multiethnic political entity. His project failed in the long run because, contrary to plan, it led to a greater fragmentation and hostility between the Mixtec domains. If we take this failure as the signpost for dividing the Postclassic, the division between the Early and Late periods would be the middle of the eleventh century, as the proponents of unification were defeated and the Mixtec ruler died in 1063. The Mixtecs dominated gold craftsmanship in the Postclassic, making jewelry that was both aesthetically and technically admirable.

Western Mesoamerica became important as the leading metallurgical area during the Postclassic. The metallurgical techniques, probably coming from Ecuador, reached the area about A.D. 800. Western Mesoamericans produced not only sumptuary gold and silver goods but also digging sticks (*coas*), axes, chisels, and other bronze tools. If the conquest had not intervened, these metallic objects would have produced a significant technological transformation in Mesoamerica. Among the most widely traded objects, as is evident by their diffusion and archaeological abundance, were the copper hawk's bells made by the lost-wax process. They became one of the most sought-after goods in both Mesoamerica and the more distant Oasisamerica.

The Postclassic in the West can be divided into two periods of very different duration. During the first period the area continued to be politically and culturally fragmented as usual. Unlike the rest of Mesoamerica, it did not develop a monumental architecture. It was a prosperous area nevertheless, its southern part having a considerable increase in population due to its possible role as a commercial corridor to Oasisamerica. The second subperiod, in the fifteenth and sixteenth centuries, corresponds to the beginning and consolidation of Tarascan power, which began in the lake region of Michoacán with the almost always forcible consolidation of numerous ethnically different domains. In a short time the Tarascans became great rivals of the Mexicas, whom they matched in military might; however, the conquest interrupted their meteoric rise.

Groups from Central Mexico came to the Gulf Area during the Postclassic. Some were driven out by the arrival of the Chichimecs, while others envisioned a conquest. In the North the Huasteca soon connected with Tula and was included in trade routes to the Pacific Coast and, from there, to the Northwest Frontier. It has also been hypothesized that there were ties between the Huastecas and the Mississippi Basin. A landmark in the Gulf Region was the abandonment of El Tajín, which was weakened in the twelfth century and abandoned in the thirteenth, leaving a power vacuum in the southern Huasteca area as the city was not replaced by another power. Prosperous centers such as Cempoala rose up in the center of area because of the agricultural production resulting from the efficient irrigation of a fertile territory. However, the wealth of this city also caused the Mexicas to conquer it and make it a tributary.

There were fundamental coincidences between events in the Lowlands and Highlands of Southeast Mesoamerica during the Postclassic. The historical driving force in both was a takeover by people with a militaristic ideology, which aided them in integrating the different peoples of the region. Some of these groups, with attire and weapons resembling those of the Toltecs of Central Mexico, are depicted in the Yucatán

Peninsula in murals and sculptures and on repoussé metal sheets. Under the regime that took power at that time, Chichén Itzá led the hegemonic powers until the middle of the thirteenth century, when it was defeated by its old ally, Mayapán, which replaced it until its own fall in 1450. The subsequent era was one of fragmentation and struggle between numerous kingdoms. The Spanish conquerors exploited this situation, conquering the Yucatec Mayas. In the Postclassic the Quichés, Cakchiquels, and Rabinals acquired political and military power in the Highlands by using force to increase their kingdoms until they became the hegemonic powers of the region. The alliance among the three powerful states concluded at the end of the fifteenth century with the fall of the Quiché king Q'uikab. As we shall discuss later in this chapter, there is disagreement among Maya scholars regarding the periods into which the Postclassic in Southeast Mesoamerica should be divided.

CENTRAL MEXICO IN THE POSTCLASSIC: THE TOLTECS

Written sources from the sixteenth century describe the features of the Mesoamerican Postclassic period, providing us with the names of various peoples, dates of migrations and conquests, biographies of famous people, and lists of rulers. In short, documents give us a new kind of information, increasing the value of information obtained through the analysis of archaeological remains. There are many documents in Central Mexico concerning the famous Early Postclassic city of Tula. In different sources we hear the names of its founders, a description of its buildings, stories of the feats of its heroes, and the account of its fall. Following Tula, every aspect of Mesoamerican history seems clearer. And still, the history of Tula and the Toltecs is a hotbed of imponderables. What is the reason for this paradox? Let us begin by considering the traditional view of the archaeological data.

The Toltec capital was established near what had been the site of Chingú in the state of Hidalgo, from which Teotihuacan had, for centuries, exploited the regional limestone quarries. Tula was located in the broad geographical and cultural zone between the lakes of Central Mexico and a large, arid northern region. A large part of the northern and eastern Toltec area is in the rain shadow of the Sierra Madre

Oriental, sharing the semiaridity of the Mezquital Valley. However, this aridity is mitigated by the streams that flow along the ravines of the Magoni, El Cielito, and La Malinche Hills during the rainy season. At the bottom of these slopes are valleys fed by the Tula and the Rosas Rivers, tributaries of the Moctezuma River. In visualizing this landscape we should not be influenced by the present sad aspect of the landscape, which has been exhausted by overcultivation. In the Postclassic Tula had prosperous cultivated fields, irrigated by a complex canal system.

A proto-Toltec era began after Chingú disappeared, but its archaeological remains cannot be tied to the information in written sources. Groups who, judging by their ceramics, came from the Northwest settled in the hills and slopes of the region during the Prado Phase (A.D. 700–800). This type of ceramic is a hybrid, in which the Coyotlatelco type is a large component. With its geometric patterns, crosses, frets, and dots, the Red-on-Buff ceramic is possibly related to pottery of the elites of North Mesoamerica, particularly the Bajío, Zacatecas, and Jalisco. Magoni is one of the important sites of this phase. Afterward, in the Corral Phase (A.D. 800–900), there was a massive multiethnic occupation covering three to five km² in this area. The center of the site was a group of civic-religious buildings called Tula Chico. Its plaza—surrounded by palaces, pyramids, and ball courts—would later be imitated by the Toltec capital. During this phase, Coyotlatelco ceramics continued to be made in the region. The Terminal Corral Phase (900–950) followed, during which, in addition to the Coyotlatelco, Red-on-Buff Mazapa ceramics decorated with parallel undulating lines were manufactured. The Terminal Corral was a transitional phase linking the inhabitants of Tula Chico with Tula Grande, the climax site.

The Tollan Phase (A.D. 950–1150), clearly identified with the zenith of the Toltecs according to written sources, had strong multiethnic roots. Tula Chico was abandoned, and the center of the city was moved 1.5 kilometers to the southeast, to the nucleus now known as Tula Grande. This site was erected on a rise between two alluvial valleys at the confluence of the Tula and Rosas Rivers. There is considerable controversy regarding the size of Tula and the number of inhabitants in the city at its peak. Estimated sizes for Tula range from 5 to 16 km² and for its population, from eighteen thousand to fifty-five thousand. What is not in doubt is that Tula was an extremely important city in its time. Its diagnostic ceramic type, Jara Polished Orange, is also called Naranja a Brochazos. The presence of two other imported ceramics, Tohil Plumbate from Soconusco and Guatemala and Fine Orange from southern Veracruz, is significant.

After the Tollan Phase a period of decadence began that ended with the final abandonment of the urban center. We still do not know the causes of the collapse, which signals the beginning of the Fuego Phase (A.D. 1150–1350). There are evidences of destruction—many of the buildings of the ceremonial center were burned. Despite the fall of the Toltec capital, however, the area continued to be occupied until the Aztec settlement in the Palacio Phase (A.D. 1350–1520).

When the heart of the city moved from Tula Chico to Tula Grande in A.D. 950, there was a substantial change in the orientation of the settlement, which moved from a strictly north-south alignment to an alignment 15° east of north. Later, during its peak (1000–1050), there was another shift to an alignment 5° west of north. In the Tollan Phase the center of the city was placed on the highest elevation of the site, Tesoro Hill. As is usually the case in Mesoamerican cities, the most important part of the ceremonial center is a wide plaza surrounded by primarily religious buildings. There is a small temple in the middle of the Main Plaza. The immense mass of Pyramid C, the largest building at the site, closes the eastern end of the plaza. Unfortunately, it is badly preserved, its revetments having been plundered many centuries later by the Mexicas. Pyramid B and the Burnt Palace are located on the north side of the plaza. Pyramid B is a building thirty-eight meters on a side and ten meters high, curiously decorated with relief-carved panels depicting fantastic creatures and carnivorous birds and mammals. This rich ornamentation is completed by monumental pilasters and columns representing warriors armed with spears and spear throwers, all attired with butterfly-shaped pectorals. Based on its iconography, Jorge R. Acosta associated the temple with Tlahuizcalpantecuhtli, "Lord of the House of Dawn," or "Morning Star," one of Quetzalcoatl's avatars. Behind the pyramid is a wall called Coatepantli ("Snake Wall"), with stepped frets and serpents carrying partly skeletonized human figures. Its merlons, shaped like conch cross-sections, also refer to Quetzalcoatl.

The adjacent building, the Burnt Palace, had no residential functions despite its name. It is a complex of three hypostyle halls, several smaller rooms, and vestibules with porticos. Long benches are attached to the walls of the halls, and sculptures of a reclining deity with an altar on its abdomen—which have been arbitrarily called *chac mool*—are also present. Large segments of the benches are covered by carved and painted slabs depicting a procession of warriors, while the cornices have a serpent motif, which has been interpreted as a reference to the gods Quetzalcoatl and Mixcoatl. Behind Pyramid B and the Burnt Palace is Ball Court #1, which was also possibly damaged by the Mexicas or their contemporaries. It is a twelve-meter-long building with four exterior staircases leading to the platform and four interior staircases leading from the platform to the playing field. Another large ball court closes the plaza to the west. The base of a *tzompantli* (a wooden rack on which sacrificial skulls were exhibited to the public) was excavated at its eastern end. The southern end of the plaza is enclosed by Building K, which is similar to the Burnt Palace and has been recently explored by Robert H. Cobean.

During the Toltec age of splendor temples were erected in other areas of Tula Grande than the Main Plaza. One of the most interesting is the so-called Temple of Ehecatl in El Corral, a complex next to the old location of Tula Chico. It is hybrid in shape, combining a pyramid with a truncated cone. Toltec monumental architecture introduced new elements that, according to Marie-Areti Hers, could have come from North Mesoamerica. The handling of space was revolutionized by the introduction of light, flat roofs supported by columns and pilasters, allowing extremely large enclosures to be produced. Sculptures, for the most part integrated into the architecture of the ceremonial center, continually showed military scenes and images of human sacrifice, including warriors, bundles of weapons, and animals devouring hearts. Among the sculptures that make Toltec art famous are the large warrior-shaped columns, small atlantes that support monolithic altars, and chac mools.

Streets and avenues subdividing the city's space radiate from El Tesoro Hill. The complex social divisions of the time are reflected in the location, size, arrangement, and building materials of the dwellings. The most important ones were built on a series of platforms extending from the Main Plaza to the river. Smaller elite residences were also built near the monumental buildings. These measure approximately thirty by thirty meters, have patios with porticos, and resemble the dwelling complexes in Teotihuacan. Most of the population lived in two different types of houses. "Apartment complexes" resemble the dwellings just described but are smaller. The most common houses are the "house groups," consisting of three or four houses grouped around a central patio. The privacy of the arrangement is secured by a narrow L-shaped access leading to the patio, a common area used for productive activities such as grinding grain and for religious functions. Each of the houses consists of several rooms.

The housing units are grouped into barrios, with a temple for collective worship at their center. It is probable that people living in the barrio, apart from their agricultural tasks, had the same productive activity. Thus, the obsidian workers' barrio was located on El Cielito hill in the southeast part of the city. Large amounts of Mazapa ceramics, which were scarce in Tula but abundant in the Teotihuacan Valley, were found next to the workshops for this industry, maybe indicating the ethnic origin of the dwellers of El Cielito. The possible existence of other ethnic groups such as Huastecs, Mixtecs, and Mayas has been inferred on the basis of particular ceramics. Written sources tell of the coexistence of two main groups: the Toltec-Chichimecs and the Nonoalcas.

Like Teotihuacan, Early Postclassic Tula obtained a large part of its revenue by exploiting the limestone mines southeast of the site. Enormous amounts of limestone, extracted during centuries, were used for the mortar that was indispensable in the building and decoration of public and private buildings. Besides limestone, the Toltecs extracted basalt and rhyolite—used in construction and in making grinding tools, scrapers, axes, and beads—from the Magoni and La Malinche Hills. Many scrapers were found in the agricultural terraces, indicating a substantial production of fibers and pulque (fermented sap) from agave. Elsewhere, workshops for the production of prismatic blades, knives, projectile points and other bifacials, jewelry, and scrapers were made possible by a local supply of flint and by the importation of obsidian, 80 percent from mines in Pachuca and 10 percent from Zinapécuaro mines. Another major industry was the making of ceramics, which, as in the rest of Mesoamerica, supplied the demand for storage, preparation, and consumption of food; the domestic manufacture of textiles (spindles and spindle whorls); and religious needs (braziers, incense burners, and figurines). Toltec potters also made tubing for the city's drainage. High-quality clay was possibly obtained from the banks of the Tula River.

The archaeologically documented sumptuary objects are ornaments and containers made from travertine; greenstone beads and plaques; disks of iron ore; and garments covered with shell plates.

Archaeological Tula, which is more decorated than beautiful, contrasts with the magnificence of the Tula described in documents. The sources speak of a marvelous city where fruits and vegetables are gigantic and the inhabitants are wonderful artificers ruled by Quetzalcoatl, a wise and virtuous priest who lives in a residence made of gold, silver, precious stones, seashells, and precious feathers. According to the documents, this saintly ruler transgressed against his asceticism by getting drunk and sleeping with a priestess. Ashamed of his conduct, he ordered the abandonment of Tula and emigrated to the East.

The lack of correspondence between documental and archaeological sources has provoked ardent controversies among scholars, who have sought to find the marvelous Tollan in the historical reality of Tula. For some, only the ruins of Teotihuacan are worthy of the glorious descriptions in the documents. Most, however, have followed Jiménez Moreno, who offered convincing arguments that identified the ruins of Tula in Hidalgo with the city cited in the sources.

Neither of these perspectives resolves the paradox posed at the beginning of this chapter. The source of the confusion is the fact that history and myth are intertwined. A mythic Tollan and several real Tulas, earthly replicas of the divine archetype, are irrevocably mixed. This can also be seen in the parallel images of the god Quetzalcoatl and the real rulers of Tula who represented the god in the human realm. Confusion arises from the political uses of myth and history. The most powerful rulers in subsequent eras called themselves descendants of the Toltecs and members of the lineage initiated by Quetzalcoatl. At least for the Mexicas, Tula in Hidalgo was the source of power—Tollan. It is probable that Tula had arrogated to itself the role of earthly replica of the mythical Tollan in order to justify its right to military expansion. We shall return to this complex issue later in this chapter.

CENTRAL MEXICO IN THE POSTCLASSIC: THE CHICHIMECS

Like the cultural development of the Toltecs, that of the so-called Chichimecs is hard to delineate. Broadly speaking, we know that, beginning in the twelfth century, multiple movements of peoples from southern Aridamerica and northern Mesoamerica toward Central Mexico occurred. These caused considerable changes in the lives of the inhabitants of Central Mexico. The problem lies in determining what caused these successive waves, the degree of social complexity of the migrants, and what impact they had in each of the regions where they established themselves. These are, without a doubt, difficult questions, given the lack of sufficient information from excavations or surface surveys. It is also difficult to outline the migrations of that time from the viewpoint of historical documents, because the pictorial and written sources referring to the period between the fall of Tula and the rise of Tenochtitlan are frequently contradictory and contain more mythological elements than had previously been supposed.

There is another problem to consider in connection with sixteenth-century documents: ambiguous terms are indiscriminately used in them to designate several of the northern groups. The veritable terminological tangle is produced largely by the ignorance and contempt of the Spaniards for the inhabitants of the wide border region. In some cases the same group is designated by many terms—its language, its ethnicity, its place of residence, its tribal deity, and the name of its ruler— which leads to many errors. The opposite is also true. The extreme case is the pejorative term "Chichimec," used to mean "barbarian." The term was applied to groups with different economic systems and patterns of organization, from the stratified agricultural societies of the Cazcans and Tecuexes to egalitarian bands that lived from hunting and gathering, such as the Guachichils and the Guamares, to culturally mixed societies such as the Zacatecs. There could be considerable ethnic and linguistic differences between these groups. We can conclude that the term Chichimec does not imply any particular technological, economic, ethnic, or linguistic identity, but only a common geographic origin— that vast territory on both sides of the border between Aridamerica and Mesoamerica known in the sixteenth century as Chichimecapan, Teotlalpan, Mictlampa, or Tlacochcalco.

The first Chichimec migrants mentioned in the sources joined with the Nonoalcas to found Tula, and new waves of Chichimecs came centuries later. One of the hypotheses that attempts to explain these movements proposes that, beginning in the twelfth and thirteenth centuries, climatic conditions conducive to agriculture deteriorated in northern Mesoamerica. These changes would have forced the sedentary peoples of the border to seek moister regions to the south. Their movements would have shrunk the northern border of Meso-america by about 250 kilometers. After the farmers had retreated the nomads would not only have filled the vacant areas; many of them, along with the farmers, would have invaded Central Mexico. Another suggestive proposal is that the great sociopolitical changes that took place in the Basin of Mexico during the twelfth century caused the sedentary nuclei of the northern area to be abandoned. The fall of Tula would have favored invasions by farmers, followed by nomad invasions. Contradicting the written sources, many contemporary schol-ars agree that the majority of the Chichimecs who emigrated to Central Mexico were farmers as well as hunter-gatherers. These peoples had some typical Mesoamerican cultural traits, such as the building of pyramids and a stratified social organization in which priests played an essential role.

Among all these groups, the Chichimecs led by Xolotl stand out. It is possible that they spoke Pame, Otomí, or Mazahua. The pictographs and sixteenth-century written sources describe them as nomadic, warlike barbarians who, when they lived in the North, survived mostly on cacti and hunting. They are usually represented in pictographs dressed in animal skins, carrying bows and arrows, in arid environ-ments symbolized by caves, mesquite trees, and prickly-pear and barrel cacti. However, researchers such as Pedro Armillas, Pedro Carrasco, and Brigitte Boehm de Lameiras deny this primitivism in the Chichi-mecs. They point out that some Chichimec activities, such as taking censuses, marking their territory, the imposition of their form of government, and the ability to distribute a recently arrived popula-tion in a vast territory, demonstrate that they had a much more complex social organization.

According to written sources, Xolotl's Chichimecs arrived in the Basin of Mexico after Tula had been abandoned. Coming from the North, they identified a resource-rich territory that they would later take over with little resistance from the local population. Archaeological evidence shows that at this time there was a sizable increase in population and large hydraulic works were undertaken. The Chichimecs bypassed the ruins of Tula, continued past Actopan, and settled temporarily in a place they called Xóloc in honor of their leader. Later, Xolotl's son, Nopaltzin, explored the territory where Acolhuacan was to be founded and continued to the Puebla Valley. He went through Teotihuacan and the area of Chimalhuacan, passed through Chalco, and arrived at Cholula. The sources affirm that the men from the North spread over a vast area, Xolotl taking over a large territory that he divided into four provinces whose borders were the Nevado de Toluca, Izúcar, Atlixco, the Cofre de Perote, Huauchinango, Tulancingo, Metztitlán, and Cuetzallan. The great northern wave was not composed simply of Xolotl's people; other Chichimec groups such as the Tepanecs, Otomazahuas, and Acolhuas came into the Basin at that time.

Meanwhile the Toltec-Chichimecs, who had abandoned declining Tula, had settled in Cholula with the consent of its inhabitants, the Olmec-Xicalancas. A short time after their arrival, the Toltec-Chichimecs seized power through treason and sought an alliance with other Chichimec groups in order to extend their territory to the slopes of the volcanoes. This resulted in the northerners' expansion and domination of the entire valley. A number of power centers were founded, which are listed in the sources as ruled by different *tetecuhtin* (lords). However, these domains were never united under a central power even though some of them attained considerable military and political strength.

On the other side of the mountains, Xolotl's descendants set up their capital successively at Tenayuca, Coatlinchan, and Texcoco. The ruling lineage consolidated its power by merging with nobles of the ancient inhabitants of the Basin of Mexico and by allowing peoples who had higher cultures than their own to settle in the region. It is interesting to note that the sources constantly reiterate the theme of a supposed transformation of the Chichimecs, due both to intermarriage with noble lineages and to learning from more civilized peoples. The sources state that after a few generations the Chichimecs were transformed from barbarians to people of a high culture, whose culmination would be the successive reigns of Nezahualcoyotl and Nezahualpilli. The transformation was so radical that, according to the sources, the fifth ruler made Nahuatl the official language, forcing his people to stop using their own language.

CENTRAL MEXICO IN THE POSTCLASSIC: THE MEXICAS

Whenever Mesoamerica is mentioned, the first image in people's minds is that of a warlike people, the Mexicas. This is not unjustified. The Mexicas ruled an immense territory and were at the height of their power when the European conquerors arrived. Furthermore, among all the Mesoamericans the Mexicas are the people about whom we have the greatest number of documents written in the Latin alphabet. After the Spanish victory over Mexico-Tenochtitlan, the Europeans set up the center of colonial domination on the ruins of the city. The conquerors used the Mexicas as their principal model in describing the beliefs, customs, and institutions of the conquered.

This perspective continues today, impairing our understanding of the cultural distinctiveness of other peoples in the Postclassic. While we would like to criticize this oversimplified view and to allude to the dangers of overgeneralizing, we know that a study of the wealth of information about the Mexicas is indispensable for an understanding of their contemporaries. If we wish to describe the daily and institutional life of a Mesoamerican people in detail, the most pertinent example is to be found in the Mexica culture. What follows, then, is a model that, although sweeping, provides a deeper look at some of the fundamental traits of one of the societies discussed in this book.

Broadly speaking, the two centuries of Mexico-Tenochtitlan's existence can be divided into four periods: the settlement of the population on an island in Lake Texcoco, where they were subject to the Tepanecs (1325–1430); the formation of a hegemonic state after the defeat of Azcapotzalco (until 1469); military expansion (until 1502); and the consolidation of territory (until the arrival of the Spanish in 1519). Written sources, however, start two hundred years before the establishment of Tenochtitlan, with a minutely detailed, although contradictory and myth-filled description of the migration of the Mexicas from Aztlan to what would be their final home.

Referring to this migration is not unjustified, and certainly not for Mesoamericans; by recounting the events of what they considered to be their "first" years, they tied their history to the myth of origin. Nor is it useless to modern historians, because in these stories we can see the way in which a society deals with its own ideology. The Mexicas, like the Chichimecs and the Tarascans, describe the transformation of a poor, wandering people into a powerful society. The question whether Aztlan was real or mythical is debated today. For some, Aztlan is a retrospectively created image of an embryonic, lacustrine Mexico located next to a place called Culhuacan. On the other hand, those who posit a real Aztlan tend to locate it in West or North Mesoamerica or even beyond the borders of this cultural superarea. The debate also encompasses whether the original economy of the Mexicas was one of hunter-gathering or sedentary farming. While we do not wish to deal with the details of the debate here, we agree with Carlos Martínez Marín that the sources clearly show that the Mexicas were well acquainted with agricultural techniques and, though a poor people, had fully Mesoamerican characteristics.

The sources show two contradictory Aztlans. On the one hand, it was linked to a myth totally or partially identified with the place of origin and became identified with or was considered adjacent to the mythic Chicomóztoc ("Place of Seven Caves"), Culhuacan ("Place of the Ancestors"), Cemícac Mixtitlan Ayauhtitlan ("Always Among Clouds and Mists"), and so forth. The migrants were said to have been left there under orders of their patron deity who, either directly or through his priests, guided his people to the promised land. On the other hand, there is the story of an almost unknown people called Aztecs who lived in Aztlan. The Mexicas, tired of being exploited by the Aztecs, escaped in search of a better life. One of the miracles of the migration was a prophetic command to the migrants to stop calling themselves Aztecs and to recover their true identity as Mexitins or Mexicas, the protégés of a god called Mexi or Huitzilopochtli.

People have tried to locate Aztlan geographically. Among the places proposed are Mezcaltitlán (an island in Nayarit) and a bend on the Lerma River southeast of Guanajuato, offered respectively by Jiménez Moreno and Kirchhoff. They emphasize that both of these places have the watery surroundings that are constantly mentioned in the historical texts of the sixteenth century.

According to the sixteenth-century sources, the migrants left Aztlan under the protection of their patron deity, Huitzilopochtli, who had promised them a glorious and prosperous future. They traveled in typical groups called *calpultin,* forming a body that underwent severe splits and recombinations during the many decades of their migration. Each *calpulli* carried an image of its particular patron deity and had its own chief. Apparently all these deities were subordinates of Huitzilopochtli. The stopovers in some places along the route were long, and frequently the local inhabitants were hostile toward the migrants. After a long trek the Mexicas arrived near Lake Texcoco and wandered around the area, settling temporarily in some localities. Finally, in 1325 (or 1340 according to some sources), they settled in their definitive residence (see map 15).

The advantages of settling the small islands in the western part of Lake Texcoco were evident. The Mexicas knew how to exploit lake resources, and they calculated that they would find an abundance of useful plants and animals there. The lake also gave them a good defensive position. There were also negative aspects to the location: scanty terrain, little potable water, a scarcity of wood and stone, and the need to build a dike in order to cultivate the swamp, as the level of the lake surface varied so much that there was the danger of an overflow of salty water from the eastern part of the lake. In addition to these ecological considerations, the situation was politically complicated. The Mexicas' long route around the Basin had acquainted them with the difficult relationships in the region, and they had occasionally suffered because of them. Numerous towns were grouped around powerful and frequently rival cities. Alliances—despite being based on ethnic ties and political pacts—shifted periodically, contributing to a general feeling of instability.

During a century of precarious equilibrium, power centers fought to extend and solidify their spheres of influence. In the North, the center of Xaltocan, on Lake Xaltocan, consolidated the Otomis and fought with its neighbors, the Chichimecs of Cuauhtitlan. Northwest of Lake Texcoco, Tenayuca was an important Chichimec center. In the eastern part of that same lake, the Acolhuas and, later, the Chichimecs were first united by Coatlinchan and later by Texcoco. In the South, Culhuacan prided itself as the foremost town with Toltec ancestry, while the settlements that cultivated the shores and swamps of the southern lakes of Calco and Xochimilco extended their territories and their influence beyond the borders of the Basin. Among these centers Chalco was dominant up to Amecamecan, at the foot of the volcanoes, and Xochimilco controlled the mountains to the south. However, the primary power in the region was Azcapotzalco, a Tepanec city with Otomi and Nahua components that ruled

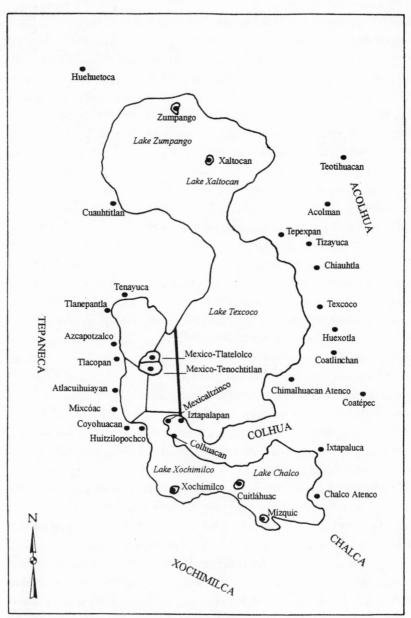

Map 15. The Basin of Mexico.

the western shore of Lake Texcoco and the Toluca and Ixtlahuaca Valleys. This situation compelled the Mexicas to establish favorable alliances.

Many Mexicas had split from the original group to join Azcapotzalco, Culhuacan, Xochimilco, Texcoco, Coatlinchan, and other cities in the Basin. On the other hand, some of the inhabitants of Mexico-Tenochtitlan were not Mexicas; part of the population was Otomi, Xochimilca, and Huexotzinca. The founders of Tenochtitlan built a temple to Huitzilopochtli and Tlaloc as well as other religious buildings in the center of the island. They divided the small island into four segments, with barrios set aside within them for settlement of the calpultin. Many of the original settlers were unhappy with the allocation of the land, however, and a split took place about 1337. The rebels moved to the adjacent islands to the north, establishing the twin rival city of Mexico-Tlatelolco.

In the beginning, life was precarious on both islands. Even though the lake provided the people with abundant plants and animals, there was a scarcity of the essential materials for building chinampas (cultivated raised fields in the swamp). The Mexicas had to pay tribute, because the islands belonged to Azcapotzalco. They were impelled to seek a connection with a royal lineage in order to solidify trade with their neighbors, to protect their existence through the patronage of one of the powerful states, and to improve their prospects of participating in the political life of the Basin. Such a connection would allow them to begin their own dynasty. The initial conflict between the Tenochcas and the Tlatelolcas meant, however, that each group sought this connection independently. The Tenochcas got their first *tlatoani* (king) from the Culhuacan lineage, while the Tlatelolcas got theirs from the Azcapotzalco lineage.

The political situation of the two Mexica settlements improved due to new ties to the powerful that came about through military alliances and marriages of convenience. For example, they were able to profit from waging joint campaigns with the ruler of Azcapotzalco. When the precarious equilibrium of the area fell apart in 1371 and the Tepanecs expanded their territory at the expense of their neighbors, the Mexicas became valuable fighting allies of the aggressive Tepanecs. Later, under King Huitzilihuitl, Mexico-Tenochtitlan conquered the Culhuas—the source of their ruler's lineage—on its own.

A political takeover disrupted relationships in the Basin. After the death of Tezozomoc, their protector and the ruler of Azcapotzalco, the

Mexicas clashed with Maxtla, his successor. After a bloody war began, the Mexicas shifted their allegiance to the Acolhuas of Texcoco and together they defeated the Tepanecs in 1430. The victors decided to reorganize the Basin of Mexico, known as the *excan tlatoloyan*, or "tribunal of the three seats". This suprastatal institution, today commonly called the Triple Alliance, proclaimed a structure imposed by the three hegemonic states. Previously, the Tepanecs had suspended the excan tlatoloyan. When Texcoco was restored, it reclaimed its title as one of these centers through inheritance from Coatlinchan. Mexico-Tenochtitlan claimed the title possessed by Culhuacan, and the title that the defeated Azcapotzalco had held passed on to the Tepanec city of Tlacopan. This arrangement excluded Mexico-Tlatelolco from the political order.

The main function of the excan tlatoloyan was to settle disputes between the different political entities under its jurisdiction, but it was also charged with maintaining security in the region and incorporating reluctant states into the coalition. Under this pretext the three capitals began a military expansion, initially intended to control the lake basin but later expanded to a large surrounding area. Another function of the excan tlatoloyan was to promote mutual assistance among the three capitals. For this reason Mexico-Tenochtitlan was able to build a dike twenty meters wide and twelve kilometers long, freeing it from untimely incursions of brackish waters from the east.

The triumph over Azcapotzalco, the wealth acquired in the first conquests, and the needs of expansionist campaigns brought about a profound change in the Tenochca State. Beginning with Itzcoatl and continuing with Motecuhzoma Ilhuicamina, measures were taken that widened the differences between nobles and commoners, centralized power, reorganized public administration, controlled and propagated militaristic ideology, strengthened the priesthood, and granted status and privileges for military prowess.

After Motecuhzoma Ilhuicamina's death in 1469, a succession of three brothers continued the expansion of the Triple Alliance. The first, Axayacatl, fought against the twin city of Mexico-Tlatelolco, which never again had its own ruler after being defeated. Axayacatl was followed by Tizoc, who had some minor military conquests. Under Ahuítzotl, the third brother, Mexico-Tenochtitlan achieved its greatest might and pushed trade to great distances. The political and commercial dominion of the excan tlatoloyan extended from the Basin of Mexico to the coasts of Veracruz, the Huasteca, Oaxaca, and a good portion of the West. Its influence also extended along a commercial corridor that took the traders of the Alliance to Soconusco, the center of cacao production. The empire of the Triple Alliance extended from coast to coast, although a few territories such as Tlaxcala, Metztitlán, Costa Chica in Guerrero, Tututepec, and the Tarascan region remained unconquered.

Ahuítzotl's expansion increased the status of merchants and placed many commoners in important administrative posts. After his death in 1502 a new austere and religious tlatoani, Motecuhzoma Xocoyotzin, was elected who, according to some interpretations, was devoted to the interests of the nobility. His predecessor's expansion had been too sudden, and Motecuhzoma intended his reign to consolidate and reorganize the state in favor of the ruling class. It was a period of splendor, which made the name of tlatoani synonymous with magnificence. It is estimated that at this time the population of the islands was between 150,000 and 300,000. Mexico-Tenochtitlan had profited from its role as the military leader of the excan tlatoloyan and had risen to political leadership. The suprastatal institution was again being weakened by the preeminence of one its components. However, it was Motecuhzoma Xocoyotzin's sad fate to face the European invasion. He was followed by two rulers—Cuitlahuac and Cuauhtemoc—who ruled for brief intervals and continued the war of resistance against the Spanish.

At their peak, having reclaimed land from the lake for two centuries, the twin cities of Mexico comprised a large urban expanse, exceeding 13.5 km², and linked to the mainland by three large causeways. Mexico-Tenochtitlan and Mexico-Tlatelolco were crisscrossed by wide streets and canals in a grid pattern. Tenochtitlan was divided into four urban quadrants that constituted the four great administrative units of the city. The quadrants were divided into barrios, one for each calpulli, filled with temples, plazas, schools, houses, and narrow cultivated strips of land. The solidly built, luxurious palaces of the nobility, often two storied, were located in the center of the city. The royal palace housed, under one roof, the royal quarters, chambers of the court, tribunals, and storage rooms. The civic-religious precinct, an enormous rectangular area surrounded by a platform, rose at the exact intersection of two principal city axes. Inside the precinct were located an enormous complex of temples, among which the pyramid topped by two chapels consecrated to the gods Tlaloc and Huitzilopochtli stood out.

The dizzying rise to power of the Mexicas affected the life of all the peoples of Central Mexico. Behind the volcanoes, in the Puebla-Tlaxcala Valley, the Chichimec conquests and settlements had grown into important power centers that coexisted, in varying political relationships, with the still powerful Cholula. The Chichimecs from Xilotepec had settled previously, on good terms with the Acolhuas, in territories belonging to Texcoco. As we have discussed, when they moved to the Puebla-Tlaxcala Valley they joined with the Toltec-Chichimecs of Cholula to defeat the previous inhabitants of the Valley, the Olmec-Xicalancas and the Zacatecs. Among the Chichimec capitals, Tlaxcala, without a doubt, had the most interesting historical development. Tlaxcala was formed by the integration of four political units that retained a large portion of their autonomy until the Spanish conquest. The first entity was Tepeticpac, founded in 1208. Eighty years later a new settlement, Ocotelulco, sprang from it. A little later Tizatlán and Quiahuiztlan were established, the former by a native group and the latter by recently arrived Chichimecs. Tlaxcala joined with other peoples in the Valley to defy attempts by the excan tlatoloyan to conquer them. The union of Tlaxcala, Cholula, Huexotzinco, and Tliliuhquitepec enabled them to resist the permanent hostilities of the Mexicas and to keep the region independent.

On the other side of the Basin of Mexico, in the Puebla and Ixtlahuaca Valleys, other Chichimec groups had achieved great economic, cultural, and political importance. These groups comprised an interesting linguistic mosaic of primarily Oto-Mangean speakers (Otomi, Mazahua, Matlatzinca, and Ocuiltec), although there were also a number of Nahuatl speakers. A constellation of minor political centers maintained unstable relationships with more important centers such as Toluca, Teotenango, Tecaxic-Calixtlahuaca, Tenantzinco, Tzinacantepec, and Xiquipilco while recognizing Azcapotzalco's leadership. When the Mexicas began their expansionist epoch, the excan tlatoloyan was able to conquer their western neighbors, who were extremely divided at that time. Subsequently, when the Tarascans and Mexicas confronted each other, the towns in the Puebla and Ixtlahuaca Valleys, which lay between them, divided their allegiance between the two.

In the twelfth century there was a massive influx of Nahuatl-speaking Chichimecs, particularly Xochimilcas and Tlalhuicas, into the southern Tierra Caliente. Among other towns, the Xochimilcas established Tepoztlan, Tlayacapan, and Tochimilco, while the Tlalhuicas numbered Cuauhnáhuac, Yauhtepec, and Huaxtepec among their capitals. From the beginning the Mexicas coveted the cotton grown in the Morelos Valley, leading them to a lengthy war with Cuauhnahuac that they eventually won. By the time of Motecuhzoma Ilhuicamina, the Mexicas dominated the region.

Social Structure

Crucial aspects of the socio-economic organization of the Mexicas and their neighbors are their family structure and the way in which domestic units organized their production and consumption. The scarcity of sources of information on this subject has been a big obstacle to scholars. Analysis of colonial documents shows that, after the conquest, family dwellings housed nuclear families (basically mother, father, and children) or extended families (two or more nuclear families headed by the one closest to the family trunk). This organization seems to date back as far as the Late Postclassic. Based on the same sources, scholars propose that most of the population lived in extended families.

Though there is more available information about the next higher level of organization, the calpulli, there are nevertheless two main interpretations of it. Pablo Escalante Gonzalbo has looked at the points of contention between the two. According to the first interpretation, espoused by Víctor Castillo F. and Alfredo López Austin among others, the calpulli was primarily a kind of kinship group that was based in part on the residential contiguity of the families composing it. Its basic characteristics were extremely old, predating the state, and were preserved due to the adaptability of the institution and its inclusion in political structures that changed as time passed. The second interpretation, championed primarily by Pedro Carrasco, emphasizes the territorial-administrative aspect of the calpulli. According to this interpretation, each calpulli represented a unit of the city, set up by the state government primarily to collect tribute and recruit workers.

It is not possible to present all the arguments supporting our position in this debate, but only to summarize here the characteristics we see in the calpulli. The key point is that the calpulli was composed of many mutually related families who acknowledged a common patron, the *calpulteotl*, or patron deity of the calpulli. According to myth, the calpulteotl gave the members of the calpulli their occupation. This trade, which was devoutly inherited from father to son, distinguished them from members of other calpultin.

The city-states of the Postclassic were divided into barrios, each occupied by a calpulli. There is no doubt that in this state context the territorial-administrative aspect of the calpulli was very important, but in no way was it the defining characteristic of the institution. Calpultin have been clearly shown to exist independently from any state government and not tied to a territory. The typical examples were the groups emigrating in the Postclassic, who moved in large numbers and traveled organized as calpultin. After a long journey the Mexicas, for example, established Tenochtitlan and divided the city according to the number of their calpultin. It is clear that the institution produced the division. Obviously, the cohesion between the members of the calpulli was strengthened by their system of common ownership of land. The land assigned to the community was divided so that certain plots were allotted for families to use and occupy, while others were destined for communal work by the calpulli members in order to pay for communal expenses, including tribute due to the central government. At the same time, in order to maintain the identity of the community, there were strong prescriptions against the use of calpulli land by outsiders.

The dual nature of the calpulli naturally produced two administrative apparatuses, one strictly internal and one that linked it to the central administration. Alonso de Zurita, the sixteenth-century author who provides the most information about this institution, says that the internal apparatus was run by the "eldest kinsman" and a group of community elders. The eldest kinsman was always a calpulli member belonging to a particular branch of the lineage and elected internally, based on his personal merits. His principal functions were to distribute lots of land among the families of the calpulli, to assure the proper use of the land, and to determine the fate of vacant lots. In order to carry out his functions, the eldest kinsman kept a communal census and a land register, maintaining "paintings of what kind they were, and the borders, and where [they were], who left them and who cultivated them, and what everyone has and which were vacant," and Zurita continued, the eldest kinsman would "always revise his paintings according to events." This administration was also responsible for the security of the barrio, the distribution of communal work, internal worship, and the running of the schools. It is probable that the administration also coordinated the reciprocal assistance that was so important to community life. The powers of the second administration, which connected the calpulli to the central government, were very different. This administration handled communal tribute payments, the calpulli's military force in times of war, the administration of justice, and overall religious participation. As we will discuss, the top administrator was a functionary appointed by the tlatoani, not the calpulli.

There were two clearly differentiated social classes: the *macehualtin,* or commoners, and the *pipiltin,* or nobles. Most production was done by the commoners, who were farmers, craftsmen, and merchants. The nobles, on the other hand, were in charge of public affairs, including public administration, the judiciary, the army, and the clergy. In both cases the roles were inherited. When the Mexicas founded Tenochtitlan, they had a problem because they had no noble class. The sources say that their first tlatoani, who came from the noble lineage of Culhuacan, married the daughters of the leaders of the calpultin to produce what would be Tenochtitlan's nobility.

There was a fundamental difference between macehualtin and pipiltin in terms of tribute. The macehualtin were freeborn producers and periodically delivered their services and their surplus production to the government. The nobles did not pay tribute; they administered landed property and were the direct beneficiaries of the wealth collected. In this way the nobles accumulated political power, wealth, and prestige. In order to justify this difference, the nobles argued that their public tasks were extremely arduous and their privileges commensurate with their efforts. In other words, they claimed that carrying out their duties was equivalent to paying tribute.

The nobles claimed that they had inherited power from two sources. The most important source, according to myth, was Quetzalcoatl, from whom they had inherited their role. They also claimed that, historically, they had descended from a long sequence of distinguished ancestors. This dual heritage was reinforced by the personal attributes of the nobles, which had been acquired through their painstaking and strict education in the *calmecac* (school primarily for nobles).

The functions the nobles carried out provided them with a permanent income. Each assignment carried a title, often given for life though not hereditary, and also included a government residence and the tributes assigned to it. Nobles could get additional benefits as rewards given by the tlatoani. There was a whole system of rewards for government service and military accomplishments, ranging from valuable objects (jewels, cloth, and feather crests) to the profits from lands called *pillalli*, "noble lands". These rewards did not accrue for the performance of any duty, but from the performance of meritorious deeds. For this reason they could be retained by the recipient, inherited, or sold.

Class differences were apparent in many aspects of society. Nobles were tried in special tribunals, could enter royal palaces, and could participate in the most important festivals and ceremonies. They had the sole right to wear certain items of clothing, such as cotton and shoes. Nobles used fine pottery and were the only people who could partake of certain foods and drinks, such as cacao. Additionally, noble men could have several wives. On the other hand, laws were stricter for nobles, and religion required some noble families to surrender their daughters to be sacrificed. Evidently, this severity legitimated the power of the nobility. The rigid social division could be breached, however. A pipiltin who broke the law or did not carry out his duties properly could be demoted to macehualtin—a penalty that affected the whole family, present and future. The reverse could also occur. A macehualtin who excelled in combat achieved an intermediate social position, because his children would be born noble.

Tlatlacoliztli, an institution that has been compared to slavery, also existed, though it was not economically important in Central Mexico. One became a *tlacotli* by not paying debts or by being penalized for committing a serious crime. A tlacotli was obligated to work for his creditor with no pay except his daily food. He did not lose his family or the ability to have property, including having a tlacotli of his own. The work was usually not excessively hard, and often there was a contract specifying the activities that the tlacotli was to do. The creditor could not transfer the tlacotli without his consent. Except in extreme cases, tlatlacoliztli was not hereditary, although the sources tell us that in Texcoco treason against the state was punished by slavery for four generations. In most instances a slave regained freedom if the debtor remitted the debt, if the debt was repaid, if the slave and the master had sexual intercourse, or if certain rituals that washed out the stain of tlatlacoliztli were carried out. Repeated disobedience made the condition of the tlacotli worse. A wooden yoke was put on him that impeded his movements, he no longer could choose his owner, and he could be bought by merchants who, after ritually washing his impurities, could offer him for sacrifice as if he were captured in war.

In the final stages of Mexica history the massive influx of war captives began to change this form of forced labor. In early times all captives were destined to be sacrificed, but as time went on some of the battle captives, particularly craftsmen or artists, began to be assigned to work for a temple or to provide service in the royal palace.

Land Tenure

According to Zurita, most of the population had land to till. Legally, land was divided into three general categories: communal lands; state lands used to support the cost of government, religion, and war; and lands intended to reward merit in battle or public service. Communal lands belonged to the calpulli, most of its parcels being distributed for family usufruct. The remaining parcels were used for communal labor to cover the expenses of the community itself. Each usufruct family was obliged to till the land itself and was forbidden to sell or rent it or to hire farm workers except in cases of widowhood, minor status, or incapacitation. It was also forbidden to stop working the land without a good reason; when this occurred, the community recouped the parcel and reallocated it to another family. In addition, workers who destroyed their own products were severely punished.

Although there was no right to family ownership of land parcels in a calpulli, the right to use them was inheritable. The sources do not tell us whether the land was divided among the children or only one son inherited the use of the land. It is probable that, as time went by, the equitable base that had been used to divide the land was lost. When the number of available parcels differed from the number of farmers needing land, the result could be calpultin that had families without land or calpultin with idle parcels. In such situations landless farmers had to rent parcels from another calpulli. The renting calpulli used the rent for collective needs. The renters continued to belong to their original calpulli, being considered strangers in the leasing calpulli. In Zurita's words, the distinction was made because "it is not proper that they should mix one with another or that they leave their lineage."

Other communal lands were cultivated by all members of the calpulli, who took turns in doing the work. The harvest was used to pay collective expenses such as the maintenance of the temples and schools of the calpultin. The internal government was also maintained by collective labor. Zurita considered this practice to be very old and independent of the central government. It is likely that some of the communal land's yield was paid as tribute to the central government. Calpultin of people who had been conquered had to cultivate additional parcels, called *tequitcatlalli,* in order to pay tribute to the conquerors.

There were two terms for usufruct families on communal lands: *calpuleque* and *teccaleque.* According to Zurita, the difference was that the former paid tribute to the tlatoani and the latter to the *tecuhtli,* a governor appointed by the ruler who lived in the calpulli and performed judicial, financial, and military tasks. His official residence or "tribunal" was the *teccali.* This small palace had parcels of land assigned for its support. Technically speaking, it was not the land that was allotted to the teccali, but the tribute that the usufruct families on those parcels would ordinarily have paid the tlatoani. The tlatoani assigned this tribute to the tecuhtli in payment for his duties. This explains Zurita's distinction between calpuleque and teccaleque. Both groups were calpulli members with equal property rights, differing only in the way their surplus was allocated. In our opinion it was easier for the central administration to pay each of their *tetecutin* with part of the revenue generated within the calpulli where he resided than to collect all the tribute centrally and then return part of it to its source in order to pay the functionary. This would be particularly important in a society in which large volumes of tribute had to be transported by humans, as there were no animals usable for transport.

The second group of lands was state owned. The *tlatocatlalli* (or *tlatocamilli*) were used to pay for royal expenses, governmental expenses, and feeding the poor and foreigners who were lodged in the palace. They were usually farmed by landless renters, tlatacotin, or people from conquered domains, as tribute. The *tecpantlalli,* lands used to support the palace and its court, were farmed by families who paid their rent by service at the palace. The *teopantlalli,* lands belonging to the temples, were cultivated by students, the faithful, and laborers. Part of their yield was used to feed the needy. Finally, the *milchimalli* were lands used to pay military expenses.

The third kind of land was used to reward meritorious conduct in battle or in public service. Its name, *pillalli* ("land of the nobles"), shows that its rewards were exclusively for the nobility. Several scholars have erroneously claimed that such land was private property. However, most agree that the rights awarded by the tlatoani were not to the parcels themselves but to the tribute owed by those occupying them. The clue to this interpretation is the name of their cultivators—*mayeque,* or "laborers." Zurita distinguishes them clearly from renters, who had temporary contracts with the landowners and paid tribute to the tlatoani. The mayeque, however, were tied to the land, lived on it as if it were theirs, and—except for military service—paid the tribute that they owed to the tlatoani to the designated nobles. This might seem to equate them with the teccaleque, but while the tecuhtli received tribute as a reward for his services, an honored noble bore no obligation for his reward. For this reason he could own the tribute given to him by the tlatoani as well as selling the right to the pillalli, as long as he sold them to other nobles.

Political Organization

We will confine our discussion of political organization to the most mature political entities of the Postclassic, the *tlatocayotl* or "kingdoms" of Mexico-Tenochtitlan and Texcoco. It is probable that these great cities of Central Mexico were models for the political organization of other power centers at the time. Nevertheless, there was such a profusion of types and levels of political organization during the period that we cannot mechanically project information from the great capitals onto smaller political units. Many Chichimec groups, for example, retained their northern organization or developed very specific adaptations to the geopolitics of Central Mexico. Xochimilco and Tlaxcala differed because of their collegial governments with, respectively, three and four rulers who represented large segments that formed the polity.

One of the biggest obstacles to understanding the political system of the Postclassic is the fact that there were two different yet harmoniously coexisting vassalage systems: territorial and kinship. To this day we do not clearly understand how these two systems overlapped or the way in which the subjects resolved their double allegiance. On the one hand they acknowledged their "natural lords" (the leaders of the corporate descent group at whatever level) and on the other they obeyed their "kings" (the tlatoque who ruled over multiethnic political units). An example may illustrate these problems. According to Fray Juan de Torquemada, Techotlala—the tlatoani of Acolhuacan—governed a heterogenous population. His subjects included Chichimec, Acolhua, Tepanec, and Culhua ethnic groups, ruled from antiquity by "natural lords." As Techotlala was afraid that the internal ethnic alliances of his subjects would weaken the unity of his kingdom, he divided each of the ethnic groups, relocating and intermingling the pieces. By this fragmentation, even though his subjects continued to acknowledge the "natural lords," he considerably diminished their power.

The basic political unit of territorial vassalage was the tlatocayotl. This unit, called a kingdom by the Spaniards, ruled over the combined destinies of the multiple ethnic groups that made up the most important cities of the time. It is interesting to note that when the territorial vassalage system was erected, it did not destroy the community corporate descent group (as Pedro Carrasco proposes) but rather based itself on that group, using the kinship structure but adapting it for its own use. In contrast to Carrasco, we are convinced that in this difficult integration process the "natural lords" went from being rulers of their communities to being bureaucrats in a multiethnic political system.

This adaptation would explain why sometimes, in sources such as lawsuits in Huexotzinco, the word *tecuhtli* means "natural lord," while in others it is the term used for functionaries appointed by the tlatoani because of services or military prowess, as described by Zurita and Torquemada. As we have seen, in more complex regimes the tecuhtli was a representative of the central government who had judicial, military, administrative, and fiscal powers; governed the calpulli in its relationships to the tlatocayotl; and set up his administrative center, or teccali, in it.

When the tecuhtli was co-opted by the central government, the corporate descent groups must have substituted another official of the same
lineage for him. In the calpulli, this official would be the "oldest kinsman" mentioned by Zurita. This phenomenon did not occur in other
societies in Central Mexico; when the Spanish arrived, the tecuhtli was
still the "natural lord."

The overlap between the two systems probably created complicated
rules for the distribution of titles and public offices, some being awarded
by descent, some for personal merit, and some because of a combination of ancestry and political career. This allowed some of the important
government posts to be filled by ennobled commoners. Each appoint-
ment could involve quite diverse functions; for example, the same individual could simultaneously be a high commander in the army, a judge,
an administrator, an executioner, and a dignitary responsible for some
religious ceremonies.

The legitimacy of the ruling body was strongly supported by the
arrangement of the cosmos. The ruling authority was considered to be
a projection of the divine order, which divided the world into two halves:
heaven/earth, light/darkness, dryness/wetness, male/female, and so
forth. If the supreme deity was the union of two manifestations, male
and female, it is logical that Mexico-Tenochtitlan was governed by two
rulers: the tlatoani and the *cihuacoatl*, who represented, respectively, the
power of the heavens and the earth.

The tlatoani was a semidivine individual representing the god Tezcatlipoca on earth, and therefore entrusted with power over life and death.
He was his people's highest military leader, high priest, and chief judge.
Mexico-Tenochtitlan's tlatoani, considered a direct descendant of
Acamapichtli, was elected from among the sons or grandsons of prior
tlatoques by a select group of nobles. The cihuacoatl, the next most
powerful official, replaced the tlatoani in his temporary or permanent
absences and could directly intervene in the administrative, fiscal, and
judicial affairs of the tlatocayotl. Both rulers appointed the highest officials. It is interesting to note that in Cholula the two supreme rulers did
not have these titles; instead, they were called "principal of the sky" and
"principal of the earth." Together, these two titles were the name of the
supreme deity. The symbol for the first one was an eagle (a celestial
symbol), and the second, a jaguar (an earth symbol).

Specialized bodies helped the tlatoani and cihuacoatl run the tlato-cayotl. The composition of these bodies varied, but the repetition of the numbers four, thirteen, and twenty leads to the supposition that they were also patterned on the cosmos. Urban affairs, for example, were handled by four functionaries in charge of the four quadrants of the city, which in turn were a projection of the plane of the four directions. These functionaries directed the tetecuhtin.

The cosmic arrangement was also projected upon the army. The supreme command was in the hands of the *tlacateccatl* and the *tlacochcalcatl,* whose names imply that they were in charge of, respectively, the troops and the weapons. The troops for the army came from the commoners in the city and from military orders composed of warriors supported by the palace. The high commanders were public officials, mostly nobles. Each calpulli formed a unit identified by a flag and a password and was commanded by its tecuhtli. The troops did not receive wages, because participating in war was a form of tribute, but they could keep booty, were rewarded with prizes, and had a kind of disability-and-death insurance.

There were also two high priests in Mexico-Tenochtitlan: Quetzalcoatl Totec tlamacazqui and Quetzalcoatl Tlaloc tlamacazqui. They were in charge of the worship of the two gods whose chapels topped the Great Temple of the city: Huitzilopochtli, the solar god, and Tlaloc, the rain god. A complicated hierarchy, with juvenile students at the bottom, supported each high priest. Depending on their titles, the clergy filled important government offices, particularly educational ones. Priestesses had a prestigious role in society and in the ecclesiastic pyramid but were not linked to important public offices.

In fiscal matters a dual arrangement divided functions between the *hueicalpixqui,* who directed all the tribute collectors, and the *petlacalcatl,* who was in charge of storing and redistributing the tribute. At the lowest level were the tetecuhtin, who received orders from the hueicalpixqui and collected tribute from the calpulli.

In each calpulli, the administration of justice began in the court called *teccalli* or *teccalco.* There, the tecuhtli handled minor matters, including divorces. If the verdicts required a severe penalty, the case was taken to the court in the royal palace, the *tlacxitlan.* The most serious cases, particularly those with the death penalty, were tried in the cihuacoatl's

Supreme Court, composed of thirteen judges. There were also several specialized courts in which palace nobles, soldiers, merchants, priests, and students were tried.

Education

When Friar Bernardino de Sahagún wrote about the customs of the Otomis, he described the Otonteocalli—a temple consecrated to Yocippa, the principal deity of these people. Children were educated in the temple amidst rituals and penance. Their harsh childhood included participating in night vigils, supplying water to the temple, fasting, and bloodletting. This rigorous education was not limited to the Otomis; there are similar descriptions of educational practices among other peoples in Central Mexico. The documents also consistently say that the temples were the schools and the priests the teachers. Even though the principal role of these centers was to provide formal education to children and young people, they also served other collateral ends. They were religious institutions and auxiliary branches of the army, and they coordinated the communal work of students.

Temple schools were public institutions with compulsory attendance for young boys and girls of the right age. A child's attendance in a school was promised in a religious vow made when the parents took children a few days old to the temple in order to offer them as its servants. Not taking a child to be offered put the child in grave danger, as the temple deity would not protect him or her otherwise. After the ceremony the parents left behind an object that they believed contained the child's animic force, acting as a pledge until the child was old enough to serve in person. The sources are contradictory concerning the children's age when they entered school. Usually, children were boarded at the school when they were between five and eight years old, although nobles enrolled later because they spent their earlier years with their tutors. Entering school was also strongly ritualistic. When girls in Texcoco joined the temple, they were elegantly dressed and wore flower garlands in their hair, while the priests received them with speeches. Boys as well as girls stayed in school until they were married.

The social division between commoners and nobles carried over into the two types of temple schools they attended. Children of the macehualtin went to the *telpochcalli*, found in all the calpulli, while children of the pipiltin went to the less numerous calmecac. The sources state that parents could choose the school their children attended. We must assume that if this freedom existed, it would have been considerably limited by economic and ideologic factors such as family loyalty to particular deities.

A basic difference between the telpochcalli and calmecac was the amount of discipline imposed, being extremely rigid in the calmecac. For example, while students in the telpochcalli could spend some time at home, which would have been very useful in times of intense agricultural activity, students in the calmecac were not allowed to leave the school. The difference in discipline was most notable in sexual matters. While youths in the telpochcalli could enjoy sporadic sexual encounters, students in the calmecac were not allowed to do this; calmecac students pledged total chastity, and any infraction was severely punished. Juan Bautista Pomar says that noble children were punished by being pierced with agave thorns, subjected to chili smoke [in the eyes], and whipped with nettles. Other sources say that youths who behaved lewdly were expelled, with great shame, after their hair was burned down to the roots.

Students in the telpochcalli fulfilled their tribute obligations by working on land that belonged to the school or going in groups to help in public works. When a youth was stronger, he went as a porter to the battlefield, where he became acclimated to warfare. If he was brave, he and his companions tried to capture an enemy; if he succeeded, he received his first promotion within the school. A student in the calmecac received more thorough military training and, after completing it, went to the battlefield accompanied by a military tutor, an experienced warrior paid by his parents.

The sources do not describe what was taught in these schools in much detail. Pomar mentions that nobles learned prestigious crafts such as silver smithing and artistic carving of wood and stone. He also mentions the study of the ritual calendar and exercises on the ball courts. We must suppose that much time was spent preparing young nobles in rhetoric, engineering, and law, which were indispensable for good government. An important skill for both common and noble boys was learning dances and songs associated with religion and war. Education of girls in the schools focused on productive activities such as weaving and spinning.

The *mexicatl teohuatzin,* an important functionary of the central admin-istration in Tenochtitlan, was the head of all the schools and determined the religious content that was taught. The complex organization's lowest rung were the "priestlings," as the beginning students were called. They began as temple servants, sweeping, carrying water and wood for the services, helping in the religious ceremonies, and so forth. The sources describe them as penitents who bathed with cold water at midnight, ritually painted their bodies black, carried flaming incense burners on their heads, and continually offered agave thorns soaked in their own blood to the gods.

What this means is that every man was a priest for a significant part of his life. Although only grown men participated in warfare, all youths served in the military, preparing them for the frequent battles in which they took part as adults. For this reason members of the military orders were also teachers, who taught dances, war songs, and playing musical instruments in the *cuicacalli.* These schools—"houses of song" where students went to get specialized instruction—were attached to temples.

Obviously, the education received in childhood and adolescence influenced adulthood, which began when the students left school and got married. In their own spheres the pipiltin and macehualtin carried out the tasks for which they had both been trained. The former, thor-oughly educated and disciplind in the calmecac, were competent to fill important public posts. The standing in the hierarchy that they acquired by their performance during their school years was their starting point in carrying out their duties to the state.

Relationships between Peoples

The climate of uncertainty in Central Mexico caused by the end of the Classic created a tense and unstable situation up to the time that the Spanish arrived. It is necessary to study the complex relationships between the peoples in the area in order to understand this permanent state of institutionalized violence. Generally speaking, the people of Central Mexico were a large heterogeneous group that—despite their ethnic, linguistic, and political differences—shared a common history that was intensely affected by trade and warfare. The extremely diverse inhabi-tants of the area came together on the basis of ethnicity among other criteria. The sources often refer to these biological ties. Some passages discuss the kinship between the patron deities of two groups; others refer to the common mythical origin of some peoples; political discourses argue that alliances and allegiances are due to a common descent. Peoples who belonged to these enormous "families" also acknowledged their "natural lords", superiors who ruled at different organizational levels.

However, the cohesion and agreement generated by this structure were significantly affected by other kinds of ties, such as the territorial vassalage that we have discussed. This authority was exercised over the various groups that lived in a particular area regardless of any kinship ties between them. The fundamental unit of the political system was the city, which, de jure, was an autonomous entity. Nevertheless, the fact that cities were territorial and political entities often made them dependent on each other. Powerful cities that owned the land allowed weaker groups to settle in their territory in exchange for a fee. One of many such historically recorded arrangements can be seen in the relationship that the Mexicas established when they founded Mexico-Tenochtitlan. Their settlement occupied the western islands of Lake Texcoco, an area belonging to Azcapotzalco. The Mexicas asked for permission to occupy them, and Azcapotzalco allowed them to do so in exchange for political fealty and the payment of periodic tribute. This was one of many such arrangements that was historically recorded. The territorial vassalage system was a wide regional network. Obviously, the coexistence of kinship and territorial vassalage systems made the relationships between peoples in Central Mexico very complicated, particularly because the most powerful rulers of the area were frequently rulers in both systems.

Although the coexistence of these two systems makes the sources difficult to understand, there is sufficient evidence to support the fact that the basis for the biggest and most powerful suprastatal institution in the Basin of Mexico—the excan tlatoloyan—was an ancient kinship vassalage. Its name literally means "tribunal of the three seats." Other names corroborate its judicial character: Hernando Alvarado Tezozómoc calls it "the tribunal of the kings" or "the Royal Court" in Spanish and *tecuhtlatoloyan* in Nahuatl. However, its role was not simply legal; it also had military functions, which is the reason why the sources call it the Triple Alliance.

The excan tlatoloyan seems to have been a response to the need for a regional suprastatal organization in the context of endemic warfare. This condition was common in the Postclassic throughout Mesoamerica, so it is not surprising that similar institutions developed among the Mayas and the Tarascans. In the Basin of Mexico the excan tlatoloyan dates back much further than the fifteenth century. Even though it is sometimes claimed that it developed after the war against Azcapotzalco in 1430, it is clear that it existed at least as far back as the Toltec era. Domingo Chimalpahin Cuauhtlehuanitzin mentions (though vaguely) an old alliance between Tollan, Culhuacan, and Otompan. In time Tollan was replaced by Coatlinchan, and Coatlinchan, in its turn, was replaced by Texcoco. Culhuacan's only heir was Mexico-Tenochtitlan, and Otompan's place was taken first by Azcapotzalco and later by Tlacopan.

When the last Triple Alliance was formed, the tlatoques of Texcoco, Mexico-Tenochtitlan, and Tlacopan became the heads of the three main ethnic groups in the Basin. In addition to their roles as territorial heads of their own cities, they now called themselves, respectively, the "Lord of the Acolhua and the Chichimec" (*acolhuatecuhtli chichimecatecuhtli*), "Lord of the Culhua" (*culhuatecuhtli*), and "Lord of the Tepanec" (*tepanecatecuhtli*).

Ideologically, the Triple Alliance paralleled the structure of the cosmos. Although there is little available information regarding this institution, we know that its archetype was the division of the cosmos into three great levels: the heavens, the surface of the earth, and the underworld. Following this model, we find elements that connect the Acolhuas and Chichimecs with the heavens, the Mexicas with the earth's surface (to which the sun belongs), and the Tepanecs with the underworld.

The excan tlatoloyan, as a replica of the cosmos, was believed to transmit its power into all its ethnic groups. The three rulers, acting as judges in a court that rotated its sessions between the three capitals, resolved disputes that arose between the elements of this great complex. Simultaneously, their military alliance put them in charge of defense against eventual external attacks. Their subjects amply repaid this guardianship and protection through subordination and tribute. Obviously, some of the neighboring peoples did not agree with the legitimacy and political demands of the three rulers. In these cases the excan tlatoloyan incorporated them by force as proof of their right to rule.

Aerial view of Tikal, Guatemala. Southeast Mesoamerica Area, Classic period. (Courtesy of Leonardo López Luján)

Maya cylindrical vessel found in Teotihuacan, Estado de México. Southeast Mesoamerica Area, Classic period. (Courtesy of Salvador Guilliem)

Tripod vase from Tomb 1, Calakmul, Campeche. Southeast Mesoamerica Area, Classic period. (Courtesy of Salvador Guilliem)

Vessel with anthropomorphic lid, Guajilar, Chiapas. Southeast Mesoamerica Area, Classic period. (Courtesy of Salvador Guilliem)

Ball court, Copán, Honduras. Southeast Mesoamerica Area, Classic period. (Courtesy of Leonardo López Luján)

Mural from the Red Temple at Cacaxtla, Tlaxcala. Central Mexico Area, Epiclassic period. (Photograph: Ignacio Guevara © *Arqueología Mexicana*, INAH)

Main ball court, Xochicalco, Morelos. Central Mexico Area, Epiclassic period. (Courtesy of Leonardo López Luján)

Relief of a mythological feline, Teotenango, Estado de México. Central Mexico Area, Epiclassic period. (Courtesy of Salvador Guilliem)

Panel from the southern ball court at El Tajín, Veracruz. Gulf Area, Epiclassic period. (Photograph: Leonardo López Luján)

Monumental columns representing armed warriors, Pyramid B, Tula, Hidalgo. Central Mexico Area, Postclassic period. (Photograph: Ignacio Guevara © *Arqueología Mexicana*, INAH)

Mexica monolith used for human sacrifice, Tenochtitlan, Distrito Federal. Central Mexico Area, Postclassic period. (Photograph: Agustín Uzárraga © *Arqueología Mexicana*, INAH)

Mexica feline sculpture used for depositing human hearts, Tenochtitlan, Distrito Federal. Central Mexico Area, Postclassic period. (Courtesy of Salvador Guilliem)

Mexica bas-relief with glyph of the ruler Ahuítzotl, Tepoztlán, Morelos. Central Mexico Area, Postclassic period. (Courtesy of Salvador Guilliem)

These ideas were consistent with the initial expansionist ambitions of the Triple Alliance. The power it gained by its victory over Azcapotzalco made it a mighty coalition from the beginning. The initial pact clearly indicated a military expansionism, because it specified the division of future booty; two-fifths to Texcoco and to Mexico-Tenochtitlan, and one-fifth to Tlacopan. The excan tlatoloyan then proceeded to conquer towns—near and far, one by one—in an expansionist process never before seen in Mesoamerica (see map 16).

Submission to the excan tlatoloyan could take place peacefully as well as by force. Militarily weaker towns surrendered without resisting after the first confrontation. In this case the assimilation treaty was benign, and their submission was limited to periodic gifts to the rulers and their gods. The fate of those who resisted and lost was different, their fate depending on the extent of their resistance. Usually, the conquered cities paid tribute acknowledging submission and were, in addition, required to allow free passage to merchants protected by the excan tlatoloyan and to help the armies of their conquerors with troops and food. However, they were allowed to retain their own legal and political systems. When resistance had been very strong, the excan tlatoloyan—besides imposing tribute—could impose their own governor or even raze the town and settle their own people in the seized territory. Despite the provisions of the assimilation treaties, all the subjugated peoples were subjected openly or subtly to intrusions by the excan tlatoloyan into their internal affairs.

The Mexicas assumed the role of military leaders in the allocation of functions among the three rulers. They used this position for their own benefit, rapidly altering the initial position of equality to which they had agreed with Texcoco. Expansionist campaigns were preferentially directed into zones that particularly benefited Mexico-Tenochtitlan. This island city, without sufficient arable land, became rich by the flow of goods that it gained in tribute. It also profited from production of crafts, long-distance trade promoted by war, and mercantile activities within the Basin. Feathers, skins, semiprecious stones, and metals requiring the specialized skill of Mexica artisans came from distant regions. Meanwhile, the food consumed in the city was produced in the Basin itself and in neighboring valleys. According to Edward E. Calnek, tribute (coming principally from the chinampa zone of Chalco and Xochimilco)

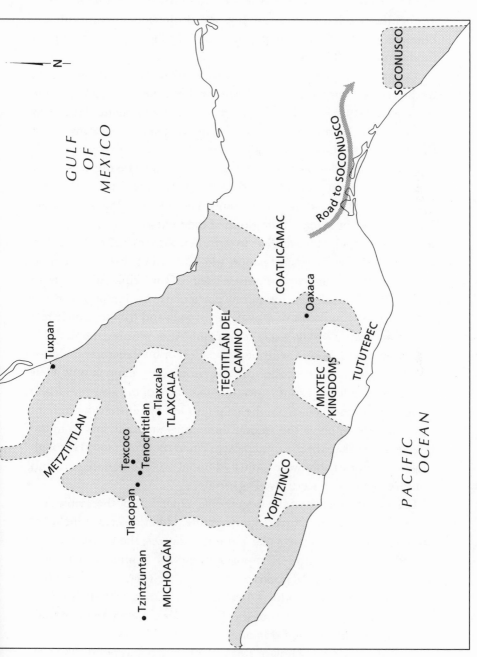

Map 16. The dominions of the Triple Alliance. (Adapted from R. H. Barlow)

would have only fed one-quarter to one-third of the inhabitants of Tenochtitlan—that is, the nobility, the professional army, and the bureaucracy. The remaining population, the majority, purchased their food commercially.

This supremacy changed the Mexicas, who proclaimed themselves to be the greatest warriors in the known world. War became, for them, the principal way to solve political problems. The development of the army was one of the fundamental enterprises of the state, and an army career the ideal way to attain other high public offices. Ideology—particularly religious ideology—was based on war. Despite this, the Mexicas never declared war against a potential foe without claiming a just cause, such as attacks on embassadors or merchants. They issued a double message. ´ To their own population, they glorified the military's role in acquiring the captives needed for sacrifice; to outsiders, they proclaimed that they were only using force against people who violated the vassalage system.

Military tactics and expansionist strategy of the Triple Alliance were shaped by technical developments, particularly by limitations in the capacity, speed, and cost of moving provisions and tribute, which had to be transported on the backs of humans. After winning the war tribute was imposed, but no army of occupation or bureaucracy was left—only the *calpixque*, or tax collectors. Garrisons were set up in only a few instances, as in border zones, meaning that most of the army was made up of nonprofessionals from the calpultin led by central-government commanders. Interspersed among these units were warriors from the military orders kept by the royal palace. When the army moved through subject territories, they were given additional provisions, transport, and reinforcements that were owed as tribute.

The main objective of the hegemonic expansion of the Triple Alliance was to obtain not territory, but tribute. Other objectives included preferential access to particular natural resources, the reorganization of trade, and the control of important markets. Sometimes tributary towns not only delivered goods produced in their own region but had to pay their debt with products they acquired in trade with their neighbors. In this way the capitals of the Triple Alliance obtained materials from regions outside their domains.

According to some scholars, this type of control was politically inadequate, lacked internal cohesion, and was based on a flawed military organization. Ross Hassig refutes this argument, pointing out that the system worked well if we take into account the true purpose of the expansion—tribute—as well as the technological level at the time. Aside from the efficacy or inefficiency of such a system for the conquerers, however, we should also consider it from the viewpoint of the conquered peoples who lived under the harsh, unstable, and insecure conditions that any institutionalized violence creates.

The enormous area controlled by the excan tlatoloyan was immediately taken advantage of by the *pochteca,* long-distance merchants who lived in the three capitals as well as in conquered cities. These merchants were organized not only in the great cities of Central Mexico—among them independent Cholula, which was famous for its commercial activities—but all over Mesoamerica. Miguel Acosta Saignes believes that they originated in the area of the Gulf of Mexico. The pochteca had a mature hierarchical organization and distinctive traditions. For example, all the calpultin of Mexica pochteca were administered by their own high officials, the *pochtecatlailotlac* and the *acxotecatl,* and in the battlefield they had their own commander, the *cuauhpoyatzin.*

The pochteca had a great deal of autonomy in organizing their commercial expeditions, and they served their tlatoque as spies, ambassadors, and—rarely—as a militia. Their wealth and the services they rendered placed them in a privileged position, with jurisdiction over the markets and the authority to set prices. The sources describe their business association with the tlatoani of Mexico-Tenochtitlan, their functioning as prominent advisors in Texcoco, and their government posts in Tlaxcala.

The pochteca were closely tied to the calpultin of the craftsmen, suppling them with the raw materials that were essential for the production of goods such as feather art, cotton textiles, and jewelry that the pochteca, in turn, would distribute throughout Mesoamerica. In cities in the Basin of Mexico, the pochteca organized joint commercial expeditions with marching columns that went through Tehuacan to Tochtepec. At this Oaxacan settlement they divided into groups, one going to Anahuac Ayotlan in the coast of the Pacific Ocean and the second to Anahuac Xicalanco in the Gulf of Mexico. In their southern branch the pochteca from the excan tlatoloyan controlled the Soconusco region, a rich source of cacao. This fruit was not only a valuable product but— together with gold powder, copper axes, and cotton mantles—was used as money. In Tabasco the pochteca from Central Mexico traded with Zoque and Maya merchants who, in turn, traded all the way to Honduras. Large transactions took place in independent neutral centers known as "ports of trade."

The greatest control over markets of the excan tlatoloyan was clearly exercised in the Basin of Mexico, particularly in Tlatelolco. Specialized markets were common. For example, slaves were sold in Azcapotzalco, fine ceramics and clothing in Texcoco, dogs in Acolman, and birds in Tepepulco. Together they acted as an interchange system that reinforced the economic symbiosis of the Basin of Mexico. Outside the Basin, the excan tlatoloyan tried to conquer and control important markets, particularly Oaxaca. Their merchants operated unfairly inside the conquered areas, and this often led to uprisings and rebellions. According to Edward E. Calnek and Frances F. Berdan, tribute, long-distance commerce, and the internal market of the Basin were tightly interconnected, forming a complex, shifting system. It is difficult to distinguish the relative importance of each one of these three components. The market was a key interactive point at the local and regional levels. Thus, sumptuary goods that the ruler received as tribute were later "given" by him to nobles and retainers as rewards for public service. In turn, the recipients used these goods to purchase essential goods in the marketplace.

The Bases of Knowledge

One of the most substantial factors in the millenial unity of Mesoamerican societies was the common development of knowledge. Agricultural knowledge, expertise in the exploitation of natural resources, formulas for computing time, and the art of medicine were all diffused, strengthened by shared experiences, and enriched by geographic diversity. Although communication between peoples and the coincidence of different practices enriched knowledge in Mesoamerica, its technology compared unfavorably with that of other peoples with similar levels of social organization, urbanism, and artistic achievement. This was the result of several deficiencies, notably the absence of beasts of burden and, concomitantly, no mechanical use of the wheel. An additional handicap was the long delay in the introduction of metallurgy. When

Mesoamericans achieved high population densities and solved their subsistence needs despite these deficiencies, it was because—in addition to their agricultural knowledge—they had a highly organized labor force and a diversified food supply.

Large areas of Central Mexico were very favorable for agriculture, having fertile soil and large bodies of water. As in the rest of Mesoamerica, most agriculture in Central Mexico used the slash-and-burn (swidden) method. In the Highlands only one crop per year was produced, using a fallow system. Palerm has defined this system as similar to the tropical swidden system, which began by cutting down all ground cover. However, in this case shorter fallow periods (the same as or less than the time during which cultivation took place) are needed than those required in tropical swiddens. Fallow agriculture was supplemented with irrigation agriculture, which required a greater collective effort by farmers in complex societies. Water was collected and distributed by canals, terraces, and dikes. With the use of irrigation, two crops a year and higher yields per crop were obtained.

In special cases—where sweet, shallow lake waters allowed it—chinampas were built. These were artificial plots of land built on a swamp, crisscrossed with canals, fertilized with mud, and watered by filtration. Chinampas had extremely high yields, but they required elaborate cultivation, continuous labor, and hydraulic works to control the level of the aquifer and to avoid contamination of sweet water by brackish water. The best-known chinampas were those in the Xochimilco and Chalco regions.

An adequate study of Mesoamerican knowledge would include an appraisal of the relationships between practice, experience, abstraction, and the systematization of information. We define knowledge as both the action and the effect of an attempt to capture an object intellectually. It is the ideal process of perception, which begins with a preconception that structures and conditions perception and is also the conceptual and structuring result of that perception. Like a serpent biting its own tail, all experience is determined by an intellectual frame and every intellectual frame is permanently changed by experience. Therefore, any area of learning is more than accumulated experiences. It is a social product produced by propositions structured by a system.

The knowledge systems of different cultural traditions can be divided (sometimes with imprecise boundaries) into two large types: macrosystems

and scientific systems. Both types are composed of diverse propositions—theories and practices both proven and hypothetical, true and
false, efficient and inefficient—but they are all validated by belonging
to a structured system. Macrosystems and scientific systems differ in their
degree of integration, potential for change, and amount of critical rigor.
The first type of knowledge system within each cultural tradition is interconnected to the degree that (as the name *macrosystem* indicates) it
becomes a far-reaching explanatory system—a cosmovision. Scientific
systems, in contrast, tend to break up and particularize their areas of
knowledge. In scientific systems there is a greater consciousness of the
social processes involved in creating knowledge and, therefore, a greater
speed of change. Finally, even though self-criticism is present in all
knowledge systems, scientists are characterized by their development of
rigorous methods of eliminating errors.

Mesoamerican knowledge systems were macrosystemic rather than
scientific. Thus, each system should be analyzed in relation to its cosmovision. This cosmovision explains cosmic processes as the effect of the
measured actions of supernatural beings with intellect, will, and the
ability to communicate. For example, Mesoamerican agricultural knowledge was based on three universal principles. The first referred to the
"heart" of earthly beings. All creatures were thought to have within their
perceptible matter an imperceptible divine substance that was the
essence of their class. Therefore, one could refer to the "heart of maize,"
the "heart of stones," or the "heart of deer" as a divine, immortal, inner
substance that transcended individuals, who were necessarily mortal.
The second principle was the division of all things into two large opposed
and complementary groups. One was composed of things whose
essence was predominantly dry, hot, male, luminous, and vital; the other
consisted of things whose essence was predominantly wet, cold, feminine, dark, and mortal. This binary division was the first taxonomic
criterion for everything that existed. The third principle was the alternation of the domination of the essences on earth. The supremacy of
opposing forces were thought to alternate, creating cycles that gave the
world its permanence.

For example, a farmer working his field in Central Mexico envisioned the annual cycle as a great struggle in which victories of the
masculine essence alternated with those of the feminine essence. During

the feminine half of the year, rains and the forces of growth ruled; the other half was ruled by the sun, which toasted the crops to a golden color. At the beginning of the first half, the world of the dead opened, releasing the waters, the powers of germination, and the "hearts of the plants," all of which had been stored during the dry season. When the rainy season was over, everything returned to its subterranean enclosure, where it rested while the sun cooked the food of humans with its rays. The farmer had to act both in the perceptible and the imperceptible realms. He cleared the land, dug into it, and collected the ears of maize, but at the same time he ritually propitiated the arrival of the different supernatural beings involved in the process, thanked them for accomplishing their functions, said good-bye to them at the end of the process, and burned the stubble, believing that by doing so he freed (in the smoke) the rainwater that had fallen on the cornfield.

The same process occurred in medicine. The human body was considered to be a complex organism composed of heavy matter and light matter. Light matter was composed of the various animic forces or essences, the most important being the "heart," an essence located in that organ. The "heart" was a part of the patron deity of the group from whom derived not only the human nature of an individual, but also the fundamental characteristics of the ethnic group protected by the god. Another animic essence was the "irradiation," or *tonalli*, which carried the individual peculiarities of a person's secret name and fate. The tonalli was a portion of the sun's rays, which had been ritually introduced into the newborn child and gave the child the fate that corresponded to the day of the ceremony. People believed that time was a divine substance that traveled regularly to the world, and, if captured and put into a child, formed part of a person. A third essence, located in the liver, controlled human passions.

The morality and health of an individual came in large part from the harmony of his or her animic forces. The last two essences (the tonalli and the essence in the liver) could leave the body temporarily. Tonalli, for example, could leave during sleep, during coitus, through using a psychotropic, or through strong fright. If it was trapped outside the body by a god, the individual would languish, sicken, and die.

The sources attribute hot or cold qualities to humans, illnesses, medicines, and foods. These are not thermal quantities, but rather refer to their classification in the dual classificatory system. Thus, there were illnesses with hot or cold origins and, correspondingly, foods and medicines that by their nature counteracted the effects of the illnesses. An individual's health required an equilibrium between hot and cold.

However, not all illnesses were caused by disharmony of the essential forces. The world was thought of as a great palette invaded by an infinity of contending deities. They overflowed and transformed everything, taking over creatures (including humans, animals, plants, and inanimate objects) temporarily or permanently. Possession of humans by deities could be harmful or beneficial. Divine possession was used to explain states of mind or health as diverse as artistic inspiration, lust, criminality, madness, and rheumatism. Thus, many illnesses were named for the supernatural being lodged in the organism. A definitive possession meant death. The invading god seized the "heart" of the possessed and took it to its domain in the beyond.

In summary, illness was a state that usually signified an imbalance or conflict among internal essential forces of beings and among those beings and their environment; the prolonged absence of one of the animic essences; or the intrusion of a supernatural being into the body. The first medical treatment was a search for the cause of the illness, which could be as different as the breaking of a moral rule, excessive sex, discourtesy to an old person, not worshipping a deity on its feast day, treating the body carelessly, or having the curse of a sorcerer. Once the cause was found, the doctor would try to return the body to equilibrium or harmony, rescue and replace the lost animic essence, or expel the invader. A doctor acted as confessor, moral guide, advisor, or participant in a religious ritual; a conjurer of illnesses; or a provider of medicines. Fully treating a patient obviously required a mixture of procedures, and had to take both the perceptible and the invisible realms into consideration. Thus, a doctor treating a bone fracture gave the patient medicine, put splints on the extremity, and prayed to the divine quail, which mythically personified the fracture.

Knowledge about and the handling of astronomical cycles are aspects of Mesoamerican knowledge that can be traced most accurately back to Preclassic times. Archaeological investigations in Mesoamerica have shown not only a preoccupation with the course of time, but also the existence of a symbolic system for its representation that continued to exist for centuries. As we have discussed, the Mesoamerican calendar involved the harmonizing of cycles of different durations. Central Mexicans used calendars with two main cycles. One consisted of 365 days divided into 18 *veintenas* (20-day months) and 5 supplementary days, which regulated seasonal activities and the most important religious feasts. The other combined two lesser cycles of 13 and 20 days to produce a 260-day divinatory calendar. There were also a divinatory calendar of 9 days that complemented the 260-day calendar but dealt with omens influenced by the powers of the night, a Venusian calendar, and a lunar calendar. Numerical combinations of these calendars produced larger cycles. The most important of these was the 52-solar-year cycle, which was equivalent to 73 260-day calendars—the Mesoamerican "century."

The manipulation of the calendar was an attempt to ascertain, by numerical calculations, the successive influence of the gods. As we have discussed, particular times were thought of as gods spreading over the world, invading it and later vacating it after leaving their imprint. God-times lived in the upper heavens and in the underworld. They traveled through the four trees that kept the earth and the sky separated, each of these trees having a characteristic color. The gods invaded the world of humans in the sequence established by the calendric cycles: first from the East, then the North, then the West, then the South. The cycle then repeated from the East, in a permanent counterclockwise rotation.

Each unit of time was a composite god made up of several deities. For example, the day 1-Death was the result of the union of the god 1 with the god Death, and this fused god-time was equated to Tezcatlipoca, the Lord of Destiny. Each god-time carried a particular force. Day 1-Death was favorable for all slaves, and while it lasted there was great danger of a radical change in luck that would impoverish those who had been prosperous until then.

One could ask whether the Mesoamerican calendar, stripped of all its religious content, was useful for agricultural activities. Clearly, a useful agricultural calendar does not require such a complex system. With the help of a few signals from nature, a simple calendar suffices for the actual needs of working the fields. However, agricultural knowledge, like any other body of information, was inextricably linked with other fields of knowledge, and the answers to the farmer's hopes, fears, and doubts were to be found mostly in the calendar wheels interpreted by specialized priests.

Myth, Religion, Magic, and Divination

Although cosmovision, as a macrosystem, shows up in the ideas pro-duced by all cultures, the great principles that humans attribute to the universal order are most clearly enunciated in myths. This does not mean that the exposition of these principles is clear and explicit in myths, but that myths refer back to the fundamental beginning of the world. In an unchanging concept of the world such as a myth, the primordial origins of beings account for their characteristics and, there-fore, the reasons for their existence on earth. That is to say, the reason for the existence of a being is to be found in its creation.

These were the concepts of the people of Central Mexico. They sought, in the time of myth, the reasons for everything that existed on earth. No single myth covers the entire process of creation. The many myths that have survived deal with pieces of this process, explaining the origin of particular creatures. It is possible, hypothetically or for heuris-tic purposes, to reconstruct the overall concept of the creation by analyzing the meaning of each of the creation tales.

The characters of Mesoamerican myths are gods—that is, supernat-ural beings with power, will, and definite personality whose actions order all the regions of the cosmos. Most of the gods in Mesoamerican religion were anthropomorphic and were usually invisible to humans, although they had frequent hierophanies, manifestations of the sacred on earth. Within the multiplicity of the pantheon, each god was restricted to certain cosmic realms and acted in very specific ways. The believers expressed the specificity of each god through a complex iconographic code. The attire and emblems of a god showed not only his or her attrib-utes but also location and role in the universe at a particular moment.

The "hearts," or essences, of earthly things were originally the gods of primeval time. Stories tell that these gods wanted to be adored and that the Divine Couple punished their pride by condemning them to inhabit the surface of the earth and the land of the dead. In their new dual home, the condemned gods were subject to the cycle of life and death. On earth these light beings were covered by heavy, hard matter, thus creating humans, animals, plants, minerals, meteors, and the heavenly bodies. As species or classes, they continued to be immortal, but as individuals, they went from life to death and from death back to life. When an earthly being—for example, a rabbit—died, the divine essence continued its cycle in the realm of death, where it awaited the time to insert itself into the womb of a pregnant rabbit in order to occupy again the body of a new individual of the same species.

Other myths refer to the setting up of the great cosmic machine, which would cause the gods to circulate as transforming forces. We have discussed the emergence of time in an orderly way from each of the colored trees at the corners of the world. Time was the fusion of opposite divine elements. The fusion of the celestial fire and water from the underworld took place within each cosmic tree trunk. In this example of the Mesoamerican concept of the union of opposite and complementary substances, the union of fire and water created time. The symbol for this encounter was war, and its visual representation was the intertwined figure of the *atl-tlachinolli* ("the water, the bonfire").

Two of the better myths on the theme of uniting opposites concern the deluge and the Sun's musicians. According to the first myth, a couple survived the great flood inside a hollow log. After the waters receded, they tried to assuage their hunger by roasting dead fish that they found in the mud. Smoke from the fire rose to the skies and angered the gods. The two malefactors were decapitated for the great sin of uniting opposites: fish (dead, aquatic, cold matter) and fire (live, dry, hot matter).

The second myth refers to the trap that Tezcatlipoca, god of the night, set for the Sun. Tezcatlipoca sent his black son, Ehecatl, to capture the celestial musicians—characters who dressed in the four colors characteristic of the cosmic trees—with his songs. The Sun forbade the musicians to answer the nocturnal emissary, but they could not resist the beauty of his song and responded with music. Because of this, one by one, they were trapped by the alternating rhythm. The union of song and music, of colors and blackness, of day and night began the festival of the world.

Myths about the origin of humans also involve the idea of combining two substances. Quetzalcoatl, the symbol of life, went to the realm of the dead and got the bones and ashes required for the creation of humans from the lord of the underworld. After encountering dangerous adventures on the way, he arrived at Tamoanchan, the generic place of origin, where he ground the bones and mixed the inert powder with blood from his own penis. Humans emerged from the resulting mixture.

Quetzalcoatl's role as the creator of humans is clearly established by this myth. However, there was still a need to explain how the respective patron gods generated the various human groups and subgroups. All humans are explained on the basis of this myth of a journey to the underworld. Variations are minimal, but significant. One of the gods, Xolotl, went down and got the cold matter of death but did not take the bones to Tamoanchan. He took them, rather, to Chicomóztoc, the place of the seven uteri, where the different human groups were born in groups of seven. Here, all the gods bled themselves to generate their respective children. Because of this, each group had their own progenitor and divine patron.

Is Quetzalcoatl's homogeneity opposed to the multiplicity of the other sacrificing gods? Not if we understand that Mesoamericans believed the gods had the ability to divide into several others or fuse into one. We saw the same phenomenon when we spoke about units of time; each unit of time was a god composed of the union of other gods. In the first myth of human origin Quetzalcoatl was the patron of all humanity. In the second myth he divided into multiple gods who individually created the human groups that would appear successively in history.

The supreme god—whom the Nahuas of Central Mexico called, among other names, Yohualli Ehecatl ("Invisible and Intangible"), Tlacatl ("The Person"), Moyocoyani ("The Arbitrary One"), and Ometeotl ("God Two")—represented the maximum fusion. The last name, God Two, is most interesting because it refers to the fusion of a male deity with a female one—a symbol of the union of two opposite and complementary substances.

From this supreme deity came a multitude of gods, individualized by their role in the cosmic dynamic. Each god had his or her own personality, powers, and attire. Generally, the great divisions of the world were dominated by pairs or larger groups of gods. For example, Tlaloc, the rain god, as well as Cihuacoatl, Tlazolteotl, Toci, and other mother goddesses associated with the earth and the moon, presided over the realm of cold. Xiuhtecuhtli, the lord of fire, and Huitzilopochtli, the solar god, controlled the realms of fire and the heavens. Four differently colored gods acted in the four posts at the corners of the world. Xipe Totec and Quetzalcoatl controlled the movements of and conflicts between the opposing substances. The gods, in turn, subdivided into avatars. Finally, the divine fragmented to such a degree that it affected the innumerable beings of the universe, so that each of them contained at least a trace of the sacred.

Mesoamericans used three approaches to the supernatural. They begged the invisible beings, making themselves inferior and dependent; they approached them on an equal or superior plane; and they immersed themselves in the mysteries of the sacred without engaging in a dialogue at all. In the first approach, humans used religion; in the second, magic; and in the third, divination. The three approaches differed in their techniques, but in practice the borders were blurred, and usually all three approaches were employed.

Because the gods were the hidden cause of things, the Mexicas as well as their contemporaries believed that the complexity of their surroundings was due to the multiplicity of the gods. Natural processes, therefore, were explained as a series of supernatural forces coming to the earth. Humans were required to receive, with dignity and using the appropriate ritual, each god whose turn it was to exert his or her power over the earth. Humans also had to contribute their efforts, and even their lives, to the continuity of cycles and the rebirth of beings. Humans and gods were collaborators.

Paralleling a strong personal worship, collective rituals—both at the level of the community and at the level of the state—reached enormous proportions. The collective rituals were one of the most significant forces for social cohesion and political action in Mesoamerica. As shown by the frequency of their feasts, their scale, and the richness of their displays, the rituals of public worship were one of the most important concerns of the inhabitants of Central Mexico.

Mesoamerican collective rituals can be divided into two groups: calendric and noncalendric. The most important calendric rituals corresponded to the 18 veintenas (20-day months) of the 365-day cycle. Ceremonies related to specific gods or groups of gods—in which they were offered food, flowers, blood, rubber-spattered paper, jewels, costumes, incense, and fire—took place in each veintena. The offerings were made amidst prayers, dances, music and song, reenactments of myth, military skirmishes, games, and eating of particular foods. Henry B. Nicholson, along with other scholars, has pointed out the correspondence of these feasts with the fertility of the earth and the various periods of the agricultural cycle. Some sort of leap-year correction was needed in order to achieve an exact correspondence between the veintenas and the agricultural periods. However, Michel Graulich has developed a complete explanation of the calendar based on the absence of a leap year. According to him, in the distant past feasts were exactly correlated with the agricultural cycle, but as time went by they began to get out of phase, until they had lost their agricultural significance. Although Graulich's ideas are suggestive, it is difficult to imagine that Mesoamericans had created an entire complex ritual calendar that would have coincided with nature during only a relatively short period.

The principal noncalendric rituals involved the most important moments in life (birth, school consecration, marriage, military honors, death), collective responses to catastrophes (defeats in war, floods, droughts, earthquakes), and supplications provoked by events considered to presage ill fortune (comets, eclipses).

Religion was used to communicate because it was thought that the gods hungered for adoration and greatly desired human goods. The most common type of relationship involved offerings. By making an offering, the worshiper asked the gods for help or thanked them for a favor received. The offering most desired by the gods was human blood, which is the reason why worshipers gave their own blood or delivered victims to be sacrificed. Human sacrifices were partly payment for divine gifts and partly intended to sustain the motion of the cosmos. In order to accomplish the sacrifices, many victims were ritually converted into vessels for divine forces and, after they were converted into god-humans, were sacrificed during feasts. Their death precipitated the cyclic rebirth of the gods, who were renewed by death. As we have discussed, particularly among the Mexicas, military expansion in Central Mexico contributed to a religious fervor, particularly for human sacrifice.

Mesoamerican religion differed from religions that emphasize condemnation/salvation, focusing instead on life on earth. Death was not seen as a passage into true existence but as the beginning of the fragmentation of what had been a whole and complete human being. According to the Mexicas, the animic force in the heart went into the beyond, to a place that varied depending on the conditions and cause of death. People who died an ordinary death went to the World of the Dead. Warriors who died in battle and women who died during their first birth went to the House of the Sun. Those who died through water (were drowned or struck by lightning, or died from dropsy, buboes, or leprosy), went to the Place of Tlaloc. Babies who had tasted no food other than mother's milk before dying went to the Nursemaid Tree Place. It was possible for the final destiny to coincide with an individual's moral behavior, but this was considered to be a consequence of entering the domain of a god, the same god that caused the death.

Magic is based on humans' coercing supernatural beings into acting. The Mexicas developed two techniques of magic that deserve special mention. The first was communication using a discourse called *nahuallatolli*, or "language of the occult," which was, and remains, extremely difficult to understand but was logical and direct in terms of what it was trying to accomplish. This discourse, to a large extent, used a nomenclature that immediately put its participants on a supernatural plane. When their imperceptible aspect was emphasized, everyone (the sorcerer, his client, the aggressors, and the helpers) was placed on the same level. Some names clearly referred directly to the time of creation, because beings were invoked by their secret name—the one that corresponded to the day on which they were created. For example, if the process involved a tree or a piece of wood, the name 1 Water—corresponding to the day in the primordial cycle on which trees were created—was used. If fire was involved, the name 4 Reed was used. The sorcerer gave himself a divine name that would give him an advantageous position. The second technique involved a journey to the world of the gods, which the sorcerer thought was accomplished by sending out one of his animic essences. This was most often done by using psychotropics. The sorcerer imagined that he was acting in the realm of the gods, with the conviction that his intervention in mythical time/space would have an effect on earth. Journeys to the other time/space were considered to be extremely dangerous and were dangerous in reality, because of the harm that could be done by ingesting drugs. Usually, this technique was used only by expert sorcerers.

Magic was used relatively often. It was used in medicine as well as in controlling weather phenomena, particularly rain and hail. Ordinary people used it in work such as planting, cutting down trees, hunting, fishing, making lime, and extracting combs from a beehive. However, they needed help from specialists in rituals such as inaugurating a new home or taking a steam bath. The most prominent and feared area was witchcraft, which was replete with specific techniques. One of these techniques—which was not always used for the antisocial purposes of witchcraft—was nahualism. Nahual sorcerers believed, for example, that one of their souls could take over the body of an animal or a ball of fire in order to move unseen around enemies.

Divination utilized four main techniques: the ecstatic voyage; isonomy— the manipulation of objects whose appearance or movements were thought to mirror, as a microcosm, the macrocosm of cosmic reality; the use of the divinatory calendar in conjunction with observing the skies; and the interpretation of dreams. Through an ecstatic voyage, the diviner believed that he would reach the upper heavens, where the eternal present reigned and it was possible to see the past, present, and future of humans. For example, during one medical procedure, called *pahini* ("he who takes the medicine"), the curer ingested a psychotropic and discovered the origin of the patient's illness while in the ecstatic state.

A variety of objects were used in divination by isonomy, some of the most common being maize kernels and knotted cords. The diviner cast kernels of maize or knotted cords onto a cloth or whirled the kernels in a container with water in the belief that the process he was trying to influence would develop in a way parallel with these objects, which he considered equivalent. In divination by casting corn, for example, the parts of the patient's body corresponded to the maize kernels, and the position they finally had on the cloth was a diagnosis of the patient's condition.

Divination using the divinatory calendar involved considerably more mathematical computation than astronomical observation. The specialist determined which gods were involved in each time unit and then weighed their actions and their powers in order to calculate the resulting fate. Sources mention the existence of books for interpreting dreams, but only small fragmens of their contents remain. Divination was a field for specialists who were often sorcerers, but the handling of the calendar was done by prestigious priests who specialized in books of omens and astronomy.

OAXACA IN THE POSTCLASSIC

Oaxaca is one of the areas of Mesoamerica in which the political fragmentation that characterized the Postclassic was most clearly evident. This process of fragmentation (called "balkanization" by some scholars because of a characteristic proliferation of small, hostile states) began between A.D. 800 and 900. The Postclassic in Oaxaca not only led to a fragmentation of territory, endemic wars, and the spreading of the system of matrimonial alliances between elites, but also to other significant events including a population explosion and cultural diversification. The cultural diversity of the area is reflected in its diverse linguistics. When the Spanish arrived, there were speakers of nine Oaxacan family languages (Amuzgo, Chatino, Chocho, Ixcatec, Mazatec, Cuicatec, Mixtec, Trique, and Zapotec) and two Mixe family languages (Mixe and Zoque), as well as speakers of Chontal, Huave, and Nahuatl, living in the Oaxaca area. This linguistic mosaic, contrary to what might be supposed, did not inhibit social contacts at the time. On the contrary, archaeology shows an unusual increase in the interchange of goods and ideas that daily transcended ethnic and political boundaries, enriching the shared cultural substratum.

Apart from these general observations about the Postclassic, we can say little with certainty about the history and geography of most of the fourteen geographic provinces of Oaxaca. In contrast with the abundant literature on the Mixtecs and Zapotecs, there are relatively few studies on the other societies at the time. The fullest archaeological information on the period between A.D. 800/900 and 1530 comes from the Oaxaca Valley (Monte Albán Phase V), the Mixteca Alta (Natividad Phase), and the Isthmus of Tehuantepec (Aguada and Ulam Phases). This information is complemented by the prehispanic Mixtec codices, the *Relaciones geográficas* written at the end of the sixteenth century, and the works of friars such as Francisco de Burgoa. Without a doubt, the most complete picture, both synchronically and diachronically, is provided by the records on Mixtec society. It is lamentable that we do not have similar information on the Zapotecs. However, we should point out that, because of their long shared history, even fragmentary Zapotec data show some political and social similarities with data on the Mixtecs.

We know that the Mixtec kingdoms, like contemporaneous societies in the Andes, were fundamentally self-sufficient because they included different territories that lay in ecosystems at different altitudes. This allowed them access to all kinds of resources from both tropical and highland zones. The total area of these kingdoms was usually small, however; a kingdom could often be traversed on foot, from one end to the other, in a day.

Even though in certain situations the Mixtec kingdoms could unite into confederations such as Tilantongo-Teozacoalco and Coixtlahuaca-Yanhuitlán, each one was an independent entity with its population settled in its capital and in satellite settlements of different sizes. Although some Postclassic capitals were located on hilltops, most were located on the lower slopes of fertile valleys, almost always close to important rivers and alluvial lands. Because these settlements were vulnerable to external attacks, fortresses were built in higher locations to guard the city.

The capital was the political, religious, and commercial seat of the kingdom, numerous classes living together there in a hierarchical system that we believe was more complex than the system that existed in Classic times. The many social classes that are mentioned in the sources can be arranged into four broad groups: the king (*yya*) and nobles (*dzayya yya*); the free people (*tay ñuu*); the tenant farmers (*tay situndayu*) and servants (*tay sinoquachi*); and the slaves (*dahasaha*).

The yya, who were at the top of the pyramid, legitimated their position of maximum privilege by claiming descent from divine warriors. According to the documents, some years after being engendered by the gods, Quetzalcoatl was sent to earth for the purpose of establishing the Mixtec dynasties. He created four divine warriors in the mythical Apoala by tearing off branches from Mexican bald cypresses that were growing by the side of a river. Then Quetzalcoatl had the warriors marry Puma Serpent and Jaguar Serpent's daughters, thus establishing four dynasties, one for each corner of the earth.

In order to continue this direct divine descent and a legitimate right to rule, a yya had to marry his sons to the daughters of another yya. Invariably, the male heir to the throne had to marry several women of equal rank, who came to live in his father's kingdom. This system of patrilocal polygyny created an intricate web of matrimonial alliances between many kingdoms while guaranteeing the autonomy of every royal house.

The yya could also have temporary liaisons with the daughters of the nobles, or dzaya yya. Once they were pregnant, the women returned to their homes and were soon married to men of their rank. The political purpose of this practice was the strengthening of vertical social ties. The king shared his semidivine nature with his "sons" and, in return, received their loyalty and their help in military, administrative, judicial, and priestly affairs. The dzaya yya were a heterogenous group, including individuals who ranged from members of the royal council to leaders of *siqui* (an institution similar to the calpulli). A dzaya yya achieved this status either by inheritance or through personal achievements for the collective good. Apparently, the dzaya yya also extended their kinship relationships to the next lower hierarchical rank by transitory sexual relationships with plebeian women.

The free commoners, tay ñuu, lived together in *siquis,* kin-based organizations whose members had a common divine ancestor and collective rights over the land they lived on as well as shared obligations toward their gods. Internally, as Rodolfo Pastor has defined it, the siqui was a clan organization composed of a number of extensive monogamous families headed by a leader whose authority came from his ancestry. Among his principal duties were organizing worship of the patron deity of the siqui and military leadership. He was paid collectively by the group.

The principal occupation of siqui members was agriculture, either irrigation or seasonal. At the same time they carried out many domestic activities as well as a characteristic trade, which involved the siqui in local and regional exchange systems. Mixtec crafts, renowned for their quality throughout Mesoamerica, included cotton cloth dyed with cochineal; polished polychrome ceramics; gold and silver jewelry; copper adornments and tools; small jadeite, rock-crystal, and travertine sculptures; turquoise mosaics; and the finest bone and shell carvings.

There is less information about the third and fourth social categories. We know that tenants and servants were people who had lost their rights over land and had to serve the nobles. The slaves (dahasaha, literally "hand-foot") were men with practically no rights, who could also be sacrificed.

We currently have a respectable amount of information about political events in the Mixtec domains and a lesser amount about events in the lives of their Zapotec neighbors. Basically, our information about the Mixtecs comes from the *Nuttall, Bodley, Selden I* and *II, Colombino, Becker I* and *II, Vindobonensis,* and *Sánchez Solís* codices as well as many other pictographic documents and relations written in colonial times. Because of the pioneering work of Alfonso Caso and his successors, such as Mary Elizabeth Smith, we can read long passages of Mixtec history with some confidence. These passages deal principally with the dynastic and military history of local rulers: births, marriages, alliances, rites of passage, conquests, political assassinations, and royal deaths.

Among all the Mixtec histories the most important, because of their implications at the regional level, are those dealing with 8 Deer Jaguar Claw (A.D. 1011–1063). This ruler was born in Tilantongo, in one of the most distinguished lineages of the Mixteca Alta, but, unfortunately, was not in the direct line of succession to the throne. Thus, according to some versions, at age nineteen he took over the kingdom of Tututepec, one of Tilantongo's dependencies, which he later converted into a strong expansionist capital. According to other versions of the story, 8 Deer had his uncle and seven other relatives executed, all of whom had legitimate claims to the throne of Tilantongo. With no further obstacles, he assumed power in Tilantongo along with that he held in Tututepec. Whichever version is accurate, at that time 8 Deer began a new stage in Mixtec history by conquering more than seventy surrounding kingdoms. Apparently, these conquests did not involve the replacement of local governments but only their acknowledgement of being subordinate and the periodic payment of tribute. When 8 Deer was thirty-three, after he defeated the prestigious kingdom of Acatepec, he went to Tollan to get a nose perforation and to place a jewel in it as a symbol of his new status as a great lord and warrior. By the time of his death, practically all the towns of the Mixteca Alta and the Coast comprised a single territory subject to Tilantongo and Tututepec. The ephemeral Mixtec unity ended when he was killed either by a nephew or by the rulers of a kingdom he wanted to conquer. His successors tried, not always successfully, to use force or the customary marriage alliances in attempts to recreate the old regime.

The Postclassic history of the Oaxaca Valley is less clear. It is surprising how many basic questions are still unanswered after several decades of intensive investigation. For example, we still do not know for certain who built well-known centers such as Mitla and Yagul; who made the G3M Grey ceramics; or the relative political strength of the Zapotecs and the Mixtecs in the region during the five hundred years of the Postclassic. The main challenge for specialists on the region is to outline events after the fall of Monte Albán and to assess the importance of cultural continuity relative to the influx of new groups into the Oaxaca Valley.

The information in the sixteenth-century *Relaciones geográficas* is not sufficient to characterize the nature of Mixtec influence. For example, one of these relaciones mentions the arranging of two marriages with nobles from the Mixteca Alta and the Zapotec kingdom of Zaachila (Teozapotlan). The first, around 1280, involved the ruler of Zaachila; the second, shortly before the conquest, the sister-in-law of one of the rulers of Zaachila. This last marriage led to the settlement of primarily agricultural Mixtecs next to the new couple at Sa'a Yucu (Cuilapan). Years later, the inhabitants of Sa'a Yucu fought with Zaachila, won, and made them change the location of the capital to the distant Tehuantepec. The sources tell us that after this victory the Mixtecs conquered almost all the towns in the Valley, including Mitla. Another relación, however, states that Mitla was a Zapotec religious center and was never conquered by the Mixtecs. What this tells us is that the natives of each place told the writer of each relación their own biased version of local history, which greatly complicates the task of modern investigators.

Archaeological data are also not conclusive. Among the many relevant finds, Monte Albán Tomb 7 and Zaachila Tomb 1 stand out. The human remains and offerings found in Monte Albán Tomb 7 probably date to the fourteenth or fifteenth century but were buried in a funerary chamber that was built much earlier, during Monte Albán's splendor. The importance of this site lies in the fact that purely Mixtec-style objects such as gold and silver jewels, carved bones, turquoise mosaics, obsidian ear spools, and so forth, were placed next to more than a dozen individuals. The Zaachila tomb, besides its rich funerary offering of Mixtec materials, was decorated with the images of two individuals whose names are repeated in the codices of the town of Zaachila. Despite these data we should be cautious, because the origin of the offerings does not necessarily correspond to the ethnic origin of the buried individuals.

The gorgeous architecture of Mitla and Yagul (see plan 9) does not shed much light on the ethnic composition of these sites. Although some

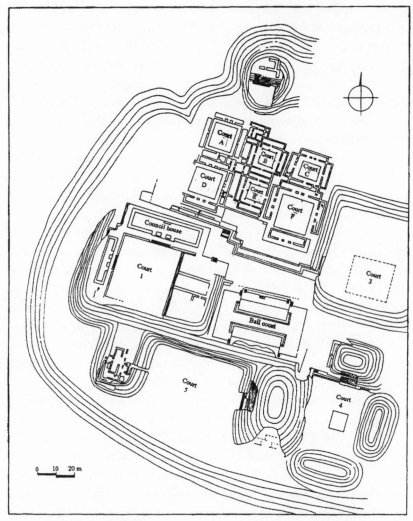

Plan 9. Yagul Archaeological Zone, Oaxaca. Oaxaca Area. Postclassic period.
(Adapted from I. Bernal)

of their characteristic elements—such as stepped frets and tableros in
"doble escapulario" (double scapulary) style—were already present in
Zapotec architecture in Monte Albán Phase II, other elements—large
columns and monolithic lintels, marvelously assembled stone mosaics,
the general arrangement of rooms, and codex-type paintings—have no
antecedents in the region. These architectural elements were not found

in the Mixteca regions either, but the murals of the Church Group in Mitla are typical of Mixtec codices.

These difficult questions about Mixtec influence in the Oaxaca Valley have led to two opposing positions, which have occasionally been debated too forcefully. On one side are authors such as Alfonso Caso, Ignacio Bernal, and John Paddock, who argue that the culture known as Monte Albán V was the result of one of several Mixtec invasions of the Oaxaca Valley. These massive settlements are seen to have eclipsed the culture of Zapotec towns, absorbing some of their characteristics and developing unique characteristics. Defenders of the opposing position, such as Kent V. Flannery and Joyce Marcus, hold that Monte Albán V is an evolutionary development from Monte Albán IV, which means that the creators of this culture were Zapotec. This second group of scholars would explain the presence of Mixtec styles and objects in the Oaxaca Valley as exchanges and imitations of fashions. In this view, the Mixtec presence was limited solely to the interchange of women among the elites.

This polemic is far from settled today. There is considerable evidence for and against each position, which suggests that the historical events were much more complicated than those proposed by either hypothesis. The Mixtec presence is undeniable in the Oaxaca Valley, but an absolute Mixtec hegemony over the Zapotecs is unsupported by the evidence. Future studies will likely lead to the formulation of more complex models of a changing time, explaining the historical and archaeological panorama in terms of intense processes of exchange, imitation, cultural hybridization, and ethnic fusion.

When the Mexicas came to Oaxaca, the final chapter of the Postclassic history of the area began. After 1450 no Zapotec or Mixtec capital was able to repeat 8 Deer's unification. The three and one-half centuries following the death of this famous ruler were a time of endless internal warfare, which rapidly sapped the strength of any kingdom that achieved supremacy. This chronic condition of fragmentation and antagonism made the Mixtecs and Zapotecs easy victims of the excan tlatoloyan. The repeated military campaigns waged after 1458 by the Mexicas and their allies had two strategic objectives. The first was to conquer the kingdoms that lay along the commercial route between Tenochtitlan and Tochtepec and to control Tochtepec, where the roads leading to Xicalanco and Soconusco crossed. The other objective was to obtain the rich Oaxacan tribute of gold, greenstones, turquoise, cochineal, and blankets and other cotton goods, in addition to the usual maize, beans, and chia (*Salvia hispanica*).

The clear superiority of the forces of the Triple Alliance was reflected in a long chain of victories over six decades. Only a few capitals were able to withstand these attacks and remain independent. Examples of these were the Mixtec kingdom of Tututepec and the Zapotec kingdom of Tehuantepec. The ruler of Tehuantepec, Cocijoeza, had to seek the support of thousands of Mixtecs from Achiotla in order to heroically defeat the Mexica armies at the famous besieged fortress of Guiengiola. When Ahuítzotl, the tlatoani at Tenochtitlan, learned of the defeat, he opted to solve the problem by marrying his daughter to Cocijoeza.

The Mexicas had difficulty collecting their tribute. The sources mention repeated refusals to pay, armed rebellions, and assassinations of Mexica merchants and ambassadors. The response to this was a brutal reprisal, which sent an enormous number of captives to be sacrificed, greatly exaggerated the tribute load, eliminated local nobles, and imposed rulers.

WESTERN MESOAMERICA IN THE POSTCLASSIC

The West is the most culturally diverse area of Mesoamerica. Due to its abundant multiple natural resources it attained a considerable population density, but its peoples were usually grouped in political units that controlled relatively small territories. Otto Schöndube blames this characteristic organization on difficulties in communication within the region as a consequence of the difficult terrain as well as on the fact that many of the units were practically self-sufficient because their ecosystems provided complementary resources.

During the Postclassic a large number of small kingdoms in the West engaged in continual warfare. Usually, the smaller settlements clustered around centers that had attained about five thousand inhabitants. Some of these centers controlled small irrigation systems and built large buildings, though they never reached the size of structures found in other Mesoamerican areas. Among these western centers were Amapa and Ixtlán on the Nayarit River, Autlán and Etzatlán in Jalisco, and El Chanal in Colima. With five large mounds and a ball court, El Chanal was almost an urban area. Some scholars, such as Weigand, point out that many settlements seem to have been hierarchically assembled into sizable political units. This seems to have been the case in the Sayula-Atoyac-Zacoalco zone and in the Atemajac Valley.

The Postclassic in the West—which some scholars believe began about A.D. 600, when the Shaft Tomb Tradition disappeared—was characterized by expanded relationships with the exterior. As a consequence of the terrible droughts that ended the Chalchihuites Culture between 800 and 900, the northern area expelled its farmers, leading to an increase in population in the West and the formation of a long frontier with the hunter-gatherers who occupied the vacated territories. The arrival of the northern farmers brought new cultures as well as demographic pressure to the West, which might have encouraged more complex political organization among groups such as the Tarascans.

West Mesoamerica also established relationships with South America. Based on analyses by Dorothy Hosler, we know that gold, silver, and copper metallurgy, probably from Ecuador, arrived in West Mesoamerica about A.D. 800. As a result, this area led Mesoamerica in metalworking. Copper was so important in the West that it was used to make not only luxury objects such as hawk bells, ornaments, and depilators but also *coas* (digging sticks), axes for hewing trees, chisels for carving wood, fishhooks, and projectile points for hunting and warfare. Bronze technology arrived, apparently from Peru, sometime later in A.D. 1200.

There were also cultural exchanges between West Mesoamerica and Central Mexico. One of the clearest examples is the beautiful polychrome decoration on ceramics that was made along a coastal strip from Sinaloa north to Jalisco. These ceramic designs include elaborate motifs of feathers, stepped frets, feathered serpents, and many other deeply symbolic religious designs, painted in as many as six colors and using the pseudocloisonné technique. Sites with large quantities of this ceramic include Guasave, at the northern end of Sinaloa, and—far to the south—Amapa, next to the Grande de Santiago River in Nayarit. Sumptuary copper goods, particularly awls, hawk bells, and rings, are found with the polychrome ceramics in both places.

These fine objects have been included in the so-called Aztatlán Complex, which is thought to have lasted for a lengthy period of time, from A.D. 600 or 900 until A.D. 1300. Its designs are similar to those found in the contemporary ceramics of Tula and Culhuacan as well as to designs in pottery from Cholula and images in the Mixtec-Puebla codices. These resemblances have led to several hypotheses. Some scholars propose migrations from Central Mexico to the Coast. Others posit the existence of a coastal commercial corridor, controlled by Central Mexico, that allowed communication between Mesoamerica and Oasisamerica. Others hold that the influence went the other way, with a West Mexican style diffusing to the other areas of Mesoamerica.

Basically, the nature of these relationships is a part of the problems associated with one of the great enigmas of the Postclassic in the West—the Aztatlán Complex. The usual explanation is that this ceramic complex was made by societies linked by the commercial route of copper from the South and turquoise from the Anasazi territory. Both ideas—the existence of the Aztatlán Complex and of the coastal corridor—are extremely suggestive and have been repeated for decades; however, they are quite flimsy. First, too many different types of ceramics have been included in the Aztatlán Complex. This means that it has been defined in terms of different manufactures, from different times, distributed over a large radius, during an enormous time period. Second, although it is probable that a Pacific coastal route existed, sufficient archaeological evidence to confirm it has not yet been found. To sum up, any explanation for these observations is premature until a thorough archaeological investigation has been completed.

Despite the political fragmentation of West Mexico, an important unifying factor developed in the second half of the Postclassic: the Tarascan State. At its peak the Tarascan State occupied 75,000 km^2, most of it in what is now the state of Michoacán, bordered by the Lerma River on the north and the Balsas Basin to the south. It is an ecologically diverse area, including timber-rich sierras; a temperate region about 2,000 meters high in the valleys surrounding Lake Pátzcuaro; a tropical region of diverse flora and fauna; and a coastal region (although only a small portion of this region was dominated by the Tarascans).

The Tarascan State was consolidated about 1470 and maintained its rule until the time of the Spanish conquest. We are familiar with its history through a document that is exceptional not only because it gives details about one of the peoples of West Mesoamerica but also because it is a text of great historiographical value. This document, the *Relación de las ceremonias y ritos y población y gobierno de los indios de la provincia de Michoacán,* was probably written by Friar Jerónimo de Alcalá about 1541. It was based on oral narrations by the Tarascans themselves and had a good number of illustrations. Unfortunately, the first part of the manuscript, which dealt with religion, was lost. The second part is the long annual peroration in which the chief priest tells the history of the Tarascans, from the remote founder of the dynasty up to the current ruler. The third part contains answers the natives gave to the Franciscan's questions about the social and political organization of the Tarascans. This work is supplemented by important sources such as the *Relaciones geográficas* of the sixteenth century and other colonial documents, among which the *Lienzo de Jucutácato*—a pictograph with Nahuatl annotations that describes the migration of a group of metal craftsmen from their mythical place of origin—stands out.

The principal political arena for Tarascan history was the Lake Pátzcuaro region, where the Uacúsechas, or "Eagles," arrived at the end of the twelfth or beginning of the thirteenth century (see map 17). Before the arrival of the Tarascans the region looked like most of West Mesoamerica during the Postclassic, with a linguistically heterogeneous population living in small independent chiefdoms that alternately participated in commerce, alliances, and war among themselves. The principal languages spoken at that time were Tarascan or Purépecha, Nahuatl, and Matlatzinca or Pirinda.

The lake and its surroundings provided its inhabitants with a wide variety of products, with exchanges between island and mainland dwellers of fishing, hunting, logging, and farming products. Xarácuaro and Pacandan were the largest island towns. The most important mainland towns were Ihuatzio, Tzintzuntzan, and Curínguaro. Elsewhere, Pareo and Záueto were famous as commercial centers where the small fish called *charal,* copper, tropical products, and salt from the Colima Coast were traded. It is likely, as Wigberto Jiménez Moreno has proposed, that the Uacúsechas came from an area near the lake that is today the division between Guanajuato, Jalisco, and Michoacán. The Uacúsechas describe themselves in their history as Chichimecs, nomadic hunter-gatherers. The *Relación de Michoacán* states that the Uacúsechas learned to farm after settling in the region. Today, some scholars doubt this Chichimec origin. There is archaeological evidence that, at least

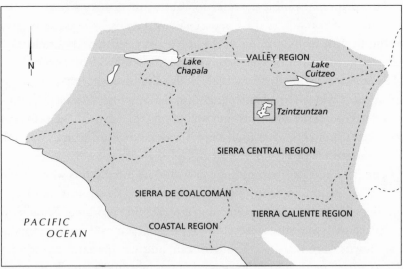

Map 17. The Lake Pátzcuaro region and the extent of the Tarascan domain.
(Adapted from D. D. Brand)

since A.D. 1300, the Uacúsechas had fully Mesoamerican agricultural settlements.

Slowly, because of their aggressiveness and battle skills, the Uacúsechas became actors in regional politics. However, they were hindered politically by their weak unification and by continual internal disputes. Their first attempt at unity was the establishment of a religious center at a location miraculously revealed by the gods. Called Pátzcuaro, it was consecrated to the patron god of the Uacúsechas, Curicaueri. This attempt at unity did not work, as Pátzcuaro itself soon became the object of disputes.

The *Relación de Michoacán* attributes the second and final attempt at unification to a heroic leader whose biography fills a good part of the document: Tanácuri. Together with his son and two nephews, Tanácuri summoned the Uacúsechas, along with other agricultural peoples, to launch an ambitious conquest. His project was aided by a resurgence of regional conflicts. Little by little, the allies conquered the lake and its surroundings. They then expanded in all directions, seeking salt works; copper, silver, and cinnabar mines; gold placers; and tropical products. The Uacúsechas fought for twenty years in the name of the powerful solar god, Curicaueri. Their forces reached Tetela del Río in the tropical South, the neighborhood of Sayula in the West, and Zacatula on the Coast.

Tanácuri, the prime mover behind the Tarascan State, died before it became a reality. When the Tarascan allies triumphed about 1450, they set up three capitals on the eastern side of the lake. Each of Tanácuri's assistants was installed in one of them as the *irecha*, or king, and the three jointly governed the vast conquered territories. Tzintzuntzan, a city protected by the lunar goddess of the old farmers, Xarátanga, was awarded to one of Tanácuri's nephews, Tangáxoan. Tanácuri's son, Hiquíngare, was awarded Pátzcuaro, which was consecrated to Curicaueri. His other nephew, Hiripan, ruled Ihuatzio, which was protected by an avatar of Curicaueri.

The proximity of the three cities, all on the shores of Lake Pátzcuaro, centralized the power of the Tarascans. The Tarascan coalition had greater political control over towns in its sphere than the excan tlatoloyan of the Basin of Mexico because, in addition to receiving tribute, the Tarascan center intervened directly in local politics. Generally, when a city was conquered, one of the captains of the winning army was appointed governor. Each governor was succeeded by a close relative who had to be confirmed by the central government. On the other hand cities that joined without a struggle kept their own natural lords, who became part of the great bureaucratic apparatus. In the new political organization four high-ranking nobles were in charge of controlling the four borders of the Tarascan State.

According to Helen Perlstein Pollard and Shirley Gorenstein, there may have been another difference between the excan tlatoloyan and the Tarascan empire. According to them, the Pátzcuaro Basin was not an urban area, because it did not have the agricultural potential to sustain that kind of population density. They calculate a population of 60,000–100,000 for the Basin when the Spanish arrived.

The Tarascan expansion was accompanied by a reorganization in land tenure. The new owner was Curicaueri, and his representatives arrogated the right to dispose of the land. Conquered farmers kept some of their fields, but only by paying tribute. In addition they had to cultivate the rest of their lands for the benefit of the temples, governors, and distinguished warriors.

In the course of their expansionist wars the Tarascans encountered the armies of the excan tlatoloyan, resulting in a confrontation between the two great powers of the time. These encounters were particularly bloody. The Tarascans had the advantages of centralized power and the use of bronze weapons, at least by their captains. The Mexicas and the Tarascans faced off, in different places, from the middle of the fifteenth century on, with one of the most famous battles at Taximaroa. Neither of the armies achieved a significant change in borders, but they left battlefields covered with corpses.

About 1480, for a variety of reasons, Tzitzispandácuare, the irecha of Tzintzuntzan, managed to become *cazonci*, or sole leader of the Tarascans, thus ending the joint rule of the three capitals. The major religious symbol of the Uacúsechas, the image of Curicaueri, was transferred from Pátzcuaro to Tzintzuntzan. The maximum concentration of political power in the Postclassic was achieved at this time.

Immediately before the Spanish conquest, the Tarascan State ruled a heterogeneous population of 750,000 to 1,300,000 people. Its capital, Tzintzuntzan, had between 25,000 and 35,000 inhabitants, in an area of almost 7 km². Its ceremonial center, located on a large natural promontory in front of the lake, had an enormous 440-by-260-meter platform supporting five *yácatas* placed in a row. Each of the yácatas, platforms combining truncated pyramids and cones, had a wooden temple on its top. The five temples were consecrated to Curicaueri, the solar god, and to his four brothers, the Tiripeme, who held up the sky at the four ends of the world: Xungápeti (yellow), Turupten (white), Caheri (black) and Cuarencha (red).

THE GULF IN THE POSTCLASSIC

There were many participants in the Postclassic history of the Gulf Area. The Huastecs had been in the northern end of the area for a long time; other groups arrived much later. Some of the new groups, such as the Otomis and Nahuas, came from Central Mexico, fleeing disturbances in the Postclassic. Quite a few of the arrivals from the West were Chichimecs, whose initial migrations had begun in distant northern lands. There were also migrants from Central Mexico, who had been displaced by northerners coming into the area. Finally, the Mexicas came, conquering the inhabitants of the Gulf and making them tributaries. The sources document invasions; occupations; noble marriages; and conquests by Toltecs, Nonoalcas, Olmec-Xicalancas, Chichimecs, Tlaxcaltecs, and Mexicas. There is also archaeological evidence of the effects of these repeated incursions on the architecture, ceramics, and sculpture of the area.

Historically, two peoples stand out among this multiplicity. The Huastecs occupied the territory from the mouth of the Cazones to the mouth of the Pánuco River as well as the mountainous region next to the coastal plain. The other, the Totonacs, also filled a wide strip of the Sierra Madre Oriental, extending from the mouth of the Tuxpan River to the Antigua River. It is probable that the Huastec and Totonac territories overlapped in the region between the Tuxpan and Cazones Rivers.

Thousands of years ago, the Huastecs had split off from the rest of the peoples in their Maya language family. For many centuries they maintained contacts with the Veracruz and Tabasco area in the South, but these diminished during the Classic, when Central Mexican influence came into the Huasteca. During the Postclassic these links, particularly links with Tula, seem to have increased, as can be seen in the architecture of Huastec sites such as Tepetzintla, Tamuín, Castillo de Teayo, and Tula, where Huastec ceramics have been found. Additionally, many commercial objects such as sumptuary copper objects, clay pipes, seals, spindle whorls, incised shells, and figurines with wheels are found along a wide corridor that passes through Tula, extending from the Gulf Coast to the Sinaloa Coast of the Pacific. The Huastecs also had contacts with the Mississippi Basin in the southeastern United States, as shown by the similarities in the motifs on luxury items in both places.

After the tenth century several Huastec sites—such as Tabuco, Tanhuijo, Cacahuatengo, and Metlaltoyuca—grew, becoming settlements with plazas, rectangular structures, and mounds up to thirty meters high. The Huastec sites attained their peak in the Las Flores Phase. There was a particular style of architecture in the Huasteca at this time that had many ceremonial buildings with circular bases, found in places such as Las Flores, Pavón, and Tancol. Despite abundant harvests of maize and cotton in the fertile Huastec lands, the population centers never grew large enough to form real states.

Huastec ceramics were also unique. They followed local styles, which were characterized by high-quality firing and cream, black and white on cherry, black on cream, and black on white. The black-on-white and black-on-cream Huastec ceramics were especially popular in the Late Postclassic. The unusual shapes of the ceramic vessels, which resembled nothing else in Mesoamerica, were like teapots with vertical spouts pointed upward and with flat, ribbonlike handles. Among Huastec fine ceramics, we should include the profusely decorated polychromes vessels with many religious symbols, which were supposedly influenced by the Mixtecs. Significant pieces of these ceramics have been found in San Luis Potosí.

However, it is in sculpture that Huastec art achieves its greatest originality and beauty. Carved stones range from freestanding pieces to slabs decorated with flat reliefs. Their stylized, linear treatment of the human body makes some of the figures appear to be those of adolescents. These figures also frequently sport extensive and complicated tatoos. Many of the sculptures have adornments identifying them with Quetzalcoatl or with death gods, such as the conical hat characteristic of wind gods and the folded paper fan that gods of the underworld wear around their necks. Some sculptures are double, with a second, often skeletal, body affixed to the figure's back. A frequent sculptural motif is a strange elderly person whose bowed body rests on a thick rod used as a cane. Despite the artistic vigor of these sculptures that are unique to the Huasteca, its stone sculpture generally showed strong influence from Central Mexico, particularly in the imagery related to deities. The religious symbols of the Huasteca also influenced the visual arts and ritual representations of the Mexicas. The most skillfully carved pieces are delicate, lacelike seashells. In sites such as Tamuín, murals on frets depict bizarre images of gods, motifs that in other cultures (among them the Mixtec) were depicted in religious codices.

The continual conflict between multiple kingdoms allowed the Mexicas—who wanted the tropical products of the Huastecas, their beautiful ceramics, and their abundant supply of fine cotton textiles— to invade the area at the beginning of the fifteenth century. Tuxpan, Tzicóac, and Temapache were conquered first, followed by Huejutla, Tamuín, Tampatel, and Oxitipa.

To the south, the imposing city of El Tajín rose between the Tecolutla and Cazones Rivers. Recent archaeological interpretations propose that the city began to decline by the twelfth century and had been abandoned by the thirteenth. What role did the Totonacs have in the history of El Tajín? The question is far from being answered. As we have discussed, there are several hypotheses regarding the relationship of the Totonacs to the city. The city's erection has traditionally been attributed to the Totonacs, but new hypotheses cast doubt on this proposal, postulating that the Totonacs, coming from the Highlands on the other side of the Sierra de Puebla, arrived late to Central Veracruz (between 750 and 800). The Totonacs then settled in the mountainous spurs as well as on the coastal plain and the coast itself, and could have occupied El Tajín about one hundred years after its abandonment, erecting only a few buildings with a different style. Based on this hypothesis, other groups such as the Huastecs have been proposed as the possible inhabitants of El Tajín during its splendor. After the fall of El Tajín no other state played such a leading role in Totonac territory. In reality, with the exception of Zacatlán, the centers of the Postclassic ruled over very small territories. This was the case for Cempoala, Misantla, Tuzapan, Cuauhtochto, Cotaxtla, Quiahuiztlan, Cacahuatengo, and Tlacolula.

Nevertheless, some centers are notable for their city plans and complex urbanization. One of them, Tuzapan, on the Chicualote plateau, had cobbled streets, drains, steam baths (*temazcalli*), and monumental architecture. The most notable site is Cempoala, which was a rich city as a result of intensive agriculture made possible by canals from the Actopan River. Cempoala had about twenty thousand inhabitants, and archaeology shows that it was divided into fenced barrios with palaces, small temples, and interior plazas. The ceremonial center of the city, delineated by stone walls, included a large precinct almost seven hectares in size where the principal religious buildings were placed (see plan 10). Among these are the Great Temple, the ridiculously named Temple of the Chimneys, and the Grand Pyramid and its subsidiaries. Outside the precinct, the Temple of the Little Faces—so named because of the small clay skulls that filled its tableros—stands out. Further evidence of the Toltec influence on the region, a mortar chac mool with a red and yellow face, was found in the Temple of the Chimneys. Canals that led to the vegetable gardens and cultivated fields ran through the city. Cempoala was one of the first places in which the Spanish confronted Mesoamerican culture. According to Bernal Díaz del Castillo, the beauty of the city and its abundant vegetation earned it the Spanish name of Villaviciosa ("Fertile Town").

Totonac architecture copied some of El Tajín's elements, among them the peculiar flying cornices, the columns, and the strips decorated with mosaic frets. Later, Tuzapan and other towns of the Highlands were influenced by the Toltecs. Walls made from boulders, clay, and stucco; houses with pounded earth floors on the inside and stucco exteriors; and ball courts with stone hoops imbedded in the walls of the court all occur frequently in Totonacapan. Funerary architecture is characterized by tombs that have a scale model of a house or a temple with a palm-leaf roof on an outside platform.

Isla de Sacrificios, Cerro Montoso, Quiahuiztlan, and Tres Picos are famous for their ceramics. The pieces are characterized by the sobriety and beauty of their geometric designs, combined with their simply and deliberately drawn, stylized but naturalistic images of mammals, fish, and centipedes.

Descriptions of Totonac religion in the sources emphasize the cruel character of their rituals, the practice of cannibalism of the sacrificed, and the use of blood to make a paste that was eaten reverently by the

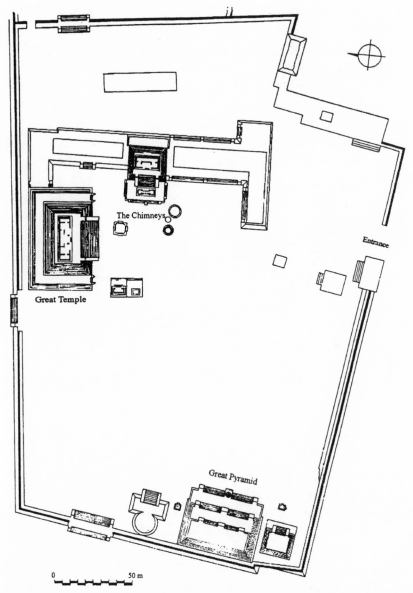

The Chimneys

Entrance

Great Temple

Great Pyramid

0 ⊢⊢⊢⊢⊢⊢⊢⊢⊣ 50 m

Plan 10. Cempoala, Veracruz. Gulf Area, Postclassic period. (Based on J. García Payón)

faithful. The principal gods were the sun, the moon, and maize dieties. A unique aspect of their funerary tradition was the burial of corpses in sacred places such as Quiahuiztlan and Isla de Sacrificios. We should point out that this practice—particularly burial in large clay pots at Isla de Sacrificios—was limited to a few corpses, probably those of very important persons. Based on this limited number, Lorenzo Ochoa claims that such sites, rather than being cemeteries, were places that preserved the remains of humans who were touched by divinity and were therefore sacred, worthy of worship, and producers of benefits for all the people.

The Totonac country was seen by the Mexicas as a tropical paradise; its wealth—the result of its exceptional production of maize, cotton, and the valuable vanilla—attracted the conquerors from Central Mexico. After their conquest Totonac multicolored textiles as well as crops from the region came as tribute to Mexico-Tenochtitlan.

SOUTHEAST MESOAMERICA IN THE POSTCLASSIC

As a result of their linguistic kinship, their contiguous territory, and their perennial interaction, the Mayas developed a cultural homogeneity that was unmatched in Mesoamerica. This does not mean that there were no significant cultural and historical differences between the Mayas of each region. In reality, the long centuries of the Postclassic were experienced differently by the inhabitants of the flat Yucatán Peninsula, the inhabitants of the sierras of Chiapas and Guatemala, and the people of the jungles of the Petén. It should be mentioned that the Petén people were not conquered by the Spanish until a century and a half after the kingdoms to the north and south of them had been defeated. Nevertheless, histories of the Maya in the Postclassic are variations of the same drama, all featuring actions of parallel characters in different scenarios, a struggle for control between groups of people with two different conceptions of power. On one side were peoples who wanted to preserve an authority based on ethnicity; on the other were innovators who, influenced by foreign ideologies, tried to put in place a broader authority that would include different ethnic groups.

We know that the first group were Mayas, but what peoples made up the second group? They were long called "Mexicans," which is not only an inadequate and confusing term but an anachronistic one. Nor are names such as Toltec, Putun Maya, or Mexica useful. We cannot use an ethnic name in the context of an event in which a great number of groups, including the Mayas, participated. For the same reason, any linguistic term would be inappropriate. We could choose a neutral term such as "westerners," based on the origin of some of these peoples, but the term would be confusing both in World and Mesoamerican histor-ical contexts. Nor can they be called "invaders," because many of them had lived for centuries in Maya territory. Thus, we find ourselves in the uncomfortable and risky position of needing to coin a new term. According to the written sources, these peoples claimed that their remote ancestors all came from the same faraway place—Zuyuá or Siwán—which, as we shall see, was mythical. Since this belief was one of their ideological pillars, however, we propose to call these peoples the Zuyuans or Siwans.

For several centuries after the end of the Classic, many waves of people migrated from the Gulf Coast to the areas of Chiapas and the Petén. Some of the clearest indications of these migrations are the early sculptures found at sites on the Pasión River, which were made by a culture that has been called hybrid (*mestiza*). J. Eric S. Thompson iden-tified their place of origin as the border area between Tabasco and Campeche and identified the invaders as Putun-Chontals, a group who were permeated by Central Mexican ideology. The invading waves followed several routes, moving toward the jungle, north to the Yucatán Peninsula, or across the course of the Chixoy River toward the high valleys of Guatemala.

Either gradually or suddenly, these people imposed a militaristic political order in which a few capitals attempted to absorb all the surrounding native cities. It was said that some of these invaders spoke a strange Maya language, practiced and preached exotic religious ideas, and had scandalous practices. In the North as well as the South the rulers of these new entities claimed to represent an individual called Feathered Serpent, and some of them actually called themselves by that name.

Because events happened in a different sequence in each of the zones of Southeast Mesoamerica, scholars focusing on the various zones have established different period divisions to describe events in each of those zones. Let us begin with the area making up most of the Yucatán Peninsula, which presents the most difficult problem in the chronology of the northern zone. Without a doubt, this is the zone for which we have the most and the best documental sources. However, the correlation between dates given in the sources and those that come from archaeological investigations poses apparently insurmountable problems. This lack of correspondence is due to a historiography that is vague, dating events unclearly. The accurate Maya Long Count system was abandoned in the Postclassic. Because power came from a different kind of relationship with the gods at that time, it was no longer necessary to record history by such an onerous and complicated method. A simplified system called "count of the katuns," in which the symbols would repeat every 256.26 years, was used instead. This calendar produced a considerable number of errors, at least in colonial documents. Even today this calendric ambiguity continues to fluster Maya scholars, whose studies contain frequent discrepancies in dates and sequences of events.

Some modern authors, based on documents from the first colonial decades, date the Early Postclassic from the arrival of the invaders, presumably Toltecs, in the tenth century to the fall of their capital, Chichén Itzá, in the middle of the thirteenth century. The Late Postclassic began at that time and lasted until the arrival of the Spanish in the sixteenth century. Miguel Rivera Dorado disagrees, seeing three periods and one transition in this zone. According to Rivera Dorado, in the first period—the Early Postclassic (1000–1200)—the strongly Toltec-influenced culture of the invaders fused with that of the Puuc region of the peninsula, Chichén Itzá predominated politically, and Sotuta ceramics were prevalent. A transitional period (1200–1300) followed, characterized by the ceramics of the Hocabá Complex. The Late Postclassic (1300–1450) followed; at that time the city of Mayapán took the place of Chichén Itzá as a hegemonic center and Tasés ceramics proliferated. Finally, according to Rivera Dorado, there was a period of cultural decline (1450–1524), beginning with the destruction of Mayapán and characterized by the definitive political fragmentation that produced numerous kingdoms in a permanent state of war. The period division promulgated in 1986 by Jeremy Sabloff and E. Wyllys Andrews is also worth mentioning. According to this system the Terminal Classic lasted for several more centuries, until the fall of Chichén Itzá. Sabloff and Andrews view Chichén Itzá as only a late northern prolongation of the Classical civilizations of the Petén, its collapse signifying a real discontinuity between them and the Postclassic societies of Mayapán and the later kingdoms.

On the basis of the contradictory colonial documents, it is believed that at the end of the tenth century the first Zuyuan wave came to the Puuc Region, occupying the formerly powerful city of Uucil Abnal (later called Chichén Itzá). The paintings and sculptures of the city show the invaders with cylindrical helmets, protected by stylized butterfly pectorals, armed with spear throwers, and adorned with dorsal disks. Some helmets have a butterfly insignia or a descending bird as a mosaic design. The spear throwers are decorated with feather tufts. In short, they are dressed like warriors from Tula. In battle scenes they are led by the Feathered Serpent, and, furthermore, the tradition associated them with a ruler called Kukulcan, which—like Quetzalcoatl—means "Feathered Serpent."

After the Zuyuans conquered the native population, the Uucil Abnals became the political power in the Puuc region. On the basis of some images of the court found in the substructure of the Temple of Warriors, we think it is possible that from that time on there was a dual Zuyuan/ Maya government. Apparently, a considerable time after the first wave, a second wave of Zuyuans arrived, made up of people called Itzás by the sources. It is difficult to determine whether they belonged to the same ethnic group as the people of the first wave. What is known for certain is that it was the second wave who changed the name of the city to Chichén Itzá. Their ruler, like was his remote ancestor, was also called Kukulkan. Some time after that, other Zuyuans established Mayapán to the west.

Another of the great puzzles of Postclassic Maya history is the existence of the famous League of Mayapán, which was composed of the three capitals that joined together to control the northern end of the peninsula: Uxmal, Chichén Itzá, and Mayapán (see map 18). Some scholars dispute the written sources, denying that the league existed, as archaeological data do not indicate that the three cities were powerful at the same time. On this basis they propose that the alliance did not involve three cities but rather three ethnic groups or dynastic lineages: Tutul Xiu, Itzá, and Cocom.

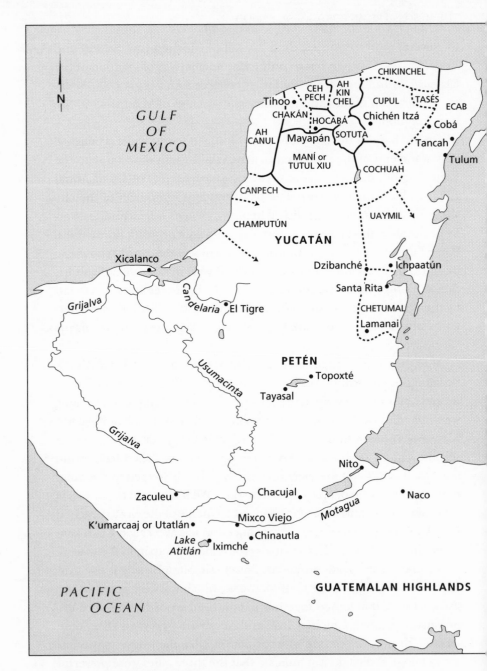

GULF
OF
MEXICO

PACIFIC
OCEAN

N

CHIKINCHEL

CEH
PECH
Tihoo
AH
KIN
CHEL
CUPUL
TASÉS
ECAB

CHAKÁN
HOCABÁ
Chichén Itzá
Cobá

AH
CANUL
Mayapán
SOTUTA
Tancah

MANÍ or
TUTUL XIU
COCHUAH
Tulum

CANPECH

UAYMIL

CHAMPUTÚN

YUCATÁN

Xicalanco
Dzibanché
Ichpaatún

Santa Rita

Grijalva
Candelaria
El Tigre
CHETUMAL

Lamanai

Usumacinta
PETÉN

Topoxté

Tayasal

Grijalva

Nito

Zaculeu
Chacujal
Naco

K'umarcaaj or Utatlán
Mixco Viejo
Motagua

Lake
Atitlán
Iximché
Chinautla

GUATEMALAN HIGHLANDS

Map 18. The Maya territory in the Postclassic period.

Whatever its nature, the league broke up because of war between its members. The Itzás of Chichén were defeated and migrated to the south, and—at the end of the thirteenth century—power passed to the Cocoms of Mayapán. Although it was a pale copy of its predecessor, Mayapán maintained its hegemony for two centuries. Architecturally, Mayapán basically copied Chichén Itzá, but it also used some purely Maya architectural elements.

Mayapán's collapse in the mid-fifteenth century clearly resulted in political fragmentation. The sources state that the Tutul Xius of Uxmal rose up against the Cocoms and that Mayapán was defeated. The political arrangement of the peninsula changed drastically, the territory splitting into seventeen kingdoms that were constantly engaged in warfare. Cultural decadence was everywhere, as the Spanish found on their arrival in Yucatán. Friar Diego de Landa's writings on Maya society correspond to this historic moment. In his *Relación de las cosas de Yucatán* he describes the use of surnames, which was not practiced by many Mesoamerican societies but which has allowed researchers to dig deeper into the social organization in the zone at that time. Surnames were derived from both the mother and the father. From the latter we know that at the time of the conquest there were approximately 250 patrilineages in Yucatán, each composed of people with quite different rank and status. The right to communal use of land was tied to patrilineage. The father's surname also regulated marriage, as two people with the same paternal surname were not allowed to marry. Furthermore, an individual could rely on assistance from anyone who had the same paternal surname, whether the two were acquainted or lived far away from each other.

The population was divided into nobles and commoners, nobles filling the most important public posts and making up the warriors and priests of higher rank. Nobles managed large-scale trade and benefited from the best lands. Some positions belonged to particular lineages. Many of the commoners were free farmers with the right to use lands of their patrilineage, but they were obligated to pay tribute, partly in the form of labor. At the lowest level were the slaves, whose status was a result of their committing a crime or being captured during war or was inherited.

Immediately prior to the conquest, authority still resided in a hereditary nobility. Almost all the political units were ruled by a king, or *halach uinich* ("true man"), who had inherited his position from his patrilineage. He was very powerful, but his prerogatives were tempered by a council of noble elders. He lived in the capital sustained by his subjects' tribute and the yield of his rich lands, some of which were cacao plantations. The halach uinich exercised control over his dependent villages through chiefs he appointed from lineages close to his own. These were the *bata-boob*, "ax holders," each aided by a council of influential men. The *batab* was the military commander of his area, although he shared command with a curious functionary who held the post for only three years, the *nacom.* During his term, the nacom observed so many dietary and sexual restrictions that it is possible he was considered to be a human/god with transitory powers. In some exceptional circumstances a batab performed the duties of a halach uinich, as occurred in Cupul and Ah Canul.

Interestingly, there was a code of elegant riddles in the language used by rulers that the halach uinich used to test his bataboob. This game provided a way to demonstrate a noble education and a knowledge of the mythical origins of nobility, who were descended from Zuyuá. The code was expressly called "the language of Zuyuá."

Despite its political fragmentation and armed conflicts, at the end of the Postclassic the Yucatán Peninsula had a lively commercial traffic, as shown by archaeological and documental sources. The eastern coast, composed at that time of the kingdoms of Ecab, Uaymil, and Chetumal as well as the islands of Cancún, Mujeres, and Cozumel, had an active commercial life. This can be seen in the prosperity of places such as Tulum, Ichpatún, Tancah, Xelhá, Akumal, Xcaret, and San Gervasio. In addition, conquerors such as Francisco de Montejo and Alfonso Dávila saw the wealth of Chetumal and Bacalar. These two cities were exchange points that benefited from the old Caribbean coastal route that linked Xicalanco and ports on the Gulf of Honduras in a coastal trade. Yucatán was the greatest producer of sea salt in Mesoamerica. It also exported cotton, honey, copal, rubber, dry and smoked fish, and slaves. It received gold and silver jewels, copper objects (hawk bells, axes, dishes), rabbit-hair yarn, and other goods from Central Mexico; precious stones and feathers from the Maya Highlands; and seashells from the Pacific Coast of Nicaragua. Cacao beans were commonly used as money.

The Zuyuan ideology can be seen in the archaeology of Yucatán, in the arrangement of their buildings and their iconography, which were responses to specific ideas regarding the cosmos, ritual rules, and political organization. Above all, both the architecture and the iconography imitated elements found in Tula in Central Mexico, which itself was the most prestigious terrestrial copy of the mythical Zuyuá.

There was a characteristic Zuyuan use of architectural space. The small, dark rooms in which the rulers of the Classic contacted the gods in an almost familiar way and the relatively small throne rooms were replaced by larger halls with flat roofs supported by columns, in which a larger number of people participated in political decisions and in the religious ceremonies of the warrior orders. Simultaneously, images of the Feathered Serpent (the mythical being that is part human, bird, and reptile), chac mools, and *atlantes* (atlantean figures), who supported the heavens or the surface of the earth above their heads, proliferated. Military power, converted into a sacred symbol, duplicated adornments, weapons, and insignias originating in the West, featuring rows of skulls, standard bearers, and images of eagles and jaguars devouring human hearts.

Even more than Tula, Chichén Itzá is a pure earthly expression of Zuyuan architecture, and it is an expression that harmoniously combines foreign and native styles. Its heart is the grand temple, identified by Landa as Kukulcan's, where Puuc stylistic elements combine with Zuyuan effigies. Called El Castillo today, it is a pyramid with serpentine balustrade stairways on all four sides. The ball court is the biggest and most impressive in Mesoamerica. The Temple of the Warriors sits on an exceptional platform with hypostyle corridors. In short, the city is a fitting earthly residence for the god Kukulkan.

The appearance of Mayapán is quite different. Above all, it is a residential city, with the nucleus completely surrounded by a wall. Only 15 percent of its structures are ceremonial. The remainder is an disordered agglomeration of dwellings that decrease in quality towards the periphery and lack a perceptible urban pattern. The wall is not a defensive structure, its small size showing that it served as a social marker. The center was occupied by the Temple of Kukulkan, a poor imitation of Chichén Itzá's temple. Some old Maya buildings replace the Zuyuan equivalents, but the combination is neither majestic nor harmonious.

Tulum is a good example of the eclectic style called East Coast. Its modest ceremonial center is protected on the east by cliffs on the

Caribbean and on the other three sides by a low wall. The murals of its Temple of the Frescoes appear to be stylistically influenced by Mixtec codices, although the gods belong to the ancient Maya pantheon.

We have excellent Native written sources of information regarding the religion of the northern zone in the Postclassic. One group consists of four amate-paper screenfold pictographic codices containing ritual and astronomical information. The most famous one, the *Dresden Codex*, is a copy of documents from the Late Classic. The other group consists of colonial documents that record a number of Postclassic beliefs and practices. The books generically called the *Chilam Balam*, with their heterogeneous contents, are particularly valuable recordings of complex myths of the origin of the world and time. Another colonial document, the *Ritual of the Bacabs*, is so named because the four gods of different colors, who were placed at the corners of the world, are mentioned in its incantations. Unfortunately, its esoteric nature still conceals many significant meanings. Comparing these documents with the information obtained by Spanish historians allows us to reconstitute a pantheon presided over by the celestial god Itzamna and his wife, Ix Chel. The singular god Hunab Ku rules over all the gods—or rather, is a fusion of all the gods.

The Postclassic syncretic religion reveals its Zuyuan roots in the mortuary cult of the nobility, which involved cremation. In addition, the Cocoms kept the fleshless skulls of their rulers, artificially replaced their features, and worshiped them. Another interesting aspect of the religion was the value given to sanctuaries, where—despite permanent warfare—all the faithful congregated. The best known was the Sacred Cenote (natural well) at Chichén Itzá, where many human sacrifices took place. Other sanctuaries are the Caves of Balankanché, consecrated to the rain god Chac, and the sanctuaries in San Gervasio in Cozumel, where the goddess Ix Chel was asked for omens regarding the future. We have already mentioned the Postclassic replacement of the Long Count by a system that only counted groups of 13 katuns in historical and prophetic accounts. The katun was a unit of time involving 20 x 360-day cycles, 13 of them equaling a unit of 93,600 days—an insignificant amount when compared to the calculations of previous eras.

The central jungle zone also has great historical significance. In the western half of this zone, archaeologists date the beginning of the

Postclassic to the appearance of the Jonuta ceramics, characterized by black vessels and beautiful molded anthropomorphic figurines. The Chontals or Putuns—the Maya ethnic group considered to be one of the most important Zuyuan peoples—resided there. For centuries the Putuns monopolized land, riverine, and maritime trade in the Southeast. Their center of operations was Xicalanco, situated in the area of the Laguna de Términos between the Usumacinta and Candelaria Rivers. Xicalanco was the exchange point between the land route of the excan tlatoloyan coming from Central Mexico and the Caribbean Sea route that reached Nito and Naco in the Gulf of Honduras. Once they reached Honduras, goods continued on to the Guatemalan Highlands. The sources describe the role of the Putun rulers as that of prime movers in trade. In order to achieve this role, noble families lived in Xicalanco, Acalan, and Nito.

The Petén of Guatemala and Belize is the eastern half of the central zone. The beginning of the Early Postclassic in the Petén is marked by the New Town Phase in Belize and the Cabán Phase in Tikal and ends with the foundation of Tayasal, which some authors place in the fourteenth and others in the fifteenth century. The Late Postclassic, characterized by monumental architecture on the islands of Lakes Petén and Yaxhá, lasted from that time until the Spanish conquest. The history of the Petén and Belize differs from that of the rest of the area. When the Itzás were expelled from Chichén Itzá by the Cocoms, they moved south and settled on several islands in lakes belonging to the Cehachés and the Mopans. In the beginning of the fourteenth century, it is possible that they founded Noh Petén, also called Tayasal, on an island on Lake Petén. The island has an area of thirteen hectares and, in its time, it might have had as many as two hundred houses in addition to temples and palaces. According to the Europeans, Tayasal was ruled by a king whose name and title were Ahau Canek; he was assisted in his rule by a priest of the same lineage, Kin Canek. As in the northern regions, the king delegated power to the bataboob and the nacom.

The Petén Itzás had the same gods that were worshipped in the Yucatán Peninsula, but according to the sources they also venerated a stone column representing the central cosmic tree, Yaxcheelcab. Even though Cortés reached Tayasal in 1524, the jungle Mayas were able to fight off the Spanish longer than any other Mesoamerican people. Tayasal was finally conquered on March 13, 1697.

We turn finally to the southern Maya zone, which had been inhabited from time immemorial by peoples who primarily spoke languages of the Maya family. Thus, in the territory of Chiapas the main languages were Chol, Tzetzal, Tzotzil, Tojolabal, and Chuj, whereas in Guatemala Mam, Aguacateco, Ixil, Chuj, Achí, Quiché, Pokomchí, Cakchiquel, Tzutuhil, Kekchí, and Pokomam were spoken. Chortí was spoken on the border between Honduras and Guatemala. Some of the few non-Maya languages in the area were Chiapanec and Pipil, found on the Pacific Coast, and another unnamed language of the Uto-Aztecan family.

Contemporary scholars disagree about the chronology of the zone, because they rely on different criteria, basically involving migrations into Guatemala. John Fox, who thinks that there were intrusive elements in the area since the Classic, defines a first phase, Pre-Acropolis (between A.D. 800/1000 and 1100). At that time continuous waves of Putun groups came to the region from the Gulf along the course of the Usumacinta River and its tributary, the Chixoy. The Putuns settled in the bottoms of the valleys, where they erected long buildings; temples with circular bases; and closed, H-shaped ball courts. Red-on-White and White-on-Red bichromatic pottery, decorated geometrically in a Mixtec-Puebla style; tripod bowls with hollow zoomorphic supports; and Thin Tohil and Fine Orange ceramics date to this period. Fox calls a second phase—in which pyramidal temples with staircases on four sides (like the staircase at Chichén Itzá and its copy in Mayapán) were built—Acropolis (1000–1250). The name of this phase indicates that the main settlements were moved to protected places atop mountains, where military defense was easier. Characteristic ceramics at this time were Tohil Plumbate and Fine Orange in tripod vessels with molded supports and spoon-shaped, decorated incense burners. Bit by bit, these foreign cultures infiltrated the northern Highlands, anticipating the arrival of the Quichés. A third phase, which Fox calls the Protohistoric (1250–1524), followed. The period corresponds to what has been called the Late Postclassic in other parts of Mesoamerica. The Protohistoric is characterized by an intensification of the patterns of the previous phase, which were also spread through the Guatemalan Highlands, primarily by Quiché groups. At that time there was also an expansion of "long houses"—buildings with multiple columns and openings in their facades.

The principal ceramics of this phase were red and brown slipped, notably Fortaleza White-on-Red and Chinauhtla Polychrome. The phase was ended by the Spanish conquest.

According to Fox, intrusions by groups from the West increased in intensity in every phase. Thus, we can suppose that in the first phase the presence of the Zuyuans did not have a lot of impact on local groups, but rather that they gradually assimilated into the Classic cultures of the Highlands. This did not mean that they lost contact with their area of origin, as they kept in touch via the natural route provided by the Usumacintas and the Chixoy.

During the second phase the trend in the history of the Highlands changed. The influence of the Zuyuans become clearer, and the relationships between the different peoples of the area were no longer peaceful. This new bellicose climate may have been the result of an attempt to create a new political order by powerful groups trying to dominate the old independent kingdoms. Signs of the times include increased trade; diffusion of cultural elements; competition for political and economic control; militarism, leading to the building of major population centers on heights shielded by ravines; and the beginning of the incorporation of larger political units. During the 250 years of this phase an apparently contradictory process was going on: on the one hand the Zuyuans assimilated with the population who had the deepest roots in the area to such a degree that the Zuyuans lost their own languages; on the other hand the Zuyuan rulers clung more tightly to the foreign ideology and styles in order to impose their own type of political organization on the areas under their control.

This process no doubt coincided with the southern peoples' development of closer commercial ties through the great trading routes. Among the most desired goods from the southern zone were obsidian, jadeite, serpentine, nephrite, amber, fine ceramics, fine woods, cacao, quetzal and cotinga feathers, skins, seashells from the Pacific, and sea and inland salt.

In the third and final phase these processes were consolidated. Written sources for this time give us the names of historical actors, capitals, and rulers and dates of the capitals' founding as well as describing alliances, wars, and even the dramas and intrigues of royal courts. In their own stories, groups claim to have originated in a mythical place that they had left a short time before in order to conquer a promised land. Bit by bit, the stories become more worldly. In this later version the Quichés and their allies are the leading actors of the Guatemalan Highlands, extending their dominion through waging war, setting up confederations, and assimilating communities.

The Quichés created a centralized state with a sociopolitical and economic organization characteristic of segmented lineages. During the thirteenth and first half of the fourteenth centuries, they developed an enormous territorial power based at one of their capitals, Jakawitz. This power relied on what María Josefa Iglesias Ponce de León and Andrés Ciudad Ruiz call a "triadic pattern." The new order was based on the existence of three great capitals: Jakawitz (the Quichés), Paraxoné (the Cakchiquels), and Tzameneb (the Rabinals). With this unusual strength their conquests reached the Soconusco, the Motagua Valley, and the lands bordering the Itzás of the Petén to the north.

Sometime later, the Quichés moved their capital to Ismachí, from which they finally controlled all of the Quiché Plateau. They established the most famous of their capitals, K'umarcaaj, also known by its Nahuatl name, Utatlan, in 1450. There, the ephemeral glory of the Quichés reached its peak. Their decline was sudden, occurring during the reign of the feared Q'uikab. Q'uikab's tyrannical rule provoked his own sons into rebelling. When they overturned him in 1493, they dissolved the alliance with the Cakchiquels and Rabinals. This split was followed by a war among the three that continued until the conquest. When the Spanish came to the area, there were a myriad northern kingdoms and four large states: the Quiché, the Cakchiquel, the Rabinal, and the Tzutuhil.

Quiché society was organized on the basis of twenty-four "great houses," the heads of patrilineages that organized the distribution of human groups as well as their social, economic, and political interactions. Each "great house," or *nim ja*, appointed leaders for several smaller units called *chinamit*. Interestingly, the Nahuatl term *chinamitl* does not refer to a human group but to the space ("the enclosure") in which a human group could dwell. However, there is no doubt as to the social rather than the spatial meaning of the word, because we know that all members of the chinamit had the same surname. The chinamit had jurisdiction over its members, organized worship, formed a military unit, and supervised organized the payment of tribute to the community.

An interesting problem arises in connection with the chinamit. Quiché society was sharply divided into nobles and commoners, but the sources say that the chinamit included both commoners and nobles living within the same jurisdiction. Does this mean that nobles and commoners belonged to the same patrilineage? Robert M. Carmack holds that they did not. He claims that several plebeian patrilineages were subordinate to a noble patrilineage within the same chinamit. Carmack argues that the plebeian lineages or "spiders" (*amak*) did not belong to the lineage of a "great house" or *nim ja*. The strange designation "spider" derives from the scattering of the farmers' houses in the fields, resembling a spider with open legs. Apropos of this, colonial documents clarify that the amak was a "kinship unit, or *calpul*." There is still some uncertainty regarding the position of the commoners of the amak. Were they only administratively a part of the chinamit, or were they a plebeian segment of a patrilineage ultimately controlled by a nim ja? In other words, could every nim ja have been divided into two groups, one a privileged ruling group and the other the common people?

As in other Mesoamerican societies, the lowest class consisted of the slaves (*alabil*), many of whom were foreign warriors—commoners captured in battle. Captured nobles, in contrast, were sacrificed to the gods.

Politically, the twenty-four Quiché "great houses" were grouped into four major lineages, and these in turn were divided into two bodies. The Cakchiquels had a similar organization, although they had ten "great houses." High-ranking members of the Quiché "great houses" inherited military, government, and religious offices and distributed them among themselves. Thus, the king, or *ah pop*, belonged to the main lineage—the Cawek; the chief advisor, or *atzij winek*, to the Sayil lineage; the oracle, or *k'alel*, to the Nijaib lineage. Each subdivision of the patrilineages provided functionaries, officers, and priests at different hierarchical levels. This type of government was attributed to the mythical ancestors, the lines of descent beginning with the four men and their wives who left Tulán Siwán to spread over the world.

The ah pop ruled with the assistance of a high dignitary, the *ah pop c'amjá*, and was also helped by the chiefs of the four main lineages and a council composed of representatives of the twenty-four "great houses." Even though all their kings were considered to be sacred, the Quichés emphasized the momentous nature of one particular king, referring to him by the name of the god Gucumatz—"Feathered Serpent" in Quiché.

The ideology of power, tied to Zuyuan military and religious values, used architecture as one of its most fitting symbolic expressions. Several authors, Carlos Navarrete among them, have pointed out the architectural prototypes that, particularly in the Late Postclassic, extended from Central Mexico to the Highlands of Guatemala, following the Mexica trade route to Soconusco. These included temple pyramids with two staircases; temple pyramids with dual chapels; temples with circular or semicircular platforms; dadoes atop balustrades; hypostyle salons; flat roofs made from beams and mortar; *momoztli,* or ritual platforms in the centers of plazas; talud bases on some facings; a *techcatl* (sacrificial stone) embedded in front of the temples; and particular mural styles. The architectural prototypes also included stylistic elements belonging to centralized Mesoamerican governments, such as the bilateral symmetry of the capitals, representing an organization based on "halves," and the "great houses," buildings in which the most important affairs of the patrilineages were discussed.

Notable capitals of the era included the Quiché K'umarcaaj, the Cakchiquel Iximché, the Mam Zaculeu, and the Pokomam Chinantla Viejo and Mixco Viejo. Almost impregnable, the capitals rose amid precipices, mountainsides, and deep ravines and were protected by walls and parapets. K'umarcaaj could only be reached by a natural path modified by humans. Structures still standing at K'umarcaaj include the Temple of Tohil ("Thunderstorm," patron of the Cawek lineage), the Temple of Hakawitz ("Fire Peak"), the Temple of the Feathered Serpent (with a round base), the Ball Court, and the "great houses" building. Iximché, northeast of Lake Atitlán, has four enormous plazas and two smaller ones, all of them surrounded by temples and platforms and a forty-meter-long ball court. Both cities lack the false arches, stelae, and stucco sculptures that continued to be produced during the Postclassic in other Maya regions. However, many typical Zuyuan elements such as chacmool images, feathered-serpent columns, atlantes, and warriors dressed in Toltec style are also missing.

Both traditions are harmoniously blended in a document found in Chichicastenango in 1701—the literary magnus opus of Mesoamerica, the *Popol Vuh.* Written by a member of the Cawek lineage between 1554 and 1558, the *Popol Vuh* describes the departure of the forefathers from the original Tulan. It also tells the beautiful myth of the ball-playing twins, who were challenged and sacrificed by the Lords of the Underworld. After their death they engendered a new set of twins in the womb of Blood Girl. These twins defeated the terrible Lords of the Underworld and, in a final apotheosis, became the Sun and the Moon. This myth is ancient Maya in origin, as evidenced by the depiction of the Hero Twins on Classic vessels from the Petén.

THE TOLTECS AND MEXICAS IN THE POSTCLASSIC

Like the Classic, the Postclassic period was visibly marked by societies from Central Mexico. Although the flow of people, goods, and ideas came from all directions, the successive footprints of the Toltecs and the Mexicas were especially deep and nearly omnipresent in Mesoamerica. It is true that the consequences of their presence were different in each area, but none were exempted from either peaceful or bellicose, direct or indirect contact with Tula and Mexico-Tenochtitlan.

No one today doubts the leading role Tula played during the first centuries of the Postclassic. Paradoxically—and despite the importance of this city—we have not yet been able to specify the area it directly dominated, the centers with which it had the most intense trade relationships, or the kind of ties it had with distant capitals in Oaxaca, Yucatán, and the Guatemala Highlands. Kirchhoff stands out among the few investigators who have tried to specify the area dominated by Tula. Using a sixteenth-century colonial pictograph, the *Historia-tolteca-chichimeca*, Kirchoff reconstructed a hypothetical Toltec tributary sphere. According to this model, Tula-Xicocotitlan was the primary center, ruling over a nearby area divided into four dependent sections occupied by the Cuetlaxtecas, Cozcatecas, Cuitlapiltzincas, and Nonoalcas. On a larger scale Tula was the center of a vast tributary dominion, with four territories themselves divided into four parts and each administered by a main town: Teotenango to the south, Colhuacan (San Isidro Culiacán) to the west, Tulancingo to the east, and a head town (the name of which we do not know) to the northeast.

For many centuries Tula had an impact through its trade that extended far beyond this supposed tributary zone. Apparently, the city controlled several prime routes leading to the Huasteca, the center of Veracruz, Morelos, Querétaro, North Mesoamerica, and various places on the coast of the Pacific from Chiapas to the Sea of Cortés. However, the most enigmatic and controversial routes are those apparently established by Tula with much more distant places on the coasts of Tabasco and Campeche and in the north of the Yucatán Peninsula, the Soconusco region, and the Guatemala Highlands. Without a doubt the most debated contact is that of Tula with Chichén Itzá.

In 1887 the question of the Tula–Chichén Itzá contact led to one of the most passionate controversies in Mesoamerican studies. That year, Désiré Charnay published a book sponsored by the French government that described his travels in Mexico and Central America. In the book, amidst outlandish anecdotes and commentaries, Charnay pointed out an important fact that had not been noticed before—that there were enormous architectural similarities between Tula and Chichén Itzá despite the hundreds of kilometers that separated them. From that time on, investigators of the caliber of Alfred M. Tozzer began to compare by Tula and Chichén Itzá through archaeological investigations and quantitative analyses, resulting in a long list of shared traits.

Comparisons between the two cities continue to be made to this day. Regarding the arrangement of the main plazas of Chichén Itzá and Tula, Lindsay Jones has pointed out the similarities in the orientation of monuments; the junction of temple-pyramids rising over an open, rectangular amphitheater-shaped patio; the correlative location of the ball court, the tzompantli, and the stands; the presence of large precincts with columns (Burnt Palace in Tula and the Group of the Thousand Columns in Chichén Itzá); and the existence of almost identical buildings (the Pyramid B in Tula and the Temple of the Warriors in Chichén Itzá).

Obviously, these parallels are not limited to architecture but include numerous cultural expressions such as artifacts, mural paintings, and—particularly—sculptures. Both places contain three-dimensional sculptures, particularly atlantes supporting lintels, or altars; chac mool sculptures; columns in the shape of descending feathered serpents; and standard bearers with animal or human characteristics. There is also an abundance of pilasters, benches, tableros, and other architectural elements decorated with bas-reliefs alluding to war and sacrifice, such as birds and felines devouring hearts; parading warriors; mythical beings that are part bird, part human, and part reptile; as well as richly attired warriors armed with spear throwers and darts.

Faced with such similarities, scholars have argued for decades, trying to explain simultaneously the kind of relationship that could have existed between two cities so far apart and the lack of these characteristic structures in intermediate points. A wide range of proposals have resulted, seeking archaeological and documental support. To mention only a few, one of the earliest and most hackneyed proposes that a great Toltec army led by Topiltzin Quetzalcoatl conquered the wise and peaceful Mayas of Chichén Itzá and afterward erected buildings there in the exact style of Tula.

Sylvanus G. Morley proposed the more complex scenario that the Itzás, a Maya group from the Petén, had built old Chichén. Later, according to Morley, this group supposedly traveled to the southwest of the Yucatán Peninsula and fused with a culturally and linguistically mayanized group of Toltec exiles. This fused group returned to Chichén Itzá to forge what Morley called "the New Maya Empire."

On the other hand, Tozzer argued that the Mayas in Chichén had been invaded, not once but three times, by people from Central Mexico who, in addition to their own architectural style, introduced human sacrifice, phallic worship, and sodomy. According to Tozzer, the first intruders were Toltecs led by Kukulcan I, who were followed by mexicanized Itzás from the Gulf Coast led by Kukulcan II, and, finally, Mexican mercenaries from Tabasco.

J. Eric S. Thompson and many others argue differently, proposing that the Putun Itzás, powerful traders and warriors from the Gulf region, dominated the coast of Yucatán and subjugated some of the capitals of the peninsula, including Chichén Itzá. At their peak in the tenth century the Putun Itzás, because of their continuous contacts with Central Mexico, had internalized many of the customs of Tula. This led them to welcome Quetzalcoatl and his armies with open arms when they fled from the Central Plateau. They forged an alliance through which the exiled Toltecs, supported by the might of the Putuns, were able to recreate a newer and more sumptuous Tula at Chichén Itzá.

All these theories, directly or indirectly, make Tula the prime mover in the process and the Maya capital the "victim" of an invasion. Some authors, such as George Kubler and Román Piña Chan, have a completely different approach. They invert the causation, arguing that groups coming from the north of Yucatán established a colony in Tula and created a modest copy of their capital there.

More recently, because of an extraordinary change in our conception of the nature of Maya society, the debaters have abandoned their traditional positions and are exploring new approaches. First, we now know that the Mayas were not that peaceful. Advances in archaeological, historical, and epigraphical information, as well as a critical reevaluation of old data, lead us to a picture of continuous conflict between power centers. Second, the Mayas did not avoid external influences. It is possible that the builders of Chichén Itzá were Mayas imitating Central Mexican models as part of a novel political strategy.

Lindsay Jones is a leading exponent of this approach. In a suggestive proposal Jones argues that the architectural and sculptural program at Chichén Itzá was carried out by local Mayas, who were very warlike and world-wise because of their commercial activities. Jones posits that the imitation of Toltec style was due more to the flow of ideas than of people. The copy, stripped of its original functions and meaning, would thus have been integrated into a hybrid cosmopolitan style that was used to legitimize ideologically a hegemony that had been recently achieved.

Faced with this array of possibilities, where do we stand? Like Jones, we feel that there was a clear intention to copy elements of a foreign style. The direction of the flow—regardless of who the historic agent was—went from Central Mexico to the Maya territory, because some of the architectural and sculptural elements (hypostyle rooms, tzompantli, military emphasis, and, perhaps, the chac mool) have northern precedents during the Classic. As we saw previously, Marie-Areti Hers discovered the cultural roots of the Toltec-Chichimecs in northern Mesoamerica.

We agree with Jones that the reasons for this imitation were political, but we do not feel that it was done simply to legitimate something, using a seductive, cosmopolitan image. On the contrary, there was a profound political and ideological motive: instituting a new conception of power. This means that the relationships between Tula and Chichén Itzá must be analyzed, both in space and time, in a much wider context. We refer to the historical process that we described earlier involving the Zuyuans, whose influence is found during the Classic in Becán, Seibal, and Altar de Sacrificios and continued to the Late Postclassic in places such as K'umarcaaj and Iximché.

To properly evaluate the Toltec presence at Chichén Itzá and in all of Mesoamerica, we must determine that which is Zuyuan; distinguish that which is Zuyuan from that which is truly Toltec; and evaluate the importance of that which is Toltec within that which is Zuyuan. As we discussed above, the Zuyuans did not correspond to a single ethnic group, language, or area of origin. Furthermore, their influence began and ended several centuries after Tula's peak. The key to the nature of Zuyuan lies in a very specific type of political action and the ideological basis for that action.

First, the behavior of the Zuyuans corresponded to a hegemonic model of political control of a large territory with an ethnically mixed population. This model spread over a large part of Mesoamerica during the Postclassic despite strong resistance from political units that held to more traditional autonomous kinds of government. Examples of activities of this type are the frequently brutal campaigns of the excan tlatoloyan in Central Mexico, of 8 Deer Jaguar Claw in Oaxaca, of Q'uikab in the Guatemalan Highlands, of Tariácuri in Michoacán, and of the Itzás and Cocoms of Chichén Itzá and Mayapán in Yucatán.

Second, ideologic support for this Zuyuan hegemonic model, as we might suppose, was evident in religious beliefs as well as in political institutions. The triple confederations in the Basin of Mexico, Michoacán, and Yucatán are key Zuyuan institutions. Leaving aside their viability as durable organizations, they claimed to be ordained to rule the world. Other notable Zuyuan institutions included military orders welded together by a common religion; rule by a sovereign incarnating the power of the Feathered Serpent—Quetzalcoatl, Kukulcan, Gucumatz, Nacxit; and royal authority legitimated by an anointing ceremony in shrines equated with the mythical place of origin. For example, 8 Deer went to Tollan, where his nose was perforated and a jewel signifying supreme authority was inserted in it. K'okib', the first Quichean ah pop, went on a pilgrimage to the East to obtain the ritual symbols of authority from Naxcit, "the Great Lord and only August Judge." The Zuyuans believed that all of their primordial ancestors came from the same mythical place called—among other names—Tollan, Zuyuá, and Tulán Siwán. Consistent with this, Zuyuan nobility, at least the Mexica pipiltin and the Mixtec yya, said that they had been expressly created by the ruler god of Tollan, the Feathered Serpent.

How did they tie together this ideology and these political activities? The answer is, through myth. Each ethnic group claimed a primordial ancestor, a "human seed" who gave them their essence, as their creator. Even though all the members of a community believed that they were the progeny of the same divine ancestor, the ruling class justified their preeminence by a supposed privileged line of descent that connected them more closely to the creator. Clearly, this ideology contributed to the cohesion of political units composed of a single ethnic group, because power came from this supposed hierarchical descent.

Without abandoning this generally held religious conviction, the Zuyuans had to develop a myth to validate an organization that would supersede ethnically based rulers. They found the answer in myths about Quetzalcoatl, the creator of all humanity. Ancient myths described Quetzalcoatl's trip to the world of the dead to get bones and ashes, which he mixed with blood from his penis to create humans. This myth emphasized the creation of all humans, overriding myths about the specific origin of each ethnic group.

What, then, about Tollan? It was the most fertile city, with birds of precious plumage soaring overhead. In Tollan the ruler, Quetzalcoatl, lived in four houses of four colors, symbols of the four trees in which time circulated. Tollan was the place where the world was ordered, and Quetzalcoatl was the source of this order, of the unity of humankind, and of power.

The myths combined to justify an authority over different ethnic groups. They did not repudiate beliefs about the primordial fathers who gave their children languages, professions, sacred images, or sacred bundles. Rather, they emphasized that all the peoples originated in mythical Tollan. Thus, in primordial times when all was darkness, all humans spoke the same language, but before they left Tollan to inhabit the world, each ethnic group received a different language, the stone and wood images of their particular gods, and their *pisom c'ac'al,* or sacred bundle.

The *Popol Vuh* says:

> The names of each one were different when they multiplied there in the East, and there were many names of the people: Tepeu

Olomán, Cohah, Quenech, Ahau, as they called those men there in the East, where they multiplied. . . . Neither the sun nor the light had yet been made when they multiplied. All lived together, they existed in great numbers and walked there in the East. . . . they did not sustain or maintain [their god]; they only raised their faces to the sky. . . . The speech of all was the same. They did not invoke wood nor stone. . . . In this manner they spoke, while they thought about the coming of the dawn. . . . Now then, the name of the place where [the four ancestors of the Quiché] Balam-Quitzé, Balam-Acab, Mahucutah, and Iqui-Balam and those of the Tamub and Ilocab went was Tulán-Zuiva, Vucub-Pec, Vucub-Ziván. This was the name of the city where they went to receive their gods. . . . And there it was that the speech of the tribes changed; their tongues became different. They could no longer understand each other clearly after arriving at Tulán. There also they separated.

Another Quiché document, *El título de Totonicapán*, tells in similar terms that: "They . . . changed their tongue in a place called Wukub Pec, Wukub Siwán, Siwán Tulan. . . . And it was the Earthly Paradise where we were formed and created by God the Great Lord. . . . They lived there before they came. . . . They came after Lord Nacxit gave them the pisom c'ac'al." The individual who gave the sacred bundles to the peoples is the "Great Lord and only August Judge" who gave K'okib' the symbols of authority: Nacxit—that is, Quetzalcoatl. Quetzalcoatl's dynasties were Zuyuan, which is why some of its kings were remembered historically as human/gods, saints, or prodigious beings incarnating the Feathered Serpent.

We do not know whether the Tollans, where 8 Deer went, or the East, where K'okib' went to ratify his authority, were real or mythical places. In any case, there is no evidence to support the existence of a great city to which all the groups of Zuyuans owed allegiance. However, we know that certain cities such as Cholula and Mexico-Tenochtitlan were also called Tollan. It is even possible that the Zuyuan culture was very old, with its roots in the multiethnic trading cities of Central Mexico in the Epiclassic. Cacaxtla and Xochicalco are good candidates for the birthplace of this ideology.

For reasons we do not know, Tula-Xicocotitlan became prestigious enough to claim to be the earthly Tollan. Tula-Xicocotitlan might have absorbed the principles of Zuyuan culture and given them particularly vigorous symbolic expression, thus becoming the exemplary earthly Tollan of its time. This would explain why its architectural and sculptural style would have spread throughout Mesoamerica and why some of the terminology of Zuyuan sociopolitical organization was in Nahuatl. In other words, Tula was not the capital of a Mesoamerican empire but rather, in its time, the principal center for the transmission of Zuyuan ideology and, perhaps, the source of some of the migrating groups of conquerors.

All sorts of people participated in the Zuyuan system. While this system was imposed in some regions by invading foreigners who seized power, in other regions it was imposed by local groups on their neighbors. The trade routes, so important to the Zuyuans, may have also functioned as ideological routes. There is a reason why Tohil pottery, made in Highland Guatemala, is diagnostic for the presence of Zuyuans. However, the principal interest of the Zuyuans was to extract tribute from their respective local territories, and they took it for themselves. They were not agents of remote powers living in enclaves; therefore, even if in the beginning some Zuyuans were invading foreigners, we can logically assume that with the passage of time they assimilated with local cultures, even to the degree of losing their original language.

Returning specifically to the relationship between Tula and Chichén Itzá, the Zuyuans—with weapons, attire, and devices identical to those of the Toltecs of Central Mexico and sometimes shown in a clearly hostile pose in Chichén Itzá—were probably foreigners. Today, it is difficult to tell whether the Zuyuans were Toltecs from Tula or Toltec-influenced Mayas. According to the sources, there were two separate invasions of Chichén Itzá. Assuming that they were Toltecs in at least one case, they must have been a group of emigres from Tula. If Tula had had direct political control of northern Yucatán, there would have been clear evidence of Maya influence there. We know that this is not the case, however.

The politics of the Mexicas fluctuated. For much of their history they tried to associate themselves with the Toltecs. They established direct dynastic ties with the Culhuas, descendants of the Toltecs. They systematically excavated the ruins of Tula in order to learn their architectural and sculptural style and to replicate it in Mexico-Tenochtitlan, and they retrieved ceramics and sculptures to take back to their capital.

This identification with the Toltecs allowed them to claim to be their legitimate successors when the last excan tlatoloyan, an institution supposedly invented in Tula, was established. Through this institution, Mexica political actions and ideology followed the Zuyuan norms.

However, the dominions of the Triple Alliance soon transcended the regional sphere and attained an extraordinary size, extending north to Xilotepec; northeast along the Pánuco River, down the Gulf Coast from Tuxpan to Lake Catemaco; west, colliding with the Tarascans; southwest, including the Pacific Coast from the region of the Balsas River to the Tlapa region; and south, including Coyolapan in Oaxaca, where a protected route to their distant enclave in the Soconusco began. Border powers such as Metztitlán to the north, the Tarascans to the west, Yopitzinco and Tututepec to the south, and Coatlicámac to the southeast were beyond their control, as were Tlaxcala and Teotitlán, which were inside their area but were independent.

This unrestrained increase, together with the Mexicas' burdensome demands on the other two members of the excan tlatoloyan, led to a slow change in the Zuyuan ideology accompanied by a large increase in human sacrifice. The Mexicas considered themselves to be the chosen children of the sun god, declaring that their destiny was to feed the sun with blood to ensure the continuation of the world. Feeling on top of the world, the Mexicas preached that as his children had conquered militarily, the time had come for their patron god, Huitzilopochtli, to rule. Huitzilopochtli became the "adoptive father" who would take under his wing (and control) all the patron deities of the world and the peoples they protected. According to this view, even the Mexicas' Texcoco and Tlacopan allies would be subject to Huitzilopochtli. The Triple Alliance, discarded by Mexico-Tenochtitlan, no longer made hegemonic political decisions.

The ideology of a god who "adopts" peoples by force initiated a political change that was interrupted by the conquest. Were the Mexicas the only ones to use this strategy? No, the Tarascans to the east were proclaiming the same policy, except that the god involved was their patron, Curicaueri.

Pyramid of Tenayuca, Estado de México. Central Mexico Area, Postclassic period. (Courtesy of Salvador Guilliem)

Pyramid of Malinalco, Estado de México. Central Mexico Area, Postclassic period. (Courtesy of Salvador Guilliem)

Tableros decorated with mosaic greques, Mitla, Oaxaca. Oaxaca Area, Post-classic period. (Photograph: Leonardo López Luján)

Lord 8 Deer Jaguar Claw with two allies, *Nuttall Codex*. Oaxaca Area, Post-classic period. (Photograph: Carlos Blanco © *Arqueología Mexicana*, INAH)

Tarascan yácatas in Tzintun-tzan, Michoacán. West Meso-america Area, Postclassic period. (Photograph: Carlos Blanco © *Arqueología Mexicana*, INAH)

Totonac Quetzalcoatl temple, Cempoala, Veracruz. Gulf Area, Postclassic period. (Photograph: Lorenzo Ochoa Salas)

Pyramid called "El Castillo," Teayo, Veracruz. Gulf Area, Postclassic period. (Courtesy of Leonardo López Luján)

Stele with the image of Tlaloc, Teayo, Veracruz. Gulf Area, Postclassic period. (Courtesy of Leonardo López Luján)

Huastec stone sculpture. Gulf Area, Postclassic period. (Photograph: Marco Antonio Pacheco © *Arqueología Mexicana*, INAH)

Codz Pop Palace, Kabah, Yucatán. Southeast Mesoamerica Area, Postclassic period. (Courtesy of Leonardo López Luján)

Atlante from the Temple of the Jaguars, Chichén Itzá, Yucatán. Southeast Mesoamerica Area, Postclassic period. (Courtesy of Salvador Guilliem)

View of Iximché, Guatemala. Southeast Mesoamerica Area, Postclassic period. (Courtesy of Leonardo López Luján)

Conclusion

THE THREE HISTORIES

Throughout this book we have noted the considerable differences in the developmental histories of Aridamerica, Oasisamerica, and Mesoamerica. An analysis of the first of these superareas clearly shows that the fate of its inhabitants was determined by its harsh and most difficult environmental conditions and by the relative isolation of the people. Although it is true that most of the inhabitants of Aridamerica subsisted primarily by gathering plants and to a lesser extent by hunting, their techniques, lifeways, and traditions varied considerably from one place to another in the vast geographical mosaic that is the North. These cultural differences might be due to the fact that their contact with each other, although continuous, did not achieve the intensity of the contacts among various societies in Oasisamerica, much less the closeness of ties among Mesoamerican societies. Aridamericans never had relationships with each other that were substantial, constant, or extensive enough to enable them to develop a vigorous shared tradition.

There was a historical unity in Oasisamerica, on the other hand, producing similar cultures with characteristics that are still identifiable in many of their descendants. The peoples of Oasisamerica had unique features, though it is probable that many of their domesticated species, agricultural techniques, ceramics, and beliefs came from Mesoamerica. Nevertheless, the desert farmers did not directly copy Mesoamerican lifeways, nor did they subsequently integrate into the great traditions to the south. Despite continuous interactions between the two superareas, the inhabitants of Oasisamerica retained their own traits because of the great distance that separated them from their more advanced neighbors as well as marked ecological differences between the two superareas. Major adjustments were required for the cultivation of crops in Oasisamerica's semiarid and arid lands and severe climates. These peoples also had a rich cultural legacy from their ancestors, the Desert Archaic tradition, which was most useful in dealing with the harsh climate of Oasisamerica.

The peoples of Mesoamerica enjoyed a common history, born in the remote times of agricultural sedentariness. In the 1,300 years before social hierarchy began, maize farmers put in place the fundamental principles of what would later be one of the most creative cultures of the continent before the arrival of the Europeans. Based on these principles, local and regional traditions and histories developed gradually, later blended by the globalizing actions of those societies we might call "leading actors." Generally speaking, the development of the Mesoamerican tradition was a long-lasting process, continuing for four thousand years without an interruption. During this very long period, the inhabitants of the superarea jointly created and recreated a shared cultural base. Though many aspects of the Mesoamerican tradition evolved through the years, its core beliefs changed so slowly that today they seem not to have changed at all.

Clearly, the specific history of each area, region, and locality of Mesoamerica was very different. Although their histories were not the product of internal factors alone, Mesoamericans were inexorably tied to local geography, economy, and politics and to the secular interaction of their ethnically, linguistically, and culturally varied inhabitants. The people participated in and were a product of these factors.

In contrast, area-wide histories, which mostly involved "leading actor" societies, produced cohesive models with broadly based supraethnic scenarios. They resembled the basic history of the great tradition and differed from specific local-regional histories. However, these area-wide histories also differed from each other. The actions of "leading actors" and the responses of "secondary players" were quite different depending on the period, the area or areas involved, the comparative strength of the participants, the type of system that was being imposed, and the historical circumstances, many of them opportunistic.

Let us look at the qualities of the principal "leading actors." It is difficult to determine exactly what the role of the Olmec culture was. As we have seen, their portrait is still cloudy. All we can say with certainty is that, judging by their traces that remain, they were involved in one of the most important processes in the superarea. Solving the puzzle of the Olmecs is one of the great tasks in the future.

We know somewhat more about Teotihuacan. Their domination of Mesoamerica was not simply military. We have emphasized the fact that research in the last few decades has destroyed the romantic image of the Classic as a period of general peace and tranquility. We now know that there were endemic wars among the Mayas and that military prowess was essential to keeping the elites in power. It is likely that Teotihuacan intervened frequently in local disputes in areas where they were involved or even that they fomented political conflicts for their own benefit. It is also possible that they eventually used force in order to impose their economic system or pursue their self-interest. However, the purpose of their system did not seem to be direct political control, nor was force the usual way they obtained power. Teotihuacan exercised its power through its trade networks, and its objectives were basically commercial. Teotihuacan was also a force for cultural diffusion, however. For several centuries, its influence was felt over all of Mesoamerica. Teotihuacan diffused styles and fashions that were copied everywhere as part of the display strategies of local elites. But despite this cultural diffusion, there is no evidence that Teotihuacan's goals were to impose all its political institutions, religious beliefs, or artistic creations on those territories included in its sphere of influence.

The Zuyuan regime was different. In contrast with Teotihuacan the Zuyuans sought direct political control, and their preferred method of obtaining it was force. The diffusion—or imposition—of their type of rule, religion, and artistic conceptions was a part of their hegemonic ideology. With respect to centralization, the Zuyuans did not try to establish an empire ruled by a single earthly capital, but, rather, to establish regional tributary systems. The Mexicas are the great exception to this approach, because, immediately prior to the conquest, they erupted out of their own region in order to expand their power and political control to an unusually large area. Their behavior could have been the precursor of a new Mesoamerican era, but it was suddenly interrupted the arrival of the Spanish.

Let us return to the three basic strands of the complex Mesoamerican fabric: a tradition produced by a common history of long duration, a local-regional history, and an area-wide history. Obviously the weaving of these three strands into a whole varied according to the time, the area, and the region. At particular periods some peoples lived area-wide history intensely, either as "leading actors" or as their interlocutors, and found themselves at the center of pan-Mesoamerican events during that time. Other peoples, in their particular periods, focused on regional events and participated to a much smaller degree in the area-wide events of their time. Still others, relatively isolated from the historical tumults of the powerful, remained at the level of the basic Mesoamerican village.

This analysis leads to a vision of a pluralistic Mesoamerica in which historical processes can marginalize peoples, regions, or even whole areas for centuries, delaying their development. However, we should make clear that area-wide history was not the sole Mesoamerican history and that—to a lesser or greater degree—there was continuous inter-communication throughout the great complex. The heterogeneity and marginalization we have described have led researchers to privilege a chronology based solely on evidence of progress. This choice has been productive, allowing us to outline and explain more fully the processes involved in regional historical evolution. However, we feel that an area-wide historical approach to a superarea would be more suitable to understanding the general development of Mesoamerica. This approach would require setting up time divisions that would be valid for all of Mesoamerica, independently of the differences in progress of the vari-ous areas and peoples included. The similarities, differences, interre-lationships, and relative marginalizations of peoples during each of these periods would all be explained on the basis of their being manifesta-tions of the same historical process.

These period divisions have been convincingly criticized. In most cases the criteria used for classification are incongruent, because subsis-tence bases, settlement patterns, degrees of centralization of power, rela-tive importance of the army, and aesthetic levels of artistic production are used indiscriminately in determining these periods. In the past we have upheld this critique and have considered it to be valid. At the same time, however, we recognize that if we tried to apply strictly coherent and uniform criteria in Mesoamerican history, we would encounter serious obstacles of a different kind. Some of the fundamental changes are very gradual, making it difficult to find dividing points. Using a single criterion would result in period divisions so large that they would be taxonomically useless. An even greater problem is the fact that there are no precise archaeological indicators that can be used to identify the sequence of fundamental historical processes.

Faced with this indisputable reality, let us reevaluate the period divisions that have been used and have crystallized into vehicles of academic communication (see table 3). We do not intend to defend their appropriateness or their terminology but only to note that they have served as practical tools and that the temporal cuts they propose correspond to real historical landmarks, although these are landmarks of different kinds. There is general agreement on the existence of four basic periods:

1. *Early Preclassic* (2500 B.C.–1200 B.C.)
2. *Middle* and *Late Preclassic* (1200 B.C.–A.D. 200)
3. *Classic* (A.D.200–900)
4. *Postclassic* (A.D. 900–1500)

These four large segments of Mesoamerican history are based on different criteria, which can be summarized as follows:

1. The Early Preclassic is based primarily on the adoption of a sedentary, agricultural way of life, archaeologically dated at 2500 B.C.
2. The Middle and Late Preclassic is based on the relations of production, with the transition from an egalitarian village existence to social stratification occurring about 1200 B.C.
3. The Classic is based on a differentiation of rural and urban due to large human concentrations that could not feed themselves. This process took place about A.D. 200.
4. The Postclassic is based on politics: the appearance of systems aiming to control regions on a supraethnic basis, beginning about A.D. 900.

There are three other intermediate historical landmarks, however; though they are not as important as the others, they signal important changes in Mesoamerican relationships. They result in the following periods:

1. Early Preclassic (2500 B.C.–1200 B.C.)
2. Middle and Late Preclassic (1200 B.C.–A.D. 200)
   2-a. *Late Preclassic* (400 B.C.–A.D. 200)
3. Classic (A.D. 200–A.D. 900)
   3-a. *Late Classic* or *Epiclassic* (A.D. 650–A.D. 900)
4. Postclassic (A.D. 900–A.D. 1500)
   4-a. *Eve of the conquest* (A.D. 1450–A.D.1500)

The three intercalated divisions have their own criteria:

2-a. Start of the Late Preclassic (about 400 B.C.). A period of competition and wars between the regional centers began, manifested by their becoming true protourban capitals. It is probable that the institutionalization of power, which concentrated it in a sector of the ruling class, created the ideology that favored monumental public architecture (including giantism), the complexity of the calendar, writing, and mathematics.

3-a. Start of the Epiclassic (about A.D. 650). The fragmentation of what seems to have been a very centralized system of economic control began. This did not radically change the Mesoamerican economy, because—even after its collapse—Teotihuacan continued to be the most important regional power of Central Mexico. Nevertheless, there are clear consequences of this fragmentation in different parts of Mesoamerica.

4-a. Fully in the Late Postclassic (about A.D. 1450). In specific areas of Mesoamerica the political ideology of supraethnic equilibrium began to break down. This was due, at least in specific cases, to the rise of an ideology that promulgated the supremacy of particular ethnic groups. The crystallization of this last phase of Mesoamerican life could not be achieved.

The European invasion ended the autonomous life of the indigenous Native societies of Mexico. Some of them were annihilated during the conquest and colonization. A large proportion of the female

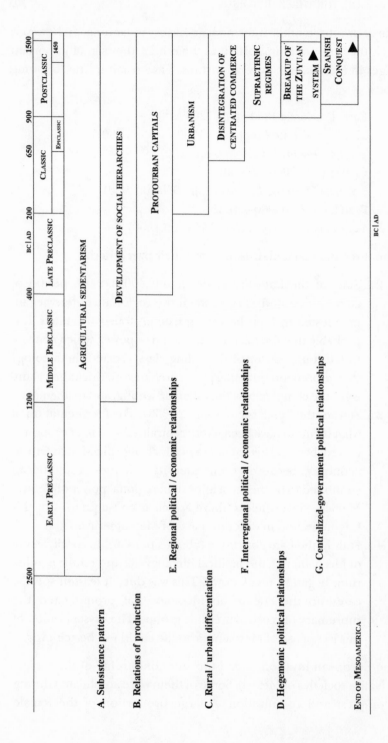

Table 3. The Different Criteria Used in the Chronological Division of Mesoamerica.

survivors married Spanish men and both changed culturally, resulting in the majority of what is called the national society of Mexico today. Another numerous contingent retained their Native languages and traditions, although they were severely affected by colonial spoliation and exploitation, political and religious intervention, and cultural neglect. Even after five hundred years, those who belong to this group continue to live under a colonial-like regime that—despite official pronouncements and supposedly academic justifications—has worsened in the last few years with the adoption of neoliberal politics that exacerbate the differences between Mexicans. Today, as in many other times in the course of their arduous history, Native peoples are rebelling against the political and economic power that keeps them in poverty, unhealthy living conditions, and neglect or that invades their territory in the name of progress and the securing of foreign capital. Native resistance has few weapons, but one of the most valuable is a part of their cultural legacy. Forged in the thirteen centuries of the Early Preclassic, it was the essence of Mesoamerica. As in the past, the rebels turn to the unifying and hopeful symbol of the man-god. It is not the prehispanic Quetzalcoatl, not the colonial Canek. Today, everywhere in the country, the image of Emiliano Zapata springs forth.

Bibliography

ABBREVIATIONS

CEMCA	Centre d'Études Mexicaines et Centraméricaines
CISINAH	Centro de Investigaciones Superiores del Instituto Nacional de Antropología e Historia
CNCA	Consejo Nacional para la Cultura y las Artes
ENAH	Escuela Nacional de Antropología e Historia
FCE	Fondo de Cultura Económica
IMNCR	Instituto Mexicano-Norteamericano de Relaciones Culturales
INAH	Instituto Nacional de Antropología e Historia
INI	Instituto Nacional Indigenista
MAEFM	Mission Archéologique et Ethnologique Française
NGASI	National Gallery of Art, Smithsonian Institution
SAENAH	Sociedad de Alumnos de la Escuela Nacional de Antropología e Historia
SECOFI	Secretaría de Comercio y Fomento Industrial
SEP	Secretaría de Educación Pública
UNAM	Universidad Nacional Autónoma de México

JOURNALS

American Antiquity, Society for American Archaeology.
Anales de Antropología, Instituto de Investigaciones Antropológicas, UNAM.
Anales del Instituto de Investigaciones Estéticas, UNAM.
Ancient Mesoamerica, Cambridge University Press.
Arqueología, Subdirección de Estudios Arqueológicos, INAH.
Arqueología Mexicana, INAH and Editorial Raíces.
Boletín INAH, INAH.
Cuadernos de Arquitectura Mesoamericana, Facultad de Arquitectura, UNAM.
Estudios de Cultura Maya, Centro de Estudios Mayas, UNAM.
Estudios de Cultura Náhuatl, Instituto de Investigaciones Históricas, UNAM.
Journal de la Société des Américanistes, Société des Américanistes.

Latin American Antiquity, Society for American Archaeology.

Mesoamérica, Centro de Investigaciones Regionales de Mesoamérica and Plumsock Mesoamerican Studies.

México en el Tiempo, Editorial Jilguero and INAH.

Mexicon, Internationalen Gesellschaft für Mesoamerika-Forschung.

Revista Española de Antropología Americana, Facultad de Geografía e Historia, Universidad Complutense de Madrid.

Revista Mexicana de Estudios Antropológicos, Sociedad Mexicana de Antropología.

Tlalocan, UNAM.

Tlatoani, Escuela Nacional de Antropología e Historia.

ARTICLES AND BOOKS

Acosta, Jorge R. 1976. "Los Toltecas." In *Los señoríos y estados militaristas,* edited by Román Piña Chan, 137–58. Mexico: INAH.

Acosta Saignes, Miguel et al. 1975. *El comercio en el México prehispánico.* Mexico: Instituto Mexicano de Comercio Exterior.

Adams, Richard E., ed. 1989. *Los orígenes de la civilización Maya.* Mexico: FCE.

———. 1991. *Prehistoric Mesoamerica.* Norman: University of Oklahoma Press.

Alcina Franch, José. 1993. *Calendario y religión entre los Zapotecos.* Mexico: UNAM.

Alvarado Tezozómoc, Hernando. 1944. *Crónica mexicana.* Mexico: Editorial Leyenda.

Armillas, Pedro. 1957. *Cronología y periodificación en la historia de América precolombina.* Mexico: SAENAH.

———. 1964a. "Condiciones ambientales y movimientos de pueblos en la frontera septentrional de Mesoamérica." In *Homenaje a Francisco Márquez Miranda,* 62–82. Madrid: Universidades de Madrid y Sevilla.

———. 1964b. "Northern Mesoamerica." In *Prehistoric Man in the New World,* edited by J. D. Jennings and E. Norbeck, 291–329. Chicago: University of Chicago Press.

———. 1967. "Tecnología, formaciones socioeconómicas y religión en Mesoamérica." In *The Civilization of Ancient America,* edited by Sol Tax, 19–30. New York: Cooper Square Publications.

———. 1969. "The Arid Frontier of Mexican Civilization." *Transactions of the New York Academy of Sciences.* Ser. 2, 3 (no. 6):6–8.

Ashmore, Wendy, ed. 1981. *Lowland Maya Settlement Patterns.* Albuquerque: University of New Mexico Press.

Aveleyra Arroyo de Anda, Luis. 1967. *Los cazadores primitivos de Mesoamérica.* Mexico: UNAM.

Aveleyra Arroyo de Anda, Luis et al. 1956. *Cueva de la Candelaria.* Mexico: INAH.

Aveni, Anthony F. 1977. *Native American Astronomy.* Austin: University of Texas Press.

————. 1980. *Skywatchers of Ancient Mexico.* Austin: University of Texas Press.

Barlow, Robert H. 1992. *La extensión del imperio de los Culhua-mexica.* In *Obras de Robert H. Barlow,* vol. 4, edited by Jesús Monjarás-Ruiz, Elena Limón, and María de la Cruz Paillés. Mexico: INAH and Universidad de las Américas.

Baudez, Claude-F. 1970. *Amérique Central.* Genève: Les Editions Nagel.

Baudez, Claude-F., and Pierre Becquelin. 1984. *Les Mayas.* Paris: Gallimard.

Bell, Betty, ed. 1974. *The Archaeology of West Mexico.* Ajijic: Sociedad de Estudios Avanzados del Occidente de México.

Benson, Elizabeth, ed. 1968. *Dumbarton Oaks Conference on the Olmec.* Washington, D.C.: Dumbarton Oaks.

————. 1973. *Mesoamerican Writing Systems.* Washington, D.C.: Dumbarton Oaks.

————. 1981a. *Mesoamerican Sites and World-Views.* Washington, D.C.: Dumbarton Oaks.

————. 1981b. *The Olmec and Their Neighbors.* Washington, D.C.: Dumbarton Oaks.

Berdan, Frances F., and Patricia Anawalt, eds. 1992. *The Codex Mendoza.* 4 vols. Berkeley: University of California Press.

Berdan, Frances F., Richard E. Blanton, Elizabeth Hill Boone, Mary G. Hodge, Michael E. Smith, and Emily Umberger. 1996. *Aztec Imperial Strategies.* Washington, D.C.: Dumbarton Oaks.

Berlin, Heinrich. 1958. "El glifo 'emblema' en las inscripciones mayas." *Journal de la Société des Américanistes* 47:111–19.

Berlo, Janet C., ed. 1992. *Art, Ideology, and the City of Teotihuacan.* Washington, D.C.: Dumbarton Oaks.

Bernal, Ignacio. 1965. "Archaeological Synthesis of Oaxaca." In *Handbook of Middle American Indians,* vol. 3, edited by Robert Wauchope, 788–831. Austin: University of Texas Press.

————. 1975. "El Valle de Oaxaca hasta la caída de Monte Albán." In *Historia general de México,* vol.2, edited by Miguel León-Portilla, 71–114. Mexico: Salvat Editores de México.

————. 1976. "Formación y desarroyo de Mesoamérica." In *Historia general de México,* vol. 1, 125–64. Mexico: El Colegio de México.

————. 1979. *Historia de la arqueología en México.* Mexico: Porrúa.

————, ed. 1974–76. *México: Panorama histórico y cultural.* 10 vols. Mexico: INAH.

Berrin, Kathleen, and Esther Pasztory, eds. 1993. *Teotihuacan: Art from the City of the Gods.* New York: Thames and Hudson and the Fine Art Museum of San Francisco.

Blanton, Richard E. 1978. *Monte Albán: Settlement Patterns at the Ancient Zapotec Capital.* New York: Academic Press.

Blanton, Richard E., Stephen A. Kowalewski, Gary Feinman, and Jill Appel. 1978. *Ancient Mesoamerica: A Comparison of Change in Three Regions.* Cambridge: Cambridge University Press.

Boehm de Lameiras, Brigitte. 1986. *Formación del estado en el México prehispánico.* Zamora: El Colegio de Michoacán.

Boone, Elizabeth H., ed. 1987. *The Aztec Templo Mayor.* Washington, D.C.: Dumbarton Oaks.

Boone, Elizabeth H., and Walter Mignolo, eds. 1994. *Writing without Words: Alternative Literacies in Mesoamerica and the Andes.* Durham, N.C.: Duke University Press.

Brand, Donald D. 1952. "Bosquejo histórico de la geografía y la antropología en la región tarasca" (first part), *Anales del Museo Michoacano,* 2ª época (no. 5):40–153.

Braniff, Beatriz. 1975a. "Arqueología del norte de México." In *Los pueblos y señoríos teocráticos,* edited by Ignacio Bernal, 217–72. Mexico: INAH.

———. 1975b. *La estratigrafía arqueológica de Villa de Reyes, S.L.P.: Un sitio en la frontera mesoamericana.* Mexico: UNAM.

———. 1994–95. "La frontera septentrional de Mesoamérica." In *Historia antigua de México.* edited by Linda Manzanilla and Leonardo López Luján, vol. 1, 113–43. Mexico: UNAM, INAH, and Miguel Ángel Porrúa.

Broda, Johanna, Davíd Carrasco, and Eduardo Matos Moctezuma. 1987. *The Great Temple of Tenochtitlan: Center and Periphery in the Aztec World.* Berkeley: University of California Press.

Broda, Johanna et al., eds. 1991. *Arqueoastronomía y etnoastronomía en Mesoamérica.* Mexico: UNAM.

Brüggemann, Jürgen Kurt. 1994–95. "La zona del Golfo en el Clásico." In *Historia antigua de México,* edited by Linda Manzanilla and Leonardo López Luján, vol. 2, 11–40. Mexico: UNAM, INAH, and Miguel Ángel Porrúa.

Brüggemann, Jürgen Kurt, Sara Ladrón de Guevara, and Juan Sánchez Bonilla. 1992. *Tajín.* Mexico and Madrid: El Equilibrista and Turner Libros.

Brüggemann, Jürgen Kurt et al. 1991. *Cempoala: El estudio de una ciudad prehispánica.* Mexico: INAH.

Byland, Bruce, and John Pohl. 1995. *In the Realm of 8 Deer: The Archaeology of the Mixtec Codices.* Norman: University of Oklahoma Press.

Cabrera Castro, Rubén, Ignacio Rodríguez García, and Noel Morelos García, eds. 1991. *Teotihuacan 1980–1982.* Mexico: INAH.

Cabrero, María Teresa. 1995. *La muerte en el Occidente del México prehispánico.* Mexico: UNAM.

Calnek, Edward E. 1972. "Settlement Patterns and Chinampa Agriculture at Tenochtitlan." *American Antiquity* 37:104–15.

———. 1978. "El sistema de mercado de Tenochtitlan." In *Economía política e ideología en el México prehispánico,* edited by Pedro Carrasco and Johanna Broda, 95–114. Mexico: Nueva Imagen and CISINAH.

Cardós de Méndez, Amalia, ed. 1990. *La época clásica.* Mexico: INAH.

Carmack, Robert M. 1973. *Quichean Civilization: The Ethnohistoric, Ethnographic and Archaeological Sources.* Berkeley: University of California Press.

————. 1976. "La estratificación quicheana prehispánica." In *Estratificación social en la Mesoamérica prehispánica*, edited by Pedro Carrasco and Johanna Broda, 245–77. Mexico: CISINAH.

————. 1979. *Historia social de los quichés*. Guatemala: Ministerio de Educación.

————. 1981. *The Quiche Mayas of Utatlán*. Norman: University of Oklahoma Press.

Carmona, Martha, ed. 1989. *El Preclásico o Formativo: Avances y perspectivas*. Mexico: INAH.

Carrasco, Davíd. 1982. *Quetzalcoatl and the Irony of Empire: Myths and Prophesies of the Aztec Tradition*. Chicago: University of Chicago Press.

————. 1990. *Religions of Mesoamerica: Cosmovision and Ceremonial Centers*. San Francisco: Harper and Row.

Carrasco, Davíd, Lindsay Jones, and Scott Sessions, eds. 1999. *Mesoamerica's Classic Heritage: From Teotihuacan to the Aztecs*. Niwot: University Press of Colorado.

Carrasco, Pedro. 1976a. "La sociedad mexicana antes de la Conquista." In *Historia general de México*, vol. 1, 165–288. Mexico: El Colegio de México.

————. 1976b. *Los otomíes: Cultura e historia prehispánica de los pueblos mesoamericanos de habla otomiana*. Mexico: UNAM.

————. 1985. *América indígena*. In *Historia de América Latina*, edited by Pedro Carrasco and Guillermo Céspedes, vol. 1, 9–266. Madrid: Alianza Editorial.

Carrasco, Pedro et al. 1986. *La sociedad indígena en el Centro y en el Occidente de México*. Zamora: El Colegio de Michoacán.

Carrasco, Pedro, and Johanna Broda, eds. 1976. *Estratificación social en la Mesoamérica prehispánica*. Mexico: INAH.

————. 1978. *Economía política e ideología en el México prehispánico*. Mexico: Nueva Imagen and CISINAH.

Caso, Alfonso. 1958. *The Aztecs People of the Sun*. Norman: University of Oklahoma Press.

————. 1967. *Los calendarios prehispánicos*. Mexico: UNAM.

————. 1977–79. *Reyes y reinos de la Mixteca*. 2 vols. Mexico: FCE.

Caso, Alfonso et al. 1967. *La cerámica de Monte Albán*. Mexico: INAH.

Castillo F., Victor. 1972. *Estructura económica de la sociedad mexica, según las fuentes documentales*. Mexico: UNAM.

Castro, Efraín et al. 1993. *El arte de Mezcala*. Mexico: Gobierno Constitucional del Estado de Guerrero.

Castro-Leal, Marcia. 1986. *Tzintzuntzan, capital de los Tarascos*. Morelia: Gobierno del Estado de Michoacán.

Centro de Estudios Históricos. 1976. *Historia General de México*. 4 vols. Mexico: El Colegio de México.

Cervantes-Delgado, Roberto, ed. 1986. *Arqueología e etnohistoria del Estado de Guerrero*. Mexico: INAH and Gobierno del Estado de Guerrero.

Chapman, Anne M. 1959. *Puertos de intercambio en Mesoamérica prehispánica*. Mexico: INAH.

———. 1976. "¿Historia o estructura? A propósito de Mesoamérica." *Boletín INAH* 2ª época (no. 19):35–38.

Chase, Arlen F., and Prudence Rice, eds. 1986. *The Lowland Maya Postclassic.* Austin: University of Texas Press.

Clark, John E. 1990. "Olmecas, olmequismo y olmequización en Mesoamérica." *Arqueología* 3:49–55.

Clark, John E., and Michael Blake. 1989. "El origen de la civilización en Mesoamérica: Los olmecas y mocayas del Soconusco de Chiapas." In *El Preclásico o Formativo: Avances y perspectivas,* edited by Martha Carmona, 385–405. Mexico: INAH.

Clendinen, Inga. 1991. *Aztecs: An Interpretation.* Cambridge: Cambridge University Press.

Coe, Michael D. 1978. *Lords of the Underworld.* Princeton: Princeton University Press.

———. 1992. *Breaking the Maya Code.* London: Thames and Hudson.

———. 1994. *The Maya.* 5th ed. London: Thames and Hudson.

Coe, Michael D., and Richard A. Diehl. 1980. *In the Land of the Olmec.* 2 vols. Austin: University of Texas Press.

Cohen, Mark Nathan. 1978. *The Food Crisis in Prehistory.* New Haven: Yale University Press.

Conrad, Geoffrey W., and Arthur A. Demarest. 1984. *Religion and Empire: The Dynamics of Aztec and Inca Expansionism.* Cambridge, England: Cambridge University Press.

Cook de Leonard, Carmen, ed. 1959. *Esplendor del México Antiguo.* 2 vols. Mexico: Centro de Investigaciones Antropológicas de México.

Cordell, Linda S. 1984. *Prehistory of the Southwest.* New York: Academic Press.

Covarrubias, Miguel. 1957. *Indian Art of Mexico and Central America.* New York: Knopf.

Covarrubias, Miguel, and Daniel Rubín de la Borbolla. *El Arte indígena de Norteamérica.* 1945. Mexico: INAH, NGASI, and IMNCR.

Culbert, Patrick T., ed. 1973. *The Classic Maya Collapse.* Albuquerque: University of New Mexico Press.

———. 1990. *Classic Maya Political History: Hieroglyphic and Archaeological Evidence.* Cambridge: Cambridge University Press.

Dahlgren, Barbro. 1966. *La Mixteca: Su cultura e historia prehispánica.* Mexico: UNAM.

Daniel, Elin, and Robert J. Sharer, eds. 1992. *New Theories on Ancient Maya.* Philadelphia: University of Pennsylvania Press.

Davies, Nigel. 1977. *The Toltecs until the Fall of Tula.* Norman: University of Oklahoma Press.

———. 1982. *The Ancient Kingdoms of Mexico.* London and New York: Penguin Books.

Di Peso, Charles C. 1974. *Casas Grandes: A Fallen Trading Center of the Gran Chichimeca.* Vols. 1–3. Flagstaff, Ariz.: The Amerind Foundation.

Di Peso, Charles C. et al. 1974. *Casas Grandes: A Fallen Trading Center of the Gran Chichimeca.* Vols. 4–8. Flagstaff, Ariz.: The Amerind Foundation.

Díaz del Castillo, Bernal. 1950. *Historia verdadera de la conquista de la Nueva España.* Mexico: Ediciones Mexicanas.

Diehl, Richard A. 1983. *Tula: The Toltec Capital of Ancient Mexico.* London: Thames and Hudson.

Diehl, Richard A., and Janet C. Berlo, eds. 1989. *Mesoamerica after the Decline of Teotihuacan: A.D. 700–900.* Washington, D.C.: Dumbarton Oaks.

Duverger, Christian. 1987. *El origen de los Aztecas.* Mexico: Grijalbo.

Edmonson, Munro S. 1988. *The Book of the Year: Middle American Calendrical Systems.* Salt Lake City: University of Utah Press.

Escalante Gonzalbo, Pablo. 1990. "La polémica sobre la organización de las comunidades de productores." *Nueva Antropología* 11 (no. 38):147–62.

Fash, William L. 1991. *Scribes, Warriors and Kings: The City of Copán and the Ancient Maya.* London: Thames and Hudson.

Flannery, Kent V. 1968a. "Archaeological Systems Theory and Early Meso-america." In *Anthropological Archaeology in the Americas,* edited by Betty J. Meggers, 67–87. Washington, D.C.: Anthropological Society of Washington.

———. 1968b. "The Olmec and the Valley of Oaxaca: A Model for Inter-regional Interaction in Formative Times." In *Dumbarton Oaks Conference on the Olmec,* edited by Elizabeth P. Benson, 79–110. Washington, D.C.: Dumbarton Oaks.

———. 1985. "Los orígenes de la agricultura en México: Las Teorías y la evidencia." In *Historia de la agricultura: Época prehispánica—Siglo XVI,* edited by Teresa Rojas Rabiela and William T. Sanders, vol. 1, 237–66. Mexico: INAH.

———. 1986. *Guilá Naquitz: Archaic Foraging and Early Agriculture in Oaxaca, Mexico.* New York: Academic Press.

Flannery, Kent V., ed. 1976. *The Early Mesoamerican Village.* New York: Academic Press.

Flannery, Kent V., and Joyce Marcus, eds. 1983. *The Cloud People: Divergent Evolution of the Zapotec and Mixtec Civilizations.* New York: Academic Press.

Florescano, Enrique, ed. 1989. *Historia general de Michoacán.* Morelia: Instituto Michoacano de Cultura.

———. 1994. *Memoria mexicana.* 2d ed. Mexico: FCE.

Foncerrada de Molina, Marta. 1993. *Cacaxtla: La iconografía de los olmeca-xicalanca.* Mexico: UNAM.

Foster, Michael S., and Phil C. Weigand, eds. 1985. *The Archeology of West and Northwest Mesoamerica.* Boulder, Colo.: Westview Press.

Fox, John. 1978. *Quiche Conquest: Centralism and Regionalism in Highland Guatemalan State Development.* Albuquerque: University of New Mexico Press.

————. 1980. "Lowland to Highland Mexicanization Processes in Southern Mesoamerica." *American Antiquity* 45:43–54.

————. 1987. *Maya Postclassic State Formation.* Cambridge, England: Cambridge University Press.

Fuente, Beatriz de la. 1977. *Los hombres de piedra: Escultura olmeca.* Mexico: UNAM.

Gamio, Manuel. 1979. *La población del Valle de Teotihuacan.* 5 vols. Mexico: INI.

García Cook, Ángel, and Beatriz Leonor Merino Carreón, eds. 1995. *Antología de Cacaxtla.* 2 vols. Mexico: INAH.

Garibay K., Àngel M. 1953–54. *Historia de la literatura náhuatl.* 2 vols. Mexico: Porrúa.

Gendrop, Paul. 1982. *Arte prehispánico en Mesoamérica.* Mexico: Trillas.

González Jácome, Alba, ed. 1987. *Orígenes del hombre americano.* Mexico: SEP.

González Lauck, Rebecca. 1984. *The 1984 Archaeological Investigations at La Venta, Tabasco, Mexico.* Ph.D. diss., University of California, Berkeley.

————. 1994–95. "La zona del Golfo en el Preclásico: La etapa olmeca." In *Historia antigua de México,* edited by Linda Manzanilla and Leonardo López Luján, vol. 1, 279–321. Mexico: INAH, UNAM, and Miguel Ángel Porrúa.

González Licón, Ernesto, and Lourdes Márquez Morfín. 1994–95. "La zona oaxaqueña en el Postclásico." In *Historia antigua de México,* edited by Linda Manzanilla and Leonardo López Luján, vol. 3, 55–86. Mexico: INAH, UNAM, and Miguel Ángel Porrúa.

González Torres, Yólotl. 1975. *El culto a los astros entre los mexicas.* Mexico: SEP.

————. 1985. *El sacrificio humano entre los mexicas.* Mexico: INAH and FCE.

————. 1991. *Diccionario de mitología y religión de Mesoamérica,* assisted by Juan Carlos Ruiz Guadalajara. Mexico: Larousse.

Gorenstein, Shirley, and Helen Perlstein Pollard. 1983. *The Tarascan Civilization: A Late Prehispanic Cultural System.* Nashville, Tenn.: Vanderbilt University.

Graulich, Michel. 1990a. "Dualities in Cacaxtla." In *Mesoamerican Dualism/ Dualismo Mesoamericano,* edited by Rudolf van Zantwijk, Rob de Ridder, and Edwin Braakjhuis, 94–118. Utrech: R.U.U.-I.S.O.R.

————. 1990b. *Montezuma.* Paris: Fayard.

————. 1997. *Myths of Ancient Mexico,* translated by Bernard R. Ortiz de Montellano and Thelma Ortiz de Montellano. Norman: University of Oklahoma Press.

Grove, David C. 1984. *Chalcatzingo: Excavations on the Olmec Frontier.* London: Thames and Hudson.

Guevara Sánchez, Arturo. 1994–95. "Oasisamérica en el Postclásico: La zona de Chihuahua." In *Historia antigua de México,* edited by Linda Manzanilla and Leonardo López Luján, vol. 3, 329–51. Mexico: INAH, UNAM, and Miguel Ángel Porrúa.

Hammond, Norman. 1982. *Ancient Maya Civilization.* New Brunswick, N.J.: Rutgers University Press.

Hassig, Ross. 1985. *Trade, Tribute, and Transportation: The Sixteenth-Century Political Economy of the Valley of Mexico.* Norman: University of Oklahoma Press.

———. 1988. *Aztec Warfare: Imperial Expansion and Political Control.* Norman: University of Oklahoma Press.

Haury, Emil W. 1945. "The Problem of Contacts between the Southwestern United States and Mexico." *Southwest Journal of Anthropology* 1:55–74.

———. 1962. "The Greater American Southwest." In *Courses Toward Urban Life,* edited by Robert J. Braidwood and Gordon R. Willey, 106–31. Chicago: Aldine.

Healan, Dan M., ed. 1989. *Tula of the Toltecs: Excavations and Survey.* Iowa City: University of Iowa Press.

Hers, Marie-Areti. 1989. *Los toltecas en tierras chichimecas.* Mexico: UNAM.

———. 1994–95. "La zona noroccidental en el Clásico." In *Historia antigua de México,* edited by Linda Manzanilla and Leonardo López Luján, vol. 2, 227–59. Mexico: INAH, UNAM, and Miguel Ángel Porrúa.

Hirth, Kenneth G., and Ann Cyphers Guillén. 1988. *Tiempo y asentamiento en Xochicalco.* Mexico: UNAM.

Hosler, Dorothy. 1988a. "Ancient West Mexican Metallurgy: A Technological Chronology." *Journal of Field Archaeology* 15:191–217.

———. 1988b. "Ancient West Mexican Metallurgy: South and Central America Origins and West Mexican Transformation." *American Anthropologist* 90:832–55.

———. 1994. *The Sounds and Colors of Power: The Sacred Metallurgical Technology of West Mexico.* Cambridge, Mass.: The MIT Press.

Iglesias Ponce de León, María Josefa, and Andrés Ciudad Ruíz. 1994–95. "Las tierras altas de la zona maya en el Postclásico." In *Historia antigua de México,* edited by Linda Manzanilla and Leonardo López Luján, vol. 3, 87–120. Mexico: INAH, UNAM, and Miguel Ángel Porrúa.

Jennings, Jesse D. 1968. *Prehistory of North America.* New York: McGraw-Hill.

———. 1986. "Prehistory: Introduction." In *Handbook of North American Indians.* Edited by William C. Sturtevant, vol. 11, 113–19. Washington, D.C.: Smithsonian Institution.

Jiménez Moreno, Wigberto. 1941. "Tula y los toltecas según las fuentes históricas." *Revista Mexicana de Estudios Antropológicos* 5 (nos. 2–3):79–84.

———. 1956. *Notas sobre la historia antigua de México.* Mexico: Ediciones de la Sociedad de Alumnos de la ENAH.

———. 1959. "Síntesis de la historia pretolteca de Mesoamérica." In *Esplendor del México Antiguo,* edited by Carmen Cook de Leonard, vol. 2, 1109–96. Mexico: Centro de Investigaciones Antropológicas de México.

———. 1977. "Mesoamérica." In *Enciclopedia de México,* edited by Rogelio Álvarez. México: Enciclopedia de México.

Jones, Lindsay. 1995. *Twin City Tales: A Hermeneutical Reassesment of Tula and Chichén Itzá.* Boulder: University Press of Colorado.

Katz, Friedrich. 1966. *Situación social y económica de los aztecas durante los siglos XV y XVI.* Mexico: UNAM.

Kelley, J. Charles. 1971. "Archaeology of the Northern Frontier: Zacatecas and Durango." In *Handbook of Middle American Indians,* edited by Robert Wauchope, vol. 11, 768–801.

————. 1985. "The Chronology of the Chalchihuites Culture." In *The Archaeology of West and Northwest Mesoamerica,* edited by Michael S. Foster and Phil C. Weigand, 269–87. Boulder, Colo., and London: Westview Press.

Kelly, Isabel. 1945–49. *The Archaeology of the Autlan-Tuxcacuesco Area of Jalisco.* 2 vols. Berkeley: University of California Press.

————. 1980. *Ceramic Sequence in Colima: Capacha, an Early Phase.* Tucson: University of Arizona Press.

Kirchhoff, Paul. 1943a. "Los recolectores-cazadores del norte de México." In *El norte de México y el sur de los Estados Unidos,* pp. 13–144. Mexico: SMA.

————. 1943b. "Mesoamérica: Sus límites geográficos, composición étnica y caracteres culturales." *Acta Americana* 1 (no. 1):92–107.

————. 1943c. "Relaciones entre los recolectores-cazadores del norte de México y las áreas circunvecinas." In *El norte de México y el sur de los Estados Unidos,* 255–58. Mexico: SMA.

————. 1985. "El Imperio tolteca y su caída." In *Mesoamérica y el Centro de México,* edited by Jesús Monjarás-Ruiz, Rosa Brambila, and Emma Pérez-Rocha, 249–72. Mexico: INAH.

Knorosov, Yuri V. 1956. "New Data on the Maya Written Language." *Journal de la Société des Américanistes* 45:210–16.

Krickeberg, Walter. 1956. *Las antiguas culturas mexicanas.* Mexico: FCE.

Kubler, George. 1961. "Chichén Itzá y Tula." *Estudios de Cultura Maya* 1:47–79.

————. 1975. *The Art and Architecture of Ancient America.* New York: Penguin Books.

Lameiras, José. 1985. *Los déspotas armados: Un espectro de la guerra prehispánica.* Zamora: El Colegio de Michoacán.

Landa, Fray Diego de. 1944. *Relación de las cosas de Yucatán.* Mexico: CNCA.

Lee, Thomas A., and Carlos Navarrete, eds. 1978. *Mesoamerican Communication Routes and Cultural Contacts.* Provo, Utah: Brigham Young University.

Lekson, Stephen H. et al. 1988. "The Chaco Canyon Community." *Scientific American* 259 (no. 1):100–109.

León-Portilla, Miguel. 1963. *Aztec Thought and Culture.* Norman: University of Oklahoma Press.

————. 1967. "El proceso de aculturación de los chichimecas de Xólotl." *Estudios de Cultura Náhuatl* 7:59–86.

————. 1968. *Tiempo y realidad en el pensamiento maya.* Mexico: UNAM.

————, ed. 1974. *Historia de México.* 11 vols. Mexico: Salvat.

Litvak King, Jaime. 1970. "Xochicalco en la caída del Clásico: Una hipótesis." *Anales de Antropología* 7: 131–44.

————. 1975. "En torno al problema de la definición de Mesoamérica." *Anales de Antropología* 12:171–95.

Lombardo de Ruiz, Sonia. 1986. "La pintura." In Sonia Lombardo de Ruiz, Diana López de Molina, Daniel Molina Feal, Carolyn Baus de Czitrom, and Óscar J. Polaco. *Cacaxtla: El lugar donde muere la lluvia en la tierra*, 209–499. Mexico: INAH, Gobierno del Estado de Tlaxcala and Instituto Tlaxcalteca de Cultura.

López Austin, Alfredo. 1973. *Hombre-dios: Religión y política en el mundo náhuatl*. Mexico: UNAM.

————. 1985. "Organización política en el Altiplano Central de México durante el Posclásico." In *Mesoamérica y el Centro de México*, edited by Jesús Monjarás-Ruiz, Rosa Brambila, and Emma Pérez-Rocha, 197–234. Mexico: INAH.

————. 1988. *The Human Body and Ideology: Concepts of the Ancient Nahuas*, translated by Thelma Ortiz de Montellano and Bernard Ortiz de Montellano. Salt Lake City: University of Utah Press.

————. 1990. *The Myths of the Opossum: Pathways of Mesoamerican Mythology*, translated by Bernard R. Ortiz de Montellano and Thelma Ortiz de Montellano. Albuquerque: University of New Mexico Press.

————. 1997. *Tamoanchan, Tlalocan. Places of Mist*, translated by Bernard R. Ortiz de Montellano and Thelma Ortiz de Montellano. Boulder: University Press of Colorado.

López Austin, Alfredo, and Leonardo López Luján. 1999. *Mito y realidad de Zuyuá: Serpiente Emplumada y las transformaciones mesoamericanas del Clásico al Posclásico*. Mexico: FCE/El Colegio de México.

López de Molina, Diana. 1986. "Arqueología de superficie y estudios urbanos: El caso de Cantona." *Revista Mexicana de Estudios Antropológicos* 32:177–85.

López de Molina, Diana, and Daniel Molina Feal. 1976. "Los murales de Cacaxtla." *Boletín del INAH* 2ª época (no. 16):3–8.

————. 1986. "Arqueología." In Sonia Lombardo de Ruiz, Diana López de Molina, Daniel Molina Feal, Carolyn Baus de Czitrom y Óscar J. Polaco, *Cacaxtla: El lugar donde muere la lluvia en la tierra*, 11–208. Mexico: INAH, Gobierno del Estado de Tlaxcala, and Instituto Tlaxcalteca de Cultura.

López Luján, Leonardo. 1989a. *La recuperación mexica del pasado teotihuacano*. Mexico: INAH and GV Editores.

————. 1989b. *Nómadas y sedentarios: El pasado prehispánico de Zacatecas*. Mexico: INAH.

————. 1994. *The Offerings of the Templo Mayor of Tenochtitlan*, translated by Bernard R. Ortiz de Montellano and Thelma Ortiz de Montellano. Boulder: University Press of Colorado.

López Luján, Leonardo, Robert H. Cobean, and Alba Guadalupe Mastache F. 1995. *Xochicalco y Tula*. Mexico: Jaca Books and CNCA.

López Mestas C., and Jorge Ramos de la Vega. 1994. "Tumba de tiro en Huitzilapa, Jalisco." *Arqueología Mexicana* 7 (Apr./May):59–61.

Lorenzo, José Luis. 1967. *La etapa lítica en México.* Mexico: INAH.

———. 1975. "Los primeros pobladores." In *Del nomadismo a los centros ceremoniales,* 15–60. Mexico: INAH.

———. 1976. "Los orígenes mexicanos." In *Historia general de México,* vol. 1, 83–123. Mexico: El Colegio de México.

———. 1978. "Poblamiento del continente americano." In *Historia de México,* edited by Miguel León-Portilla, vol. 1, 27–54. Mexico: Salvat.

Lorenzo, José Luis, and Lorena Mirambell, eds. 1986. *Tlapacoya: 35,000 años de historia del Lago de Chalco.* Mexico: INAH.

Lowe, Gareth W., Thomas A. Lee, and Eduardo Martínez, 1982. *Izapa: An Introduction to the Ruins and Monuments.* Provo, Utah: Brigham Young University.

MacNeish, Richard S. 1958. *Preliminary Investigations in the Sierra de Tamaulipas, Mexico.* Washington, D.C.: American Philosophical Society.

———. 1964a. *El origen de la civilización mesoamericana vista desde Tehuacán.* Mexico: INAH.

———. 1964b. "The Food-Gathering and Incipient Agriculture Stage of Prehistoric Middle America." In *Handbook of Middle American Indians,* edited by Robert Wauchope, vol. 1, 413–26. Austin: University of Texas Press.

———. 1970. *The Prehistory of Tehuacan Valley.* 5 vols. Austin: University of Texas Press.

Mangelsdorf, Paul C. 1986. "The Origin of Corn." *Scientific American* 22 (no. 2):72–79.

Manrique Castañeda, Leonardo, ed. 1988. "Linguistica." In *Atlas Cultural de México.* Mexico: SEP, INAH, and Editorial Planeta.

Manzanilla, Linda, ed. 1993. *Anatomía de un conjunto residencial teotihuacano en Oztoyohualco.* 2 vols. Mexico: UNAM.

———. 1994–95. "La zona del Altiplano Central en el Clásico." In *Historia antigua de México,* edited by Linda Manzanilla and Leonardo López Luján, vol. 2, 139–73. Mexico: INAH, UNAM, and Miguel Ángel Porrúa.

Manzanilla, Linda, and Leonardo López Luján, eds. 1989. *Atlas histórico de Mesoamérica.* Mexico: Ediciones Larousse.

———. 1994–95. *Historia antigua de México.* 3 vols. Mexico: INAH, UNAM, and Miguel Ángel Porrúa.

Marcus, Joyce. 1983. "Lowland Maya Archaeology at the Crossroads." *American Antiquity* 48:454–88.

———. 1992. *Mesoamerican Writing Systems: Propaganda, Myth, and History in Four Ancient Civilizations.* Princeton, N.J.: Princeton University Press.

———. 1995. "Where is Lowland Maya Archaeology Headed?" *Journal of Archaeological Research* 3:3–53.

Marcus, Joyce, and Kent V. Flannery, 1996. *Zapotec Civilization: How Urban Society Evolved in Mexico's Oaxaca Valley.* London: Thames and Hudson.

Marquina, Ignacio. 1970. *Proyecto Cholula.* Mexico: INAH.

———. 1990. *Arquitectura prehispánica.* 2d ed. Mexico: INAH.

Martínez Marín, Carlos. 1963. "La cultura de los mexicas durante la migración: Nuevas ideas." *Cuadernos Americanos* 4 (July/August):175–83.

Mastache, Alba Guadalupe, and Robert H. Cohen. 1985. "Tula." In *Mesoamérica y el Centro de México*, edited by Jesús Monjarás-Ruiz, Roas Brambila, and Emma Pérez-Rocha, 273–307. Mexico: INAH.

Mastache, Alba Guadalupe, Jeffrey H. Parsons, Robert S. Standley, and Mari Carmen Serra Puche, eds. 1996. *Arqueología mesoamericana: Homenaje a William T. Sanders*. Mexico: INAH and Arqueología Mexicana.

Mathien, Frances Joan, and Randall H. McGuire, eds. 1986. *Ripples in the Chichimec Sea: New Considerations of Southwestern-Mesoamerican Interactions*. Carbondale: Southern Illinois University Press.

Matos Moctezuma, Eduardo. 1975. *Muerte a filo de obsidiana*. Mexico: SEP.

———. 1982a. "El proceso de desarrollo en Mesoamérica." *Boletín de Antropología Americana* (Mexico, Instituto Panamericano de Geografía e Historia) 5:117–31.

———, ed. 1982b. *Proyecto Tula*. Mexico: INAH.

———. 1988. *The Great Temple of the Aztecs: Treasures of Tenochtitlan*. London: Thames and Hudson.

McClung de Tapia, Emily, and Judith Zurita. 1994–95. "Las primeras sociedades sedentarias." In *Historia antigua de México*, edited by Linda Manzanilla and Leonardo López Luján, vol. 1, 209–46. Mexico: INAH, UNAM, and Miguel Ángel Porrúa.

McGregor, John C. 1977. *Southwestern Archaeology*. Chicago: University of Illinois Press.

McGuire, Randall, and William Rathje. 1982. *Prehistoric Southwest: Hohokam and Patayan Archaeology*. New York: Academic Press.

Medina, Andrés, Alfredo López Austin, and Mari Carmen Serra Puche, eds. 1986. *Origen y formación del Estado en Mesoamérica*. Mexico: UNAM.

Mendizábal, Miguel Othón de. 1946. "De la prehistoria a la Conquista." In *Obras completas*, vol. 3, 119–41. Mexico: Talleres Gráficos de la Nación.

Michelet, Dominique. 1984. *Rio Verde, San Luis Potosí (Mexique)*. Mexico: CEMCA.

———. 1994–95. "La zona nororiental en el Clásico." In *Historia antigua de México*, edited by Linda Manzanilla and Leonardo López Luján, vol. 2, 205–21. Mexico: INAH, UNAM, and Miguel Ángel Porrúa.

Michelet, Dominique, ed. 1992. *El proyecto Michoacán 1983–1987*. Mexico: CEMCA.

Miller, Arthur G., ed. 1983. *Highland-Lowland Interaction in Mesoamerica. Interdisciplinary Approaches*. Washington, D.C.: Dumbarton Oaks.

Miller, Mary Ellen. 1986. *The Art of Mesoamerica: From Olmec to Aztec*. London: Thames and Hudson.

Miller, Mary Ellen, and Karl Taube. 1993. *The Gods and Symbols of Ancient Mexico and the Maya: An Illustrated Dictionary of Mesoamerican Religion*. London: Thames and Hudson.

Millon, Rene. 1973. *Urbanization at Teotihuacan.* Austin: University of Texas Press.

———. 1981. "Teotihuacan: City, State, and Civilization." In *Supplement to the Handbook of Middle American Indians, Vol. 1, Archaeology,* edited by Victoria Reifler Bricker, 198–243. Austin: University of Texas Press.

Monjarás-Ruiz, Jesús et al., eds. 1985. *Mesoamérica y el Centro de México.* Mexico: INAH.

Morley, Sylvanus G. 1946. *The Civilization of the Maya.* 2d ed. Stanford: Stanford University Press.

Morley, Sylvanus G., George W. Brainerd, and Robert J. Sharer. 1983. *The Ancient Maya.* Stanford: Stanford University Press.

Mountjoy, Joseph B., and Donald L. Brockington, eds. 1987. *El auge y la caída del Clásico en el México Central.* Mexico: UNAM.

Müller, Florencia. 1978. *La alfarería de Cholula.* Mexico: INAH.

Nalda, Enrique. 1981. "México prehispánico: Origen y formación de las clases sociales." In *México: Un pueblo en la historia,* edited by Enrique Semo, vol. 1, 45–165. Mexico: Universidad Autónoma de Puebla y Editorial Nueva Imagen.

———. 1990. "¿Qué es lo que define Mesoamérica?" In *La validez teórica del concepto de Mesoamérica.* Mexico: INAH and SMA.

Nárez, Jesús. 1992. *Balcón de Montezuma.* Mexico: INAH.

———. 1994–95. "Aridamérica y Oasisamérica." In *Historia antigua de México,* edited by Linda Manzanilla and Leonardo López Luján, vol. 1, 75–111. Mexico: INAH, UNAM, and Miguel Ángel Porrúa.

Navarrete, Carlos. 1976. "Algunas influencias mexicanas en el área maya meridional durante el Clásico Tardío." *Estudios de Cultura Náhuatl* 12:345–82.

Nicholson, Henry B. 1957. *Topiltzin Quetzalcoatl of Tollan: A Problem in Mesoamerican Ethnohistory.* Ph.D. diss., Harvard University.

———. 1971. "Religion in Pre-Hispanic Central Mexico." In *Handbook of Middle American Indians,* edited by Robert Wauchope, vol. 10, 395–446. Austin: University of Texas Press.

———. 1978. "West Mesoamerica, A.D. 900–1520." In *Chronologies in New World Archaeology,* edited by R. E. Taylor and W. Meighan, 285–329. New York: Academic Press.

Niederberger, Christine. 1976. *Zohapilco: Cinco milenios de ocupación humana en un sitio lacustre de la Cuenca de México.* Mexico: INAH.

———. 1979. "Early Sedentary Economy in the Basin of Mexico." *Science* 203:131–42.

———. 1987. *Paléopaysages et archéologie preurbaine du Bassin de Mexico.* Mexico: CEMCA.

Noguera, Eduardo. 1965. *La cerámica arqueológica de Mesoamérica.* Mexico: UNAM.

Noguez, Xavier. 1994–95. "La zona del altiplano Central en el Posclásico: La etapa tolteca." In *Historia antigua de México,* edited by Linda Manzanilla and

Leonardo López Luján, vol. 3, 189–224. Mexico: INAH, UNAM, and Miguel Ángel Porrúa.

Ochoa, Lorenzo. 1979. *Historia prehispánica de la Huaxteca*. Mexico: UNAM.

———, ed. 1989a. *Comercio, comerciantes y rutas de intercambio en el México antiguo.* Mexico: SECOFI.

———. 1989b. *Huaxtecos y totonacos: Una antología histórico-cultural.* Mexico: CNCA.

———. 1994–95. "La zona del Golfo en el Posclásico." In *Historia antigua de México*, edited by Linda Manzanilla and Leonardo López Luján, vol. 3, 11–53. Mexico: INAH, UNAM, and Miguel Ángel Porrúa.

Olivé Negrete, Julio César. 1958. *Estructura y dinámica de Mesoamérica*. Mexico: SAENAH.

Oliveros, Arturo. 1973. *Excavaciones de dos tumbas de tiro en el Opeño, Michoacán.* M.A. thesis, Escuela Nacional de Antropología e Historia, Mexico.

Oppelt, Norman. 1989. *Guide to Prehistoric Ruins of the Southwest.* Boulder, Colo.: Pruett.

Ortiz, Alfonso, ed. 1979. *Southwest.* In *Handbook of North American Indians.* Washington, D.C.: Smithsonian Institution.

Ortiz de Montellano, Bernard R. 1990. *Aztec Medicine, Health, and Nutrition.* New Brunswick, N.J.: Rutgers University Press.

Paddock, John, ed. 1966. *Ancient Oaxaca.* Stanford, Calif.: Stanford University Press.

———. 1990. *Un milenario oaxaqueño.* Oaxaca: Casa de la Cultura Oaxaqueña.

Palerm, Ángel. 1973a. *Agricultura y sociedad en Mesoamérica.* Mexico: SEP.

———. 1973b. *Obras hidráulicas prehispánicas en el sistema lacustre del Valle de México.* Mexico: CISINAH.

Palerm, Ángel, and Eric Wolf. 1972. *Agricultura y civilización en Mesoamérica.* Mexico: SEP.

Parsons, Lee A. 1986. *The Origins of Maya Art: Monumental Stone Sculpture of Kaminaljuyu, Guatemala and the Southern Pacific Coast.* Washington, D.C.: Dumbarton Oaks.

Pastor, Rodolfo. 1987. *Campesinos y reformas: La Mixteca, 1700–1856.* Mexico: El Colegio de México.

Pasztory, Esther, ed. 1978. *Middle Classic Mesoamerica: A.D. 400–700.* New York: Columbia University Press.

———. 1983. *Aztec Art.* New York: Harry N. Abrams.

Piña Chan, Román. 1967. *Una visión del México prehispánico.* Mexico: UNAM.

———. 1972. *Historia, arqueología y arte prehispánico.* Mexico: FCE.

———. 1976. *Un modelo de evolución social y cultural del México precolombino.* Mexico: INAH.

———. 1980. *Chichén Itzá: La ciudad de los brujos de agua.* Mexico: FCE.

———, ed. 1975. *Teotenango: El antiguo lugar de la muralla. Memoria de las excavaciones arqueológicas.* 2 vols. Mexico: Gobierno del Estado de México.

Pollard, Helen Perlstein. 1980. "Central Places and Cities: A Consideration of the Protohistoric Tarascan State." *American Antiquity* 45:677–96.

Pomar, Juan Bautista. 1941. *Relación de Tetzcoco y de la Nueva España*, 1–64. Mexico: Editorial Chávez Heyhoe.

Powell, Phillip. 1977. *La guerra chichimeca (1550–1600)*. Mexico: FCE.

Proskouriakoff, Tatiana. 1950. *A Study of Classic Maya Sculpture*. Washington, D.C.: Carnegie Institution.

————. 1960. "Historial Implications of a Pattern of Dates at Piedras Negras, Guatemala." *American Antiquity* 25:454–75.

————. 1964. "Historial Data in the Inscriptions of Yaxchilan (Part II)." *Estudios de Cultura Maya* 4:177–202.

Rattray, Evelyn Childs. 1988. "Nuevas interpretaciones en torno al Barrio de los Comerciantes." *Anales de Antropología* 25:165–82.

Reilly, F. Kent. 1991. "Olmec Iconographic Influences on the Symbols of the Maya Rulership: An Examination of Possible Sources." In *The Sixth Palenque Round Table, 1986*, edited by Virgina M. Fields, 151–66. Norman: University of Oklahoma Press.

Relación de las ceremonias y ritos y población y gobierno de los indios de la Provincia de Michoacán (1541). 1977. Mexico: Balsal Editores.

Reyes García, Luis, and Lina Odena Güemes. 1994–95. "La zona del Altiplano Central en el Posclásico: La etapa chichimeca." In *Historia antigua de México*, edited by Linda Manzanilla and Leonardo López Luján, vol. 3, 225–64. Mexico: INAH, UNAM, and Miguel Ángel Porrúa.

Rivera Dorado, Miguel. 1985. *Los mayas de la antigüedad*. Madrid: Editorial Alhambra.

————. 1986. *La religión maya*. Madrid: Alianza Editorial.

Rojas, José Luis de. 1986. *México Tenochtitlan: Economía y sociedad en el siglo XVI*. Mexico: El Colegio de Michoacán and FCE.

Rojas Rabiela, Teresa, ed. 1991. *La agricultura en tierras mexicanas desde sus orígenes hasta nuestros días*, 15–138. Mexico: CNCA.

Rojas Rabiela, Teresa, and William T. Sanders, eds. 1985. *Historia de la agricultura: Época prehispánica-siglo XVI*. Mexico: INAH.

Ruz Lhuillier, Alberto. 1968. *Costumbres funerarias de los antiguos mayas*. Mexico: UNAM.

————. 1982. *El pueblo maya*. Mexico: Salvat Mexicana de Ediciones.

Sabloff, Jeremy A. 1990. *The New Archaeology and the Ancient Maya*. New York: Scientific American Library.

Sabloff, Jeremy A., and Gordon R. Willey. 1967. "The Collapse of Maya Civilization in the Southern Lowlands: A Consideration of History and Process." *Southwestern Journal of Anthropology* 23:311–36.

Sabloff, Jeremy A., and E. Wyllis Andrews V, eds. 1986. *Late Lowland Maya Civilization: Classic to Postclassic*. Albuquerque: University of New Mexico Press.

Sabloff, Jeremy A., and John S. Henderson, eds. 1993. *Lowland Maya Civilization in the Eighth Century A.D.* Washington, D.C.: Dumbarton Oaks.

Sahagún, Fray Bernardino de. 1989. *Historia general de las cosas de Nueva España.* 2 vols. Mexico: CNCA and Alianza Editorial Mexicana.

Sanders, William T., and J. W. Michels. 1969. *The Pennsylvania State University Kaminaljuyú Project 1968 Season. Part 1: The Excavations.* Philadelphia: Pennsylvania State University.

Sanders William T., and Deborah L. Nichols. 1988. "Ecological Theory and Cultural Evolution in the Valley of Oaxaca." *Current Anthropology* 29:33–52, 69–80.

Sanders, William T., Jeffrey R. Parsons, and Robert S. Santley. 1979. *The Basin of Mexico: Ecological Processes in the Evolution of a Civilization.* New York: Academic Press.

Sanders, William T., and Barbara J. Price. 1968. *Mesoamerica: The Evolution of a Civilization.* New York: Random House.

Santley, Robert S. 1984. "Obsidian Exchange, Economic Stratification, and the Evolution of Complex Society in the Basin of Mexico." In *Trade and Exchange in Early Mesoamerica,* edited by Kenneth Hirth, 43–86. Albuquerque: University of New Mexico Press.

Scarborough, Vernon L., and David R. Wilcox, eds. 1991. *The Mesoamerican Ballgame.* Tucson: University of Arizona Press.

Schele, Linda, and David Friedel. 1990. *A Forest of Kings: The Untold Story of the Ancient Maya.* New York: William Morrow.

Schele, Linda, and Mary Ellen Miller. 1986. *The Blood of Kings: Dynasty and Ritual in Maya Art.* Fort Worth: Kimbell Art Museum.

Schöndube Baumbach, Otto. 1969. "El horizonte Clásico." In *Culturas de Occidente: Artes de México* (Mexico) 119:23–46.

———. 1975. "La evolución cultural en el Occidente de México: Jalisco, Colima y Nayarit." *Actas del XLI Congreso Internacional de Americanistas* (Mexico), vol. 1, 332–37.

———. 1980. "La nueva tradición." In *Historia de Jalisco,* edited by José María Muriá, vol. 1, 213–58.

Seler, Eduard. [1902–1903] 1960–69. *Gesammelte Abhandlungen zur Amerikanischen Sprach-und Altertumskunde.* 5 vols. Graz, Austria: Akademische Druck.

Serra Puche, Mari Carmen. 1988. *Los recursos lacustres de la Cuenca de México durante el Formativo.* Mexico: UNAM.

Sharer, Robert J., and David Grove, eds. 1989. *Regional Perspectives on the Olmec.* Cambridge, England: Cambridge University Press.

Sociedad Mexicana de Antropología. 1944. *El norte de México y el sur de los Estados Unidos.* Mexico: SMA.

———. 1948. *El Occidente de México.* Mexico: SMA.

———. 1972a. *Religión en Mesoamérica.* Mexico: SMA.

———. 1972b. *Teotihuacan.* Mexico: SMA.

————. 1976. *Las fronteras de Mesoamérica*. 2 vols. Mexico: SMA.

————. 1990. *La validez teórica del concepto Mesoamérica*. Mexico: INAH.

Sodi Miranda, Federica, ed. 1990. *Mesoamérica y el norte de México, siglos IX–XII*. 2 vols. Mexico: INAH.

Solís, Felipe. 1991. *Gloria y fama mexica*. Mexico: Smurfit Cartón y Papel de México.

Soustelle, Jacques. 1956. *Daily Life of the Aztecs*. Stanford, Calif.: Stanford University Press.

————. 1984. *Los Olmecas*. Mexico: FCE.

————. 1993. *La familia otomí-pame del Centro de México*. Toluca: Gobierno del Estado de México, Universidad Autónoma del Valle de México, Ateneo del Estado de México, and Instituto Mexiquense de Cultura.

Spinden, Herbert J. 1933. "Origin of Civilization in Central America and Mexico." In *The American Aborigines: Their Origin and Antiquity*, edited by Diamond Jenness, 217–46. Toronto: Fifth Pacific Science Congress.

————. 1975. *A Study of Maya Art: Its Subject Matter and Historical Development*. New York: Dover.

Spores, Ronald. 1984. *The Mixtecs in Ancient and Colonial Times*. Norman: University of Oklahoma Press.

Stone, Doris. 1948. "The Basic Cultures of Central America." In *Handbook of South American Indians*, edited by Julian H. Stewart, vol. 4, 169–93. Washington, D.C.: Smithsonian Institution.

Stresser-Péan, Guy. 1977. *San Antonio Nogalar*. Mexico: CEMCA.

Sturtevant, William G., ed. 1978–86. *Handbook of North American Indians*. Washington, D.C.: Smithsonian Institution.

Taladoire, Eric. 1981. *Les terrains de jeu de balle: Mésoamérique et Sud-Ouest des États-Unis*. Mexico: MAEFM.

Taladoire, Eric, and Brigitte Faugère-Kalfon. 1995. *Archéologie et art précolombiens: La Mesoamérique*. Paris: École du Louvre, Réunion des musées nationaux and La Documentation française.

Thompson, J. Eric S. 1954. *The Rise and Fall of Maya Civilization*. Norman: University of Oklahoma Press.

————. 1960. *Maya Hieroglyphic Writing*. Norman: University of Oklahoma Press.

————. 1970. *Maya History and Religion*. Norman: University of Oklahoma Press.

Tolstoy, Paul. 1975. "Settlement and Population Trends in the Basin of Mexico: Ixtapaluca and Zacatenco Phases." *Journal of Field Archaeology* 2:331–49.

Tolstoy, Paul, and Luise I. Paradis. 1971. "Early and Middle Preclassic Culture in the Basin of Mexico." In *Observations of the Emergence of Civilization in Mesoamerica*, edited by Robert F. Heizer and John A. Graham, 2–28. Berkeley: University of California Press.

Torquemada, Fray Juan de. [1615] 1969. *Monarquía Indiana*. 3 vols. Mexico: Porrúa.

Townsend, Richard Frazer. 1979. *State and Cosmos in the Art of Tenochtitlan.* Washington, D.C.: Dumbarton Oaks.

Tozzer, Alfred M. 1957. *Chichen Itza and Its Cenote of Sacrifice: A Comparative Study of Contemporaneous Maya and Toltec.* 2 vols. Cambridge: Peabody Museum, Harvard University.

Trombold, Charles D. 1990. "A Reconsideration of Chronology for the Quemada Portion of the Northern Mesoamerican Frontier." *American Antiquity* 55:308–24.

Urcid Serrano. Javier. 1992. *Zapotec Writing Systems.* Ph.D. diss., Yale University.

Wauchope, Robert, ed. 1964–71. *Handbook of Middle American Indians.* 16 vols. Austin: University of Texas Press.

Weaver, Muriel Porter. 1993. *The Aztecs, Maya and their Predecessors: Archaeology of Mesoamerica.* 3d ed. New York: Academic Press.

Webb, Malcolm C. 1978. "The Significance of the 'Epiclassic' Period in Mesoamerican Prehistory." In *Cultural Continuity in Mesoamerica,* edited by David L. Browman, 155–78. The Hague: Mouton Publishers.

Weigand, Phil. 1993. *Evolución de una civilización prehispánica.* Zamora: El Colegio de Michoacán.

Weigand, Phil et al. 1977. "Turquoise Sources and Source Analysis: Mesoamerica and the Southwestern USA." In *Exchange Systems in Prehistory,* edited by J. E. Ericson and T. K. Earle, 15–34. New York: Academic Press.

Whitecotton, Joseph W. 1977. *The Zapotecs: Princes, Priests, and Peasants.* Norman: University of Oklahoma Press.

Wilkerson, Jeffrey K. 1987. *El Tajín: Una guía para visitantes.* Mexico: Universidad Veracruzana.

———. 1989. "Presencia huasteca y cronología cultural en el norte de Veracruz Central, México." In *Huaxtecos y totonacos: Una antología histórico-cultural,* edited by Lorenzo Ochoa, 257–79. Mexico: CNCA.

Willey, Gordon R., Gordon F. Ekholm, and Rene Millon. 1964. "The Patterns of Farming Life and Ancient Civilization." In *Handbook of Middle American Indians,* edited by Robert Wauchope, vol. 1, 446–98. Austin: University of Texas Press.

Willey, Gordon R., and Phillip Phillips. 1955. "Method and Theory in American Archaeology." *American Anthropologist* 57:723–819.

Willey, Gordon R., and Dimitri B. Shimkin, 1987. "The Maya Collapse: A Summary View." In *Essays in Maya Archaeology,* edited by Gordon R. Willey, 19–58. Albuquerque: University of New Mexico Press.

Williams, Eduardo, and Robert Novella, eds. 1994. *Arqueología del Occidente de México.* Zamora: El Colegio de Michoacán.

Winfield Capitaine, Fernando. 1988. "La Estela 1 de Mojarra, Veracruz, México." *Research Reports on Ancient Maya Writing,* no. 16. Washington, D.C.: Center for Maya Research.

Winter, Marcus C. 1989. *Oaxaca: The Archaeological Record.* Mexico: Editorial Minutiae Mexicana.

————. 1990. "Oaxaca prehispánica: Una introducción." In *Lecturas históricas del Estado de Oaxaca,* edited by Marcus C. Winter, vol. 1, 31–219. Mexico: INAH and Gobierno del Estado de México.

Wolf, Eric R. 1959. *Pueblos y culturas de Mesoamérica.* Mexico: Era.

————, ed. 1976. *The Valley of Mexico: Studies in Prehispanic Ecology and Society.* Albuquerque: University of New Mexico Press.

Zantwijk, Rudolph van. 1985. *The Aztec Arrangement: The Social History of Pre-Hispanic Mexico.* Norman: University of Oklahoma Press.

Zurita, Alonso de. 1941. *Breve y sumaria relación de los señores . . . In Relaciones de Texcoco y de la Nueva España,* Juan Bautista Pomar et al. Mexico: Editoral Chávez Hayhoe.

Index